RED ZONES

In *Red Zones*, Marie-Eve Sylvestre, Nicholas Blomley, and Céline Bellot examine the court-imposed territorial restrictions and other bail and sentencing conditions that are increasingly issued in the context of Canadian criminal proceedings. Drawing on extensive fieldwork with legal actors in the criminal justice system, as well as those who have been subjected to court surveillance, the authors demonstrate the devastating impact these restrictions have on the marginalized populations – the homeless, drug users, sex workers, and protesters – who depend on public spaces. On a broader level, the authors show how red zones, unlike better-publicized forms of spatial regulation such as legislation or policing strategies, create a form of legal territorialization that threatens to invert traditional expectations of justice and reshape our understanding of criminal law and punishment.

Marie-Eve Sylvestre is Dean and Full Professor at the Faculty of Law (Civil Law Section) of the University of Ottawa. Her research focuses on the criminalization and regulation of poverty and social conflicts in urban public spaces, as well as their alternatives. She is also involved in criminal law reform and advocacy, challenging discriminatory practices against Indigenous people and other marginalized groups. She is a founding member of the Ottawa Hub for Harm Reduction and of the Observatory on Profiling (Observatoire des profilages), and an elected member of the Global Young Academy and the College of New Scholars, Artists and Scientists of the Royal Society of Canada.

Nicholas Blomley is Professor of Geography at Simon Fraser University. He is interested in the spatiality of legal practices and relationships, and the worldmaking consequences of such legal geographies. Much of his empirical work concerns the often oppressive effects of legal relations on marginalized and oppressed people. He is the author or co-editor of five books, including *Law, Space, and the Geographies of Power* (1994) and *Rights of Passage: Sidewalks and the Regulation of Public Flow* (2011).

Céline Bellot is Director of the Social Work School at the Université de Montréal and Director of the Observatory on Profiling (Observatoire des profilages). She is the Chair of the Center on Poverty and Social Exclusion (Centre sur la pauvreté et l'exclusion sociale) and the Committee on the State of Homelessness. She holds a Ph.D. in criminology and her research focuses on issues of criminalization of poverty, including homeless populations, Indigenous populations, drug users, and street youth.

Red Zones

CRIMINAL LAW AND THE TERRITORIAL
GOVERNANCE OF MARGINALIZED PEOPLE

MARIE-EVE SYLVESTRE
University of Ottawa Faculty of Law

NICHOLAS BLOMLEY
Simon Fraser University Department of Geography

CÉLINE BELLOT
University of Montreal School of Social Work

CAMBRIDGE
UNIVERSITY PRESS

University Printing House, Cambridge CB2 8BS, United Kingdom

One Liberty Plaza, 20th Floor, New York, NY 10006, USA

477 Williamstown Road, Port Melbourne, VIC 3207, Australia

314–321, 3rd Floor, Plot 3, Splendor Forum, Jasola District Centre, New Delhi – 110025, India

79 Anson Road, #06–04/06, Singapore 079906

Cambridge University Press is part of the University of Cambridge.

It furthers the University's mission by disseminating knowledge in the pursuit of education, learning, and research at the highest international levels of excellence.

www.cambridge.org
Information on this title: www.cambridge.org/9781107184237
DOI: 10.1017/9781316875544

First published 2019

Printed in the United Kingdom by TJ International Ltd. Padstow Cornwall

A catalogue record for this publication is available from the British Library.

Library of Congress Cataloging-in-Publication Data
NAMES: Sylvestre, Marie-Eve, author. | Blomley, Nicholas K., author. | Bellot, Céline, author.
TITLE: Red zones : criminal law and the territorial governance of marginalized people / Marie-Eve Sylvestre, University of Ottawa, Faculty of Law; Nicholas Blomley, Simon Fraser University Department of Geography; Céline Bellot, University of Montreal School of Social Work.
DESCRIPTION: Cambridge, United Kingdom ; New York, NY : Cambridge University Press, 2019. | Includes bibliographical references and index.
IDENTIFIERS: LCCN 2019017893 | ISBN 9781107184237 (hardback : alk. paper) | ISBN 9781316635414 (pbk. : alk. paper)
SUBJECTS: LCSH: Discrimination in criminal justice administration. | Criminal justice, Administration of–Social aspects. | Criminal law–Social aspects. | Marginality, Social. | Law and geography. | Regional planning–Law and legislation. | Regionalism.
CLASSIFICATION: LCC K5001 .S95 2019 | DDC 345.008–DC23
LC record available at https://lccn.loc.gov/2019017893

ISBN 978-1-107-18423-7 Hardback
ISBN 978-1-316-63541-4 Paperback

We dedicate this book to all the women who supported us, and our children, who make the future bright; and to the poor and marginalized, who confront a legal system that too often harms them, rather than strengthens them.

Contents

Figures

Maps

Tables

Acknowledgments

We first express our immense gratitude to all the anonymous participants in this study, who graciously committed time and provided invaluable information and insights for this project. Thank you for sharing your stories, experiences, and perceptions of (in)justice and (mis)encounters with the criminal justice system. Your courage and endurance in the face of daily violence and adversity have carried us through this book.

We are also grateful to the Vancouver Area Network of Drug Users (VANDU), How U Survive this Life Everyday (HUSTLE) at Health Initiative for Men (HiM) and Pivot Legal Society in Vancouver (DJ Larkin, former legal director, responsible for housing and homelessness issues, and Douglas King, former staff lawyer responsible for police accountability), as well as the Réseau d'aide aux personnes seules et itinérantes de Montréal (RAPSIM) and the Clinique droits devant (Bernard St-Jacques, Executive Director and Isabelle Raffestin, social worker), Cactus Montréal (Roxane Beauchemin, Clinical Director and the community members of PLAISIIRS), Stella – l'amie de Maimie (Emilie Laliberté, former executive director, as well as Jenn Clamen and Tara Santini), the Legal Committee of the Association pour une solidarité syndicale étudiante (ASSÉ), the Collectif contre la brutalité policiere (COBP), the Centre communautaire juridique de Montréal (Legal Aid Montreal), Prostitute of Ottawa and Gatineau, Work, Educate and Resist (POWER) (Frédérique Chabot, former board member and Director of Health Promotion, Action Canada for Sexual Health and Rights), Dr Mark Tyndall of the BC Centre for Disease Control and formerly from the University of Ottawa, and the members of Participatory Research Ottawa: Understanding Drugs (PROUD) for their help in recruiting participants, their important contributions and knowledge, and their invaluable support throughout the study.

We also extend our thanks to the Vancouver Downtown Community Court (DCC), the Public Prosecution Service of Canada (PPSC) (George Dolhai,

Deputy Director of Public Prosecutions, and Robert Prior, former Chief Federal Prosecutor of the B.C. Regional Office), the judges of the Quebec Provincial Court – Cour du Québec, criminal division, and of the Municipal Court of Montreal (Honorable Danielle Côté, former Associate Chief Justice, Criminal Division, and Honorable André Perreault, former Associate Chief Justice, Municipal Courts), as well as the prosecutors of the City of Montreal (Me Gaétane Martel, former Director of Social Programs), for their generosity and openness to research as well as for their participation, support, and important insights.

We thank the Court Services Branch (CSB) of the Ministry of Justice of British Columbia and the Information Technology Services at the City of Montreal (STI) for their help and assistance in providing access to court record data and for their work. In particular, we thank Kathryn Thomson, Legal Policy and Technology Advisor, Mike Scarrow, Senior Business Information and Project Analyst, and Caroline Shandley, Business Information and Project Analyst at the CSB as well as Yves Briand, director of the Court Services Division, Chantal Thériault, Senior Advisor and Information Manager at the Municipal Court of Montreal, and Julie McDuff and Sylvain Meloche from STI at the City of Montreal.

We acknowledge the excellent work of our research coordinators, Véronique Fortin (Montreal) and William Damon (Vancouver). Will completed his MA during our study and provided additional interview data from his thesis (William G. Damon, "Spatial Tactics in Vancouver's Judicial System", Department of Geography, Faculty of Environment, Simon Fraser University, 2014: http://summit.sfu.ca/item/14152) while Véronique completed her Ph.D. dissertation "Taking the Law to the Streets: Legal and Spatial Tactics Deployed in Public Spaces to Control Protesters and the Homeless in Montreal", University of California, Irvine, 2015, drawing in part from her work as a research coordinator. We also thank our wonderful research assistants, including Dominique Bernier, Francis Villeneuve-Ménard, Jessica Gaouette, Brigitte Savignac, Élizabeth Paradis, Nicholas Lamb, Emily Symons, and Katherine von Meyl, as well as Alexandre Duchesne-Blondin, Jacob Lavoie, Sean Spinney, and Kristine Gagnon Lafond for their analysis of the quantitative data.

We also thank Michael Sawada, Director of the Laboratory for Applied Geomatics and GIS Science at the University of Ottawa, Brian Bancroft from the University of Ottawa, and John Ng from Simon Fraser University for creating the maps based on our data.

Parts of this project have benefited from feedback from many people, including presentations at community gatherings in Vancouver's Downtown Eastside (2017) and at the Forum droits devants in Montreal (2018), meetings of the Quebec Provincial Court and the Quebec Bar, as well as in numerous academic circles, including the Harvard Criminal Justice Roundtable (2018), the Constituting Cities Seminar at the University of New South Wales (2018), the International Conference on the Criminalization of Social Problems at the Université de Rouen (2018), the American Bar Foundation in Chicago (2018), the Biennial Canadian Conference on Criminal Law and Criminal Justice in Quebec City (2017), the International Conference on Critical Perspectives on Criminology and Criminal Justice in Winnipeg – Placing Justice (2016), the Law and Society Association Meetings in Seattle (2015) and Toronto (2018), the Association of American Geographers Meetings in San Francisco (2016) and New York (2012), the Onati International Institute for the Sociology of Law – workshop series (2013), and the Canadian Association of Geographers Conference in Vancouver (2015). Specifically, we would also like to express our gratitude to the following people who have provided constructive feedback on our work throughout the years and supported us in different ways: Rachel Barkow, Anne-Marie Boisvert, Adam Crawford, Abby Deshman, Julie Desrosiers, Aaron Doyle, Margarida Garcia, Aya Gruber, Kelly Hannah-Moffat, Bernard Harcourt, Kurt Iveson, Manon Lapointe, Lucie Lemonde, Randy Lippert, Tracey Meares, Marilu Melo Zurita, Luke McNamara, Cintia Quiroga, Alice Ristroph, Terry Skolnik, Carol Steiker, Mariana Valverde, and, last but not least, Joao Gustavo Vieira Velloso.

Marie-Eve Sylvestre also thanks her co-authors for a terrific working relationship: Nick, for being such a dedicated and inspiring colleague and friend, and, Céline, for longstanding support and friendship and her commitment to community-based research.

Special thanks also go to my daughters, Emilia and Anais Sylvestre Velloso, who have lived and grown alongside this project foremost or all of their lifetime, for being an infinite source of joy and motivation.

We also thank Monique Lafond, Marie-Eve's mother, for the powerful painting on the book cover, and for her overall support.

Finally, we are grateful to the Social Sciences and Humanities Research Council of Canada (SSHRC) for their financial support and to the Faculty of Law, Civil Law Section of the University of Ottawa and the Department of Geography of Simon Fraser University for administrative support.

Cases

Legislation

Canadian Legislation

Criminal Code, R.S.C., 1985, c. C-46 – p. 1, 13, 49, 52, 60–62, 65, 68–70, 73, 84–87, 98, 113, 124, 138, 143, 146–148, 150, 158, 162, 188, 213, 219–221, 223

Protection of Collectivities and Exploited Persons Act, S.C. 2014, c.25 – p. 1

Bail Reform Act (S.C. 1971, 19–20 Eliz. II, c. 37) – p. 52, 103, 221

Canadian Charter of Rights and Freedoms, s. 8, Part 1 of the Constitution Act 1982, being Schedule B to the Canada Act 1982 (UK) 1982, c. 11 – p. 1, 64, 70, 102, 187, 205

An Act to Amend the Criminal Code, the Youth Criminal Justice Act and other Acts and to make consequential amendments to other Acts (Bill C-75) – p. 102, 219–224

United Kingdom Legislation

Criminal Justice Act of 1967 (c.80) – p. 50

Magistrates' Courts Act (15 & 16 Geo. 6 & 1 Eliz 2, c. 55) – p. 51

Indictable Offences Act 1848 (11 & 12 Vict., c. 42, s. 23) – p. 53

Criminal Justice Act 2003 (c.44) – p. 84, 116

Bail Act 1976 (c.63) – p. 220

Legal Aid, Sentencing and Punishment of Offenders Act 2012 (c.10) – p. 220

American Legislation

Bail Reform Act of 1966 (18 U.S.C. §3146) – p. 51

Bail Reform Act of 1984 (18 U.S.C. §§ 3141–3150) – p. 51–52

Pretrial Services Act of 1982 (18 U.S.C. § 3152) – p. 52

1

Navigating the Territories of the Law

MONTREAL, QUEBEC

Located on an island on the St Lawrence River, the city of Montreal is the second largest in Canada (Statistics Canada, 2016) and the largest French-speaking city in North America. A vibrant and festive city, the city of Montreal also has its share of social problems and income disparities: 25 per cent of its residents live below the poverty line and 70,000 individuals use food banks on a monthly basis (Massé et al., 2017).

When we first met Martine[1] in 2013, she was a skinny woman in her thirties bound by a probation order. The mother of a twenty-year-old young adult, she had just moved into an apartment in Montreal after spending several years on the streets. Using drugs, living with HIV, and working as a part-time sex worker, Martine hung out at Cactus, a community organization working with inhaling and injecting drug users and engaged in the prevention of blood-borne and sexually transmitted infections.

Martine was first charged with communication for the purposes of prostitution contrary to s. 213c) of the Canadian Criminal Code[2] in 2002. She subsequently pled guilty and was sentenced to a $250 fine. It took another six years before she was charged again with the same offence. Her personal

---

[1]   All names are altered to ensure anonymity.

[2]   L.R.C. (1985) c. C-46, "C.C.C." S. 213(c) was held unconstitutional by the Supreme Court of Canada in *Canada (Attorney General)* v. *Bedford* (2013) SCC 72 because it violated the rights of "prostitutes" to security of the person in a manner that is not in accordance with the principles of fundamental justice as protected in s. 7 of the Canadian Charter of Rights and Freedoms. In 2014, the Parliament of Canada repealed s. 213(c) and replaced it by s. 213 (1.1) creating the offence of communicating with any person – for the purpose of offering or providing sexual services for consideration – in a public place, or in any place open to public view, that is or is next to a school ground, playground or daycare centre: Protection of Collectivities and Exploited Persons Act, S.C. 2014, c. 25.

situation as a homeless youth did not change much during that period, but she reported not having too many problems with the police in the early 2000s. This started to change for her in 2008.

After being arrested by a police officer and released on a promise to appear in April 2008,[3] she was soon found in breach of her conditions of release and held in custody until her first appearance where she was remanded awaiting her bail hearing. She appeared three days later before a provincial court judge. At the time, Martine had been held in an overcrowded facility for four days in a row and had started to develop severe symptoms of withdrawal. She thus readily agreed to the release conditions "suggested" by the prosecutor and approved by the judge. The bail order required her to "keep the peace and be of good behaviour", to "notify of any change of address" and "not to be found within the perimeter formed by Berri St. (West), Sherbrooke St. (North), Viau St. (East) and Notre-Dame St. (South)". This area, or "red zone" as they are often colloquially known, encompassed large parts of the Ville-Marie and Hochelaga-Maisonneuve boroughs. While Ville-Marie borough is located in the south-eastern part of downtown, Hochelaga-Maisonneuve is a little further east of the island. Numerous community organizations and health and social services, including an important HIV clinic and a university hospital, are located in these boroughs. The Montreal police have also consistently targeted both areas for the sex trade (Map 1.1).

Standing before the judge, Martine did not think to mention that she usually worked and lived in a hotel on St Hubert Street, that she regularly went to pick up groceries at the Fondation d'aide directe SIDA Montreal, a food bank for people living with HIV, or that she sometimes met with social workers at the community group Méta d'âme, all located within her red zone. She just accepted her conditions because she was eager to be released: "you just want to get out, you say 'yes, yes'", recalled Martine.

Her trial was scheduled for the following July. By then, Martine was struggling to stay alive, and since she was not keeping a diary on a regular basis she did not show up in court. She was thus charged with failure to appear and a warrant was issued. Known by the police, Martine decided to leave the area.

The police found her nearly a year later, in 2009, and immediately sent her into custody. After spending forty-eight hours in detention, she appeared before a judge and pled guilty to three offences, including communicating for the purposes of prostitution, failure to comply with her bail order, and

---

[3]   All court records have been checked for accuracy. We sometimes changed the months slightly to ensure anonymity, but we have not modified the overall time period or order duration.

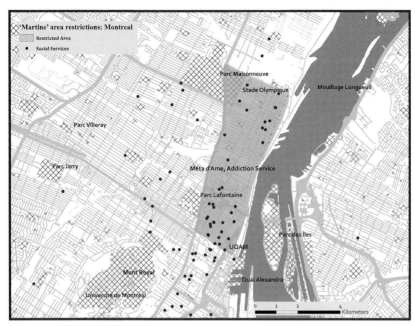

MAP 1.1: Martine's area restrictions (Montreal).
Sources: Esri, HERE, Garmin, USGS, Intermap, INCREMENT P, NRCan, Esri Japan, METI, Esri China (Hong Kong), Esri Korea, Esri (Thailand), NGCC, © OpenStreetMap contributors, and the GIS User Community

failure to appear. She was sentenced to thirty days in jail followed by a one-year probation order that maintained Martine's exclusion from most of the south-eastern part of Montreal. By the end of 2009, Martine temporarily left the city to follow her boyfriend in the suburbs.

A few days before the end of her probation order, Martine was found communicating for the purposes of prostitution by an undercover agent in Montreal. After hearing that Martine had recently moved out of Montreal, the police officer chose to include a complete ban from the Island of Montreal[4] in her promise to appear with an undertaking. He also added a prohibition to consume alcohol or drugs. Martine now faced two new charges: communicating for the purposes of prostitution and breach of a probation order. Her appearance was set for September 2010.

---

[4] The City of Montreal is located on an Island in the St Lawrence River. Before 2002, the Island was divided into 22 municipalities, including Montreal. Most of these municipalities merged in 2002 to form the new City of Montreal although they remained divided in boroughs. Martine's order refers to the Island of Montreal, which now also means that she is prohibited from going into the City as a whole.

However, in August 2010, she was found by the authorities on the Island of Montreal, thus failing to comply with the police undertaking. She appeared in custody and her conditions were revoked pending her bail hearing. Four days later, when she returned to court, she pled guilty to three offences and was released pending her sentencing hearing. In the meantime, she was required not to be found on the Island of Montreal, to reside at all times in a drug-treatment facility on the south shore of Montreal and to obey the rules and regulations of that facility that included a curfew. Martine never showed up at the treatment facility and did not come back in court for her sentence either. She was again charged for failure to comply and failure to appear and a warrant was issued. She disappeared for a while.

In 2011, Martine's mother, who lived in Montreal, died. Martine had to come back in town to empty her mother's apartment and was recognized by a police officer working for the vice unit. Unmoved by her situation, the officer detained her. She appeared in court the following day, immediately pled guilty to two offences, and was sentenced to fifty-five days of incarceration followed by a two-year probation that maintained her exclusion from the Island of Montreal and required that she attended the meetings of Narcotics Anonymous.

Her area restriction was finally lifted fifteen months later in December 2012 as she showed evidence of good behaviour and agreed to renewed conditions to follow a drug treatment and comply with a curfew. She was slowly settling in Montreal when we met her. "Why did you decide to come back?", we asked, during the interview. "Because I'm starving on the south shore", she replied.

And, indeed, in addition to being under police surveillance and carrying a heavy criminal record, during that five-year period Martine was impeded from accessing important community resources, essential to her life, health, and security, located on the island of Montreal, including food banks, shelter, medical services, and community support: "when I refer to being denied access to resources," she said, "I'm not talking about getting a manicure or having a free haircut! I mean eating, getting some food". Moreover, since she could not get HIV treatment in the suburbs, she obtained the court's permission to attend a doctor's office on the island of Montreal while her area restriction was maintained. In order to do so, however, she had to obtain evidence from public health services that the treatments needed were not offered elsewhere and she had to find transportation from the Montreal Volunteer Bureau who drove her from a subway station off the Island to the doctor's office so she could not be found walking on the streets of Montreal at any time. Martine's conditions also led to absurdities. Once, she was stopped by a police officer while she was hitchhiking on the highway on the south shore trying to get to court on time. While the officer agreed that the situation was untenable – having to go to court in Montreal while being banned from the Island – he decided to drive her up to the middle of the bridge in order to comply with her area restriction. "But how should I get to court?", Martine asked him, completely outraged. "Am I supposed to go in a helicopter and jump into the building?"

Meanwhile, Martine reported feeling considerably stressed and anxious. The spatiotemporal controls she experienced were so controlling, she joked bitterly that: "I will soon have to start walking on my hands. They are about to tell me that I am not allowed to walk on my feet".

As Martine was imposed stricter spatial conditions, as she moved from being on bail to probation and then back on bail, generating more breaches of her conditions (and more work for the court) but yet committing only one additional substantive criminal offence, there was no question raised about her fundamental rights or about the impact of breaches management on the criminal justice system. No one seemed to care, for instance, about keeping in custody such a non-threatening offender for minor offences over long periods of time and about the impact of doing so on the likelihood of her pleading guilty and accepting unreasonable and unrealistic conditions. And before we considered doing it ourselves for the purposes of this study, no one other than people like Martine had ever thought about the geographical aspects of such conditions and how they constrained mobility within the city, and access to live-saving resources.

VANCOUVER, BRITISH COLUMBIA

On April 12, 2013, the police arrested Paul on East Hastings Street, in the Downtown Eastside of Vancouver (DTES). Founded on the traditional unceded territories of the Musqueam, Squamish, and Tsleil-Waututh First Nations, the city of Vancouver is experiencing an important housing crisis amidst increasing income disparities (Hulchanski, 2016; Cheung, 2018). Vancouver's housing market is the most unaffordable in Canada (Mayor's Task Force on Housing Affordability, 2012). The Downtown Eastside is the most visible expression of these systemic fault lines, a concentration of marginalized and criminalized individuals, many of them Indigenous, struggling with addiction, mental illness, poverty, and homelessness (Carnegie Community Action Project, 2016; Pauly, Cross and Weiss 2016).[5] Highly policed, dominant

---

[5]   Carnegie Community Action Project, 2016. *Out of Control*, Carnegie Community Action Project's 2016 hotel survey and housing report.

representations of the DTES as "Vancouver's Gulag"[6] erase a long and proud history of community organizing and activism (Blomley, 2004; Lupick, 2017a).

Paul had lived on and off the Downtown Eastside for about twenty years. When we last checked the British Columbia (B.C.) court services system for criminal and traffic offences under his name, we hit 54 different entries, some going back as far as 1996 (Paul also had 46 entries in civil and family courts). Paul had had encounters with the criminal justice system for most of his adult life, having been charged for several offences including drug possession, drug trafficking, possession and trafficking of illegally obtained property under $5,000, theft under $5,000, driving while his driver's licence was suspended, driving under the influence of drugs, with multiple breaches of bail, probation, and parole orders, for which he was consistently found guilty and typically sentenced to a few months of jail time followed by a probation period.

In 2013, when we first met him, Paul had lived in Vancouver for the last seven years, including the Downtown Eastside. He was regularly using opiates, and on a typical day he spent most of his time at the intersection of Hastings and Main Street, living in front of InSite, the first supervised drug injection site in North America. He frequently visited VANDU, the Vancouver Area Network of Drug Users, a local grassroots organization of drug users and former users committed to give their members a political voice and to make sure they live healthy and meaningful lives (Lupick 2017a).[7] He also sometimes stayed overnight at the New Fountain shelter near Cordova Street.

For Paul, a typical cycle of his many interactions with the police and the criminal justice system goes as follows. One day in April 2013 he was charged with one count of possessing a controlled drug/substance for the purpose of trafficking and two counts of carrying a concealed weapon, prohibited device, or any ammunition. The police officer decided to detain Paul in custody overnight and he was released on bail the following day by a justice of the peace under a recognizance of $500 and a requirement to comply with the following six conditions, including a red zone (condition #2), which encompassed VANDU's offices located at 380 East Hastings (Map 1.2):

1   To keep the peace and be of good behaviour.
2   Not to be within the 300 block of East Hastings Street in the City of Vancouver.

---

[6]   Hopper, 2014.
[7]   See www.vandu.org/. According to Osborn and Small (2006: 71), VANDU's purpose is "changing the circumstances of drug users and challenging the global nightmare of drug prohibition".

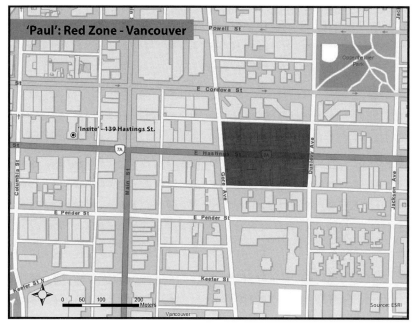

MAP 1.2 Paul's first red zone (Vancouver).
Sources: Esri, HERE, Garmin, USGS, Intermap, INCREMENT P, NRCan, Esri Japan, METI, Esri China (Hong Kong), Esri Korea, Esri (Thailand), NGCC, © OpenStreetMap contributors, and the GIS User Community

3   Not to possess any weapons.
4   Not to possess any knives except for the preparation or consumption of food.
5   Not to possess any firearm or ammunition.
6   Not to possess any cellular phones, pagers, Blackberries, or other wireless handheld devices.

Later the same day, Paul was rearrested in his red zone and charged with two counts of breach of recognizance. After spending the night in remand, he was released on bail under a renewed recognizance of $500 and with the same six conditions plus another:

7   You will upon reasonable request of a police officer submit to a pat down search when found in any public place to determine that you are in compliance with the previous conditions.

Two weeks later, on May 1, 2013, Paul was arrested, detained in custody, and charged with two additional counts of breach and one more count of possession of drug/controlled substance. The justice of the peace renewed his seven conditions and added a curfew:

8 You are to be inside your residence between the hours of 9 p.m. and 6 a.m., seven days per week.

9 You are to present yourself at the door or your residence when any police officer or staff member of the correctional branch is checking up on you for your curfew.

Five days later, on May 6, 2013, Paul was arrested again and charged with two additional counts of breach. By then, Paul resided at InSite,[8] and the justice of the peace changed his conditions to include house arrest and compliance with the rules and regulations of the treatment facility:

6 You are to be inside your residence at all times unless you are accompanied by a member of InSite or such other residence as you may move to.

7 Should you not be at InSite or any other treatment facility, you must be inside your residence between the hours of 9 p.m. and 6 a.m., seven days a week.

9 You are to reside at InSite, 2nd floor, or such other treatment facility that may be approved by your bail supervisor and obey all the rules of that residence.

Finally, on June 21, 2013, he was arrested and charged with his seventh breach of recognizance. On July 17, Paul finally pled guilty to six counts of breach and one count of possession for the purpose of trafficking and he was sentenced to seventeen months and ten days in jail and a lifetime prohibition to carry any weapon. The Crown stayed the remaining five charges.

Two years later, Paul was released from custody. On October 16, 2015, he was rearrested in the Downtown Eastside.

We met with Paul in the spring of 2013 while he was on bail and red zoned from the street corner where he used to live at Main and Hastings. We asked him why he kept coming back to his red zone and he simply replied that it was "because [he] was wired on drugs". "Someone like me," he said, "if you tell me I can't do anything, I'm gonna do it". However, living with a red zone meant always being fearful that the police could stop you, he noted: "You're not so free, you constantly got to wonder if you're going to be arrested that day, if they are going to call you in . . .". While the police sometimes let him go, at

---

[8] InSite has a detox facility on the second floor (called OnSite) and a transitional recovery housing facility on the third floor.

other times they brought him back in custody and to court, making him sick as a result of withdrawal: "Sometimes the cops just take my dope and let me go, but sometimes they hold me overnight or for a couple of days to ... I don't know ... to make me sick or something". Four years before, he told us, the guards beat him while he was in remand: "They pulled me off the top bunk and broke my five, six, seven and eight [ribs]. I had to go in for surgery. I have a rod and screws in my neck. I had to relearn my walk. It's pretty harsh. I have a lawsuit pending with them. But that doesn't look good on my file because when the cops read that I'm suing them it hurts my situations with everything else".

During one of his numerous bail hearings, Paul's lawyer had tried to prevent the imposition of a red zone given that he was living in the area and needed to have access to important resources. The judge, as Paul remembered it, was unforgiving, suggesting that, "I guess he's going to have to move". But what if someone told the judge *he* had to move, Paul mused, on similarly arbitrary grounds: "Your BMW is the wrong colour, you have to move, or whatever". But moving was not such an easy task for Paul, even when putting aside all the drug-related issues. As it turned out, the Vancouver red zone was not the only one on his record. In the past, Paul had also been red zoned from downtown Kelowna and downtown Kamloops, two B.C. cities located within 350 and 400 km of Vancouver respectively. More recently, he had been banned from going to any Money Marts in the province of British Columbia as a result of a theft charge. In the past 20 years, Paul had shuttled through more than ten cities and 14 courthouses in Vancouver and its surroundings, including Victoria, Abbotsford, Surrey, Port Coquitlam, Richmond, Prince George, Revelstoke, and Penticton.

As Paul went through these numerous cycles of fear, pain, and violence, whether in the streets or in the criminal justice system, we were not only struck by the futility and ineffectiveness of his bail conditions in terms of dealing with drug addiction and poverty, but also shocked by their harmful impact on his life. And as the police and the courts carved out new territories from which he was either excluded or confined, pushing him around from one city and one official to the next, we wondered about legal actors' roles in the management and monitoring of poor people who lived in public spaces.

TORONTO, ONTARIO

Now, meet Zora, a young woman arrested on June 26, 2010, during the protests at the G20 Summit held in Toronto. During that period, downtown Toronto became a militarized zone and many civil liberties were suspended.

She was one of the 1,118 persons arrested in the largest mass arrests in Canadian history.

A full-time graduate student, Zora had been involved in a number of anti-poverty projects as well as community activism for many years. She participated in the 2010 anti-Olympics movement in Vancouver and helped organize the anti-G20 in Toronto. On the morning of the 26th, a friend of Zora who had just witnessed the arrest of some common friends at her house warned her that a warrant had been issued under her name and that the police were coming after her. After speaking with a lawyer, Zora decided to turn herself in and was taken to a detention centre.

Zora remained in custody for three weeks before she could secure bail. She was released under nine conditions and a recognizance with sureties of several thousands of dollars. Her conditions originally included that she move out of her student residence and remain under house arrest at a relative's residence, and "be amenable to the rules and discipline of that household", except for a series of circumstances including travelling to receive emergency care, meeting with counsel, attending school, or in the direct company and supervision of sureties. Her conditions of release included a non-association condition with a series of individuals with pending cases, including her own boyfriend, and a "prohibition to attend, participate or help plan any demonstrations" as well as to "possess any wireless telecommunication device" or to use the Internet. Not surprisingly, she felt like she "couldn't be anywhere". Further, her living space started to shrink: confined in a relative's house in Toronto, she felt physically distanced from the city, and ended up not wanting to leave her bedroom.

Zora experienced her bail conditions as extremely punitive. They created a loss of employment, serious physical and mental health problems, feelings of isolation and disconnection, including from her boyfriend with whom she could not communicate, and fear of being watched, followed, and persecuted. Naturally extroverted months after her bail conditions ended, Zora found herself hiding from social interactions. At a political level, the conditions constrained her participation in political and democratic life to the point where she felt she had been "silenced, shut down completely". She even reported that had she had "less trauma response" while being held on remand, and more time to think about it, she would have chosen to do "more jail time to gain less restrictive conditions".

Bail conditions amounted to a severe form of punishment. Importantly, in her case, and that of multiple protesters under similar forms of control, conditions were the only form of punishment, given that she was ultimately released free of criminal charges some 17 months after her arrest when the Attorney General of Ontario concluded an agreement with the defence.

As Zora's political activities were completely neutralized over a significant period of time or as she was confined in her surety's house, however, there were no questions raised by the authorities about the nature and timing of punishment, presumption of innocence, or, more generally, about the role of legal actors in the silencing of democratic voices during highly contested political times.

* * *

This book explains how such punitive consequences are possible. While these three cases are embedded in different contexts and reflect different experiences, they share several commonalities: the nature of the legal instruments involved and their reliance on the criminal process, the role of judicial actors in monitoring marginalized people's behaviour in certain public spaces over extended periods of time, the overarching consequences on the lives and rights of those who use public spaces to live, work, or protest, the relative absence of rights challenges, and the shifting nature of criminal law and punishment.

Martine, Paul, and Zora's experiences of bail and sentencing conditional orders are by no means unique. As we demonstrate, such court-imposed conditions play an increasingly important role in contemporary criminal justice and occupy a significant amount of judicial resources in Canada, where probation is the most common sentence imposed in adult criminal court, and conditional release at bail has become the only available alternative to remand. As a result, these conditions have a far-reaching impact both on poor and marginalized people's lives and rights (e.g. the rights to life, security, liberty, physical and mental health, equality/non-discrimination, as well as fundamental freedoms of expression and association and the right to housing and to a decent income) and on the criminal justice system – in particular as individuals repeatedly breach their conditions and are managed by courts. Specifically, they reveal the significance of conditional orders that rely heavily on the judicial regulation of space and time. The orders direct us to the technicalities of the legal tools involved and their repetitive character, the routinized work of the courts, and the dramatic, often life-threatening consequences on the embodied lives and rights of people subject to them.

Despite their scope and significance, conditional orders have not received the scholarly and policy attention that they deserve. In this, they can be distinguished from better-publicized forms of spatial regulation, such as legislation or policing strategies (Herbert, 1996; Sanchez, 2004; Sylvestre et al., 2015). Most immediately, therefore, our goal is to document, describe, and analyze conditional orders with spatial and temporal dimensions. While marginalized people are all too aware of their presence, reach, and effects, scholars and policy-makers seem largely oblivious to them, noting only their secondary effects, such as the significant growth in the remand population, or misrepresenting them – for example, through anxieties regarding "repeat offenders", who may often simply reflect "repeat breachers" (i.e. those who end up violating their court-imposed conditions).

This book focuses more specifically on four categories of conditions with spatial and temporal dimensions imposed on different groups of marginalized people who use public spaces in Canada's cities, including people who are experiencing homelessness, street-involved sex workers and drug users, and demonstrators.[9] Given this particular focus, the conditions of particular interest include:

(a) *Area restrictions (or "red zones") and "no-go" conditions.* "Area restrictions", more commonly referred to as "red zones" by marginalized people,[10] can take different forms, but they refer to prohibitions to be found within specific perimeters, such as stretches of streets, blocks, place-specific radiuses, and even entire neighbourhoods or cities, whereas "no-go" conditions are targeted bans from specific sites such as parks, restaurants, or bars, supermarkets, or other public or private spaces;

(b) *No-contact/non-association/non-communication conditions* require that people abstain from communicating or getting in touch with a

---

[9] Demonstrators are not primarily or exclusively marginalized for economic reasons, although there are often some overlaps, but we treat them as socially and politically marginal based on their political beliefs and occupation of public spaces. While they occupy public spaces for reasons that are different than those of street populations, they also do so "for purposes that go beyond transit or leisure" (Fortin, 2018: par. 10), and they attract similar punitive responses.

[10] As the title of this book indicates, "red zone" conditions occupy a central position in our study. The exact origins of the colloquial term "red zone" are unknown, although it could be related to their association with sex workers in red light districts in the late 1970s (see Ross, 2010). While during our fieldwork legal actors in both British Columbia and Ontario generally preferred using the term "area restrictions" (see e.g. *R. v. Powis* (1999) BCCA 179), we found several references to "red zone" in B.C. court decisions starting in the 1990s. In these cases, however, the "red zone" refers to a designated zone in specific B.C. cities and not to individualized red zone conditions. The most notorious of such cases is *R. v. Reid* (1999) B.C.P.C. 12, which refers to a designated red zone in the city of Victoria systematically asked for by the federal Crown in every case of trafficking and possession for the purpose of trafficking drugs and "covering most of the downtown, one of the seven square miles that comprises the City of Victoria" (par. 50). See also *R. v. Satterthwaite* (1993) 24 B.C.A.C. 146 (BCCA), *R. v. Harland* (1995) B.C.J. no. 2085 (BCCA), *R. v. Andres* (2006) B.C.P.C. 372 and *R. v. Glendinning* (2018) B.C.S.C. 1575 (all referring to the Kelowna "red zone", "notorious for drug activity"). Interestingly, in Montreal, both marginalized people and court actors refer to area restrictions as "quadrilaterals" from the French word *quadrilatères*, a polygon with four sides, referring to the particular geography of the city of Montreal that follows a grid pattern (see Bellot, 2003 and *R. v. Valbrun* (2005) J.Q. no. 12422 (Q. S.C.), *R. v. Casimir* (2005) J.Q. no. 17170 (Q.S.C.), *R. v. Grandmaison* (2008) Q.C.C.A. 1393, *R. v. Têtu* (2009) QCCS 6549, *R. c. Jensen* (1989) J.Q. no. 625 (Q.C.C.A.) and *R. v. Prud'homme* (2007) QC.C.S. 7103).

complainant, witness, or co-accused; these may also include restrictions on the use of Internet, cell phone, or other communication devices;

(c) *Residential conditions*, including house arrests, fixed address and curfews; and

(d) *Demonstration-related conditions*, such as prohibitions to demonstrate or to participate in certain kinds of demonstrations, meetings, and assemblies (e.g. non-peaceful or illegal assemblies).

We refer to these collectively as territorial conditions. Some of these conditions specifically rely on a geographical area (e.g. red zones or no-go orders, prohibitions to demonstrate in specific areas) or time (e.g. curfews, prohibitions to demonstrate during a certain, often strategic, time, and, more generally, the orders themselves which are time-specific), while others have significant, if sometimes unexpected, spatial and temporal effects (curfews not only prohibit the occupation of public spaces during certain hours, but they also limit the distance one can cover within a single day; no-contact orders, which may require that people abstain from going to certain places during certain times when they are likely to encounter complainants, witnesses, or co-accused, etc.).

The book will suggest that such conditions of release are striking examples of how law, time, and space can combine to create powerful techniques of regulation and governance directed at marginalized people. We will also suggest that the use of conditional orders has enduring systemic effects on the criminal justice system and our understanding of criminal law and punishment, inverting traditional expectations of justice. However, we also argue that this particular type of regulation appears particularly resistant to challenges based on fundamental rights.

LEGAL CONTEXT

In Canadian law, conditions of release, including spatial restrictions, can be generated at different stages of criminal proceedings, by different actors and under various provisions of the Criminal Code of Canada. They can be imposed at both the pre-trial (bail) or post-trial (sentencing) stages. At the pre-trial stage, police officers can impose conditions in a promise to appear delivered to a person after his or her arrest in order to compel his or her appearance in court. Justices of the peace can also issue such conditions as part of bail, while the accused are awaiting trial, based on an agreement between the Crown and the defence, or after a bail hearing.

Judges can also impose conditions post-trial as part of sentencing after the accused pled or was found guilty, in a probation order or a conditional sentence order (CSO), which is a jail sentence served in the community. Alternatively, conditions can be imposed during parole or independently from criminal proceedings in preventive orders to keep the peace following information but independent from criminal charges.

Our particular focus in this book is on court-imposed conditions of release issued at bail and post-sentencing (probation and CSOs). We emphasize the role of legal actors, including prosecutors, defence lawyers, and justices of the peace and judges, as opposed to law enforcement personnel, such as police officers or bail supervisors, in enacting and enforcing conditions of release. Yet, as we will show, the work of the courts is intrinsically intertwined with that of law enforcement, and, as a result, we will also touch upon the legal framework governing arrest and community supervision insofar as it enlightens or constrains the powers of prosecutors and judges. Because of our focus on criminal courts, we have also left aside conditions of release issued in the context of parole as they are imposed and governed following a completely different normative framework and handled by administrative tribunals (i.e. the Parole Board of Canada and provincial parole boards), and have not included preventive orders, although these can also overlap in some context with criminal proceedings.

METHODOLOGY

We draw on a rich and original dataset. This book is grounded in extensive fieldwork conducted primarily in two Canadian cities (Montreal and Vancouver), together with additional interviews in Toronto and Ottawa, with different groups of marginalized people who occupy public spaces, as well as legal actors operating at various stages of criminal proceedings. We used a multidisciplinary (law, geography, and criminology) frame and both qualitative and quantitative analysis.

We first draw from a substantial case law database on bail and sentencing conditions issued to marginalized groups of people (homeless, sex workers, drug users, and protestors) in Canada, comprising approximately 120 cases between 1970 and 2015. This database contains information on the nature of the conditions imposed, their impact, as well as the relative absence of rights claims.

We also conducted fieldwork in Montreal and Vancouver from November 2012 to April 2014, including interviews with individuals subject to court orders and legal actors (including judges, justices of the peace, prosecutors, and defence lawyers), analysis of court records, court observations, and additional secondary sources. In Montreal, interviews were largely conducted in French (translated into English in this text). We also conducted additional interviews in Toronto and Ottawa in the fall of 2013. These additional interviews and court files gave us more information on the nature of conditions used across jurisdictions and their specific impact on individuals' lives and rights. They also allowed us to have a stronger and more diverse sample of demonstrators and street-level drug users/sex workers.

We met with 46 people subject to conditions of release associated with bail or probation through individual interviews or focus groups (12 in Montreal; 18 in Vancouver; 11 in Ottawa; and 5 in Toronto). In Vancouver, Will Damon also interviewed another 18 individuals as part of his MA research (Damon, 2014) and we were able to draw from these data as well. Overall, we reached 64 individuals. We obtained the court records of 22 interviewees across all cities, primarily to ensure the accuracy of their legal trajectory. We also interviewed 18 legal actors (12 in Montreal and 6 in Vancouver) directly involved in the imposition or negotiation of conditions of release and completed over 50 hours of court observations in both cities. Using geographical information systems (GIS), we produced interactive maps for 15 of our participants. These data were produced in the GIS Research Lab at the Department of Geography of the University of Ottawa and maps were drawn at the Department of Geography at Simon Fraser University.

Finally, we obtained extensive quantitative data from the Municipal Court of Montreal and the Justice Information System (JUSTIN) administered by the Court Services Branch of the Ministry of Justice of B.C. documenting all adult criminal court cases either sentenced to probation or a conditional sentence, or cases not necessarily sentenced but granted bail (Vancouver), and data for all adult criminal cases sentenced to a form of probation or a conditional sentence (Montreal). In total, our datasets document over a million conditions of release.

The strength of our methodology lies in its multiple sources and mixed methods allowing for triangulation (Mertens and Hesse-Biber, 2012). For instance, interviews provide confirmation of a more systematic phenomenon (issuance of bail and probation conditions) that we are able to document in quantitative terms through our datasets and case law analysis, while also adding some qualitative background and details. Moreover, court files ensure accuracy and validity to the interviews.

The disparities between our two case studies in terms of numbers and individuals interviewed are related to access issues in each city. For instance, in Vancouver, we tried to get access to the Vancouver Police Department, the Provincial Crown Prosecutors, and to Correctional Services, but were unsuccessful. In Montreal, after lengthy negotiations, the Provincial Crown prosecutors also refused to participate in our study.

Our focus is on the Canadian experience. However, we also bring together resources from other jurisdictions, notably Great Britain and the U.S.A., in order to point to comparable processes. Our book thus speaks to patterns of punishment and governance that go beyond the confines of Canada. Indeed, we hope that our conclusions will not only be relevant to scholars and students in other countries for comparison purposes, but also that they will stimulate a wider, systemic, and urgently needed conversation about an under-examined phenomenon in the criminal law.

If our immediate goal is to document the form, scope, and effects of the hitherto poorly documented issue of conditional orders issued in criminal proceedings, our second aim in this book is to make sense of the spatiality and temporality of these conditions. In order to understand their complex and often contradictory effects, their uptake by legal actors, as well as their apparent immunity from rights-based critiques, we argue that it helps to conceptualize these court orders as forms of territorialization – that is, the strategic attempt to govern people and social and political relationships by asserting control over a certain spatiotemporal configuration (Sack, 1983; Herbert, 1997; Brighenti, 2006).

While "territory" may appear as a predominantly spatial concept, it is only because scholarship has too often been oblivious to the ways in which temporalization affects spatialization, and vice versa (Valverde, 2015). While conditions of release are clearly spatial tactics (Low and Lawrence-Zúñiga, 2003; Sylvestre et al., 2015), they also rely on and organize time, we demonstrate. Time and space are, of course, closely intertwined (Massey, 2004; Braverman et al., 2014; Valverde, 2015). In fact, we cannot distinguish between governance processes that spatialize and those that temporalize (Valverde, 2015: 33). Conditional orders have important temporal dimensions that are intrinsically related to their spatiality. For instance, technically speaking, geographical restrictions often include time (e.g. when combined with curfews) and are of limited duration. They are connected to the timespace of surveillance (policing and the streets) and of incarceration (Moran, 2015). Further, on a systemic level, marginalized people are managed over time through their engagement with the criminal justice system.

While territories are important regulatory tools, however, they are not absolutely imposed on marginalized people. They are resisted and subject to interpretation and negotiation through everyday practices and interactions with the police and legal actors. In this book, we thus attend to map both the quotidian and systemic space/time relations produced by law and legal actors to regulate how marginalized people use public spaces.

ROADMAP

The book is divided in three parts.

In Part I – *Foundations*, we situate these conditional orders in theoretical and historical terms.

In Chapter 2, we establish the theoretical and conceptual grounds on which our study lies, arguing that we can usefully conceive of spatial conditions of release through the lens of critical legal geography, emphasizing the work of law in producing powerful spatiotemporal arrangements and representations that act upon the social world. We characterize spatial conditions of release as a form of legal territorialization, or a strategic attempt at structuring socio-legal relations through the configuring of space and time. By territorializing a set of legal commands, we suggest, legal actors aim to communicate, classify, enforce, and legitimize. Focusing on the practical work of spatial conditions of release directs us to the work they do in organizing socio-legal relations. In particular, we note the complex and simultaneous relational work of "cutting" and "joining" they entail. Red zones, for example, "cut" alleged offenders from particular spatial-temporal contexts, "joining" them up to legal networks of oversight and control. Such cuts and joins, however, often violently act on the lived bodies of people such as Zora, Paul, and Martine.

Chapter 3 delves into the historical context surrounding the ancient practices of bail and the origins of probation, as well as contemporary developments in Canada, the U.S.A., and the U.K. We delve in to the "antiquities of bail" (De Haas, 1940) and the origins of probation in order to contextualize and understand better the legal framework that govern them today. In particular, we trace the history of judicially imposed conditions of release, trying to identify how and when they came to be included in bail and sentencing practices. We find that in order to trace the origins of conditions of release and of their intricate connection with the regulation of the poor, one has to follow the history of another important instrument of law enforcement, namely recognizances to keep the peace and peace bonds.

This historical incursion allows us to make a series of observations with respect to conditions of release, laying the foundations for arguments developed later in the book. First, recognizances did not apply to everyone; the governing class typically used them to control the poor and migrants coming into town. Highly versatile and discretionary, these evolving bail and sentencing practices have primarily developed to reflect state interests and territories instead of protecting individual rights and liberties. Imposed as an alternative to another space and territory, the prison, conditions of release have finally never completely escaped its shadow. This chapter thus shows how legal actors have throughout the history of English common law used the criminal process to create and enforce territories, directly governing people's uses of spaces.

Part II – *Expansion* focuses on the shifting terrain of criminal justice management and how conditions of release contribute to the expansion and transformation of the criminal justice system.

In Chapter 4, we explore recent trends in the administration of justice, using our extensive court data from Montreal and Vancouver. This chapter also provides the opportunity to explain in some detail the current legal framework governing bail and community sentences in Canada and contrast it with legal practices. The data reveal the widespread prevalence of conditions of release at all stages of criminal proceedings, including at bail, where they should by law be exceptional. Spatial restrictions are among the most frequent conditions imposed. These, in turn, generate numerous breaches, which constitute criminal offences against the administration of justice. In fact, failures to comply with a bail order and breaches of probation orders have been the top two most common offences in adult criminal courts for at least a decade in Canada, amounting to approximately 25 per cent of all criminal cases. Echoing the concept of "net widening" (Cohen, 1979; 1985), we suggest that conditions of release have thus directly contributed to a form of "judicial territory widening". First, such breaches have led to the enlargement of the criminal justice system, increasing the courts' workload as legal actors have been involved in manufacturing crime (Murphy, 2009) and expanding the boundaries of their own jurisdiction. Secondly, bail, probation, and even conditional sentences, initially conceived as alternatives to incarceration, have gradually become the norm and a supplement to other punitive measures, increasing the criminal justice system's grip on marginalized populations.

In Chapter 5, we show that conditions of release have also contributed to the transformation of the criminal justice system into a self-perpetuating *disposition* system (Feeley, 1992 [1979]) with managerial and preventive characteristics (Kohler-Hausmann, 2018; Ashworth and Zedner, 2014). Through a particular strategy of territorialization, i.e. by imposing stringent and unrealistic conditions of release against the backdrop of incarceration to marginalized people who then repeatedly breach them, the criminal justice system has created a self-generating cycle of surveillance and institutional recidivism. This transformation, we suggest, displays and relies upon a specific spatiality and temporality that departs from more traditional expectations of justice. For instance, justice and power have now shifted to the streets, with judges and lawyers losing authority over justices of the peace and police officers with

often-unchecked discretionary powers. The pace of criminal justice administration is also particular, characterized by both speedy interactions in courts
and long-time supervision. Finally, the process becomes more circular than
linear as individuals are brought back to the courts for continuously breaching
their conditions. The same can be said about punishment, which is sometimes administered at the pre-trial stage in a bail order without being labelled
or recognized as such, only to be extended through interchangeable probation
orders. These changes directly impact marginalized peoples' rights and their
possibilities to resist legal violence.

Part III – *Territorialization and Its Consequences* presents both how court
orders are enacted and shaped and how they are lived, perceived, and resisted.

Chapter 6 explores the institutional context in which the work of territorialization is performed, its rationale, and its relational logic of cutting and
joining. We first introduce the context in which conditions of release are
imposed and how legal actors practically choose and design these conditions,
relying on internalized institutional norms and practices as well as information
on the interactions between the accused and the spaces where the offence is
(allegedly, at first) committed.

We then present the competing state interests pursued by different legal
actors (from the police to Crown prosecutors and judges) during the criminal
process. We focus particularly on the shifting rationalities of bail. According to
the law, bail must pursue one of three principal objectives. We show that legal
actors insist on the first two, namely ensuring the accused's presence in court,
and, most importantly, crime prevention and the likelihood that the accused
will reoffend regardless of the offence. However, there are also new interests
and rationalities at play, including therapeutic and policing issues related to
the surveillance and monitoring of marginalized populations and the neutralization of political dissenters. Moreover, the fact that legal actors consider
conditions of release as the only alternative to incarceration plays a crucial role
in their imposition. This chapter illustrates how legal actors mobilize both
space and time to achieve their different goals.

In Chapters 7 and 8, we argue that the lived impact of these orders is often
overwhelming, affecting marginalized peoples' (Chapter 7) and demonstrators' (Chapter 8) lives at many levels (Beckett and Herbert, 2010a; b). The
spatial and temporal dimensions of these orders are particularly consequential.
By spatially and temporally isolating the individuals subject to such orders,
orders put people's safety, security, and lives at risk, impede successful reintegration, and create further social and economic barriers and constraints for
individuals who are already socially and economically marginalized (McNeil
et al., 2015; Sylvestre, Bernier, and Bellot, 2015). Certain court orders are

imposed in a temporal fashion as they neutralize individuals who challenge the social and political order during political events or provide temporary relief to a community, and they tend to ramp up over time (Sprott, 2015). The restrictions are compounded when an individual is forced to comply with multiple conditions, at multiple places, simultaneously and over time. We conclude this part in suggesting that there is an important and often unacknowledged mismatch between the legal orders and the lived experience of street people.

In the conclusion, we discuss avenues of reforms. After a summary of our most important contributions, we make specific proposals to change legal practices and discuss why red zones and conditions of release have become such a rights-free zone despite the enormous consequences on people's lives.

PART I

Foundations

2

Law and Territory: A Legal Geography

In order to understand the red zone, and spatial conditions of release, we draw from the insights of critical legal geography. Legal geography is a flourishing interdisciplinary intellectual project (Forest, 2009; Braverman et al., 2014). It not only poses the reciprocal influences of law and space (e.g. law shapes our understanding and experiences of certain spaces and, conversely, geography and space account for evolving legal norms) but it also emphasizes that it is often difficult, indeed impossible, to analyze these two dimensions of social life independently, given their intrinsic interconnections (Blomley, 2003). Legal phenomena are always situated: they play out in a spatial context that is highly consequential in legal terms. The ways in which legal actors assess and understand certain spaces play a key role in the determination of facts and their legal characterization (Blomley and Bakan, 1992). Space is not an inert surface, but is actively constituted by legal institutions and practices (Braverman et al., 2014).

The question of power is central to critical legal geography, and in particular the insight that legal practice routinely encodes and organizes space in ways that both structure and conceal oppressive relations of power. As Soja puts it, "We must be insistently aware of how space can be made to hide consequences from us, how relations of power and discipline are inscribed into the apparently innocent spatiality of social life, how human geographies become filled with politics and ideology" (1989: 6). The spatializations, or "splices" of law (Blomley, 2003), are not simply an outcome of such power relations: in other words, but are a means through which legal power is realized, on the principle that "spatiality makes a difference to the effects that power can have" (Allen, 1999: 212).

While there is a modernist tendency to view space as abstract and prepolitical, "as the dead, the fixed, the undialectical, the immobile" (Foucault, 1980: 70), we argue for its lively and consequential politics. Most immediately, space is a resource through which we encode the world, allowing us to differentiate between things, people, and practices, including the process of territorialization whereby:

> [w]e draw a line, we establish an inside and an outside, a this side and a that side: we assign a set of If ... Thens to precise locations with respect to the line or to the act of crossing the line ... Through acts of spatial dichotomization, we thereby project a sense of clarity and certainty onto events, onto situations, onto social relationships, onto the play of power in the world.
>
> (Delaney, 2010: 138)

Such spatial classifications structure a normative landscape, constituting beliefs about what is appropriate by virtue of where something is, what is "in place" and "out of place", like the homeless person who sleeps in the "public" park. Space does much of our thinking for us. As such, the power to specify the meanings of space is profound. However, as with law, the work of space is hard to see, by virtue of the way in which it is imagined. As with law, there is a closure to space: it is imagined as an abstract and prepolitical surface, "a world of passivity and measurement" that is deemed separate from society (Soja, 1989: 37).

LAW AND THE REGULATION OF MARGINALIZED PEOPLE

The spatiality of law takes many forms (Ford, 1999). Of importance to our project, critical scholars and activists have long noted the manner in which the legal regulation of marginalized populations has entailed the strategic use of space, whether in the form of discretionary restrictions, zoning, or design tools. This is evident within criminology and geography on the spatiality of crime and criminal justice (e.g. Crawford, 2010; Hayward, 2012). For example, the police routinely use informal forms of territorial control in their management of inner-city populations (Herbert, 1997). In efforts to locate, surround, or isolate street sex work, they sometimes tolerate soliciting in red light districts while preventing it from moving to upper-class neighbourhoods (Hubbard and Sanders, 2003; Matthews, 2005). The police further rely on displacement strategies, ranging from orders to disperse (Crawford, 2008; Walby and Lippert, 2012) to transportation out of town, and sweeps to move on vagrants, while adopting containment techniques, such as the creation of hard and soft zones where protesters are prevented from accessing the target of their grievances, free-speech zones where protests can legally occur (Gilham, 2011; Gilham, Edwards, and Noakes, 2013), the resort to "kettles" (police surrounding protesters), mass arrests, and the erection of fences (Starr and Fernandez, 2009; Dupuis-Déri, 2013) to control demonstrators.

In turn, local authorities rely on different forms of spatial banishment or segregation in order to manage the homeless (Mitchell, 1997; Wacquant, 2008) or to inhibit protests and limit traffic disruption (Fernandez, 2008; Blomley, 2010). For instance, municipalities have tried to control street sex work and window working through increased renting fees (Hubbard and Sanders, 2003), or confining body rub parlours and escort services through zoning or licensing restrictions (Craig, 2011; Matthews, 2005). Cities have also embarked on revitalization programs (Caldeira, 2000; Lippert, 2007; Ross, 2010), urban planning initiatives, and architectural changes, including the redesigning of subway stations (Duneier, 2000), the closing of public places, and changes to street furniture (Davis, 1990), as well as the enforcement of by-laws regulating public order and safety to control activities performed in parks, sidewalks, and streets (Sylvestre, 2010a). Don Mitchell (1997) argues that the result is often the "annihilation of space by law" via the adoption by many U.S. cities of "a legal remedy that seeks to cleanse the streets of those left behind by globalization ... by simply erasing the spaces in which they must live" (305).

In order to withstand constitutional scrutiny, the tendency has been to use more finely tuned "time, place, and manner" regulations rather than blanket bans that criminalize activities or status (Esmonde, 2002; Zick, 2006; Beckett and Herbert, 2010b). As such, spatial tactics are often (though not always) reliant on the designation of specific spaces as off-limits to particular actions, at certain times. Examples include the use of "protest pens" allowing protestors to gather only at designated locations (McPhail McCarthy, and Martin, 2004; Zick, 2006; Gilham, 2011), prostitution-free zones (Sanchez, 2004) in many U.S. cities, or public drinking exclusion zones in the U.K. (DeVerteuil, May, and von Mahs, 2009; Johnsen and Fitzpatrick, 2007). In the Canadian context, they also include the adoption of by-laws limiting protest material, regulating face coverings, or requiring that protesters submit their route to the police for approval beforehand (Fernandez, 2008; Dupuis-Déri, 2013), as well as statutes regulating panhandling by prohibiting it in designated zones, such as at bus stops, or bank machines (Hermer and Mosher, 2002; Collins and Blomley, 2003; O'Grady, Gaetz, and Buccieri, 2013).

Of particular relevance to our focus, some scholars have finally begun to focus on "individualized spatializations" (Moore, Freeman, and Krawczyk, 2011: 168), noting that spatial tactics do not only focus on specific places or populations, but also on individuals. In an important article, Merry (2001) was among the first to discuss the development of temporary restraining orders in domestic violence cases in the U.S. in the 1970s. She noted how this legal mechanism was embedded in everyday criminal and civil processes and practices and exposed some of the difficulties raised by this (then) unusual type of intervention for the courts, including the lack of legal representation and legal guarantees given the civil nature of the order, their limited enforceability, and the possibility of being charged with a misdemeanour punishable by a jail sentence or a fine in case of violation of the conditions of the protective order. More recently, Moore et al. (2011) documented the use of geographical restrictions imposed at bail in several Canadian drug treatment courts, focusing specifically on legal actors' representations of certain urban spaces known for drug use or vending as bad or unhealthy, and Turnbull and Hannah-Moffat (2009) analyzed the impact of house residency conditions imposed to offenders under parole. Yet this scholarship is scarce and largely limited to a specific set of measures (e.g. Munn, 2011 on parole conditions or MacDonald, 2012 on bail conditions) or to a specific context, such as specialized courts (e.g. Hannah-Moffat and Maurutto, 2012). It also fails to consider the importance and effects of the legal context in which these orders are embedded.

We seek to contribute to and advance this literature. While there has been a great deal of scholarship on the specific role of the police and of legislatures in regulating public spaces, very little has been written on the ways in which courts and legal actors working within the criminal justice system (e.g. judges, justices of the peace, prosecutors, and defence lawyers) contribute, directly or indirectly, to the production of spatial governance (Sylvestre et al., 2015).

TERRITORIALIZATION

In order to reflect legal actors' active role in the production of space, we choose to focus on the particular role of territorialization in criminal law. We argue that it helps to conceptualize court orders as territories, that is as imagined spatiotemporal configurations strategically enacted by legal actors in order to regulate people and social and political relationships (Sack, 1983; Herbert, 1997; Brighenti, 2006).[1] We define a territory as a bounded space that

---

[1] Beckett and Herbert (2010a: 18) trace the combined effect of off-limits orders, parks exclusions ordinances, and trespass admonishments in Seattle, it being argued that the combined effect is "resolutely territorial: they attempt to remove perceived disorder from particular geographic locations". They also trace the contingent history of such spatial tactics, as well as the manner in which they frequently combine civil and criminal law in overlapping ways, the effect very often being to diminish due process rights. Beckett and Herbert's account is closer to our own

inscribes powerful meanings – in particular, related to spatial access or exclusion – onto defined segments of the world (Delaney, 2005: 14). We view it as a
social and political construct, serving to organize, enforce, and communicate
a set of social and political relations within a determined space (Paasi, 2003).
Territory is thus far from a self-evident or pre-given object. Territory can be
understood as a "bounded space", put another way, only if "'boundaries' and
'space' are taken as terms worthy of investigation in their own right as a
preliminary step" (dell'Agnese 2013; Elden, 2010: 13).

As such, we resist the prevalent tendency to view space simply as a topo-
graphical surface. Rather we follow a productive line of thinking that invites us
to think of the social through a relational lens (Emirbayer, 1997; Dépelteau,
2018). Rather than substantialist thinking that deals in essences, or "things"
first and their subsequent relations second, relational thinking begins from the
presumption that "the units involved in a transaction derive their meaning,
significance, and identity from the (changing) functional roles they play
within that transaction. The latter, seen as a dynamic, unfolding process,
becomes the primary unit of analysis rather than the constituent elements
themselves" (Emirbayer, 1997: 287). From this perspective, "entities take their
form and acquire their attributes as a result of their relations with other
entities" (Law, 1999: 3). A city or a place, from this perspective, is best thought
of not as a singular detached unit of space but as the product of connections
that may extend beyond a particular site. Places are not an enclosure, with a
clear inside or outside, but "articulated networks of social relations and
understanding" (Massey, 1991: 28). The same injunction applies to territory.
Rather than thinking of territory simply as a bounded and homogenous unit of
geographical space, we think of it as inherently relational. Following Painter
(2010), territory can be thought of as "the effect of networked relations" (1093)
or as a "portion of relational space" (dell'Agnese 2013). However, it can easily
become imagined in social action and consciousness as an actionable unit of
space through a process of abstraction (Paasi, 2003), reliant on particular
modernist conceptions of space (Elden, 2005). Territory's relationality, in
other words, can easily disappear from view.

Territory is a product of relations, but also a means by which relations are
organized. Territory is thus relational in a second sense. The territory of the

in some regards. However, it should be noted that the three legal forms they focus on are all
recent innovations rather than routinized forms of criminal law. Apart from trespass
admonishment, they all apply, moreover, as sentencing conditions, or as conditions of
probation or parole, rather than as pre-trial measures, as in our case.

red zone can be thought of as a "legal technology" (Paasi, 2003; Bryan 2012) that aims to establish a particular "economy of bodies, objects and places" (Brighenti, 2006: 65). Territory is, in this sense, fundamentally strategic (Sack, 1983). Once territories take shape, are communicated and enforced, they help to regulate who is included or denied access to a specific space and by whom. It is easy to think about the spatial effects of red zones and other conditions of release in those terms. Judicially imposed and enforced, conditional orders have a direct impact on individuals' use of public spaces, restraining access to resources and prohibiting certain types of behaviour within those spaces. Conditions are also connected to other territories, such as the streets, the courtroom, remand centres or prisons, which all yield different relations of power (Moran, 2015).

Power relations, of course, can be expressed and realized in many ways. If, as Allen (1999: 212) argues, spatiality "makes a difference" to the workings of power, then it may follow that to territorialize is to configure power in a particular manner. Following Sack (1983), we argue that territory is a highly efficient resource in the organization of legal power. First, territory involves classification, signalling when a thing or a person is out of bounds, reliant on a sharp inside/outside distinction. Territories are also useful communication tools, inscribing desired behaviour within or outside their boundaries. Thirdly, by territorializing a set of relations between people, and making power visible, forms of control become easier to enforce, on the assumption that boundaries are clearly defined.[2] Moreover, to the extent that territories, as a form of spatialization, may appear neutral, inert, and empty (Zick, 2006), their use may serve to deflect attention from the relationship between the controller and the controlled and to displace it to an apparently impersonal relationship in which territory itself appears to be the source of control. Extending Cresswell, territories "appear to have their own rules, not the rules constructed for them" (1996: 159). This is relevant in relation to the depoliticization of conditions of release.

In this sense, conditional court orders issued in the context of criminal proceedings work through and depend on a territorial logic based on:

---

[2] Territory's role in enforcing legal power is longstanding. Sextus Pomponius was a second-century Roman jurist, whose definition of territory is included in the *Corpus Juris Civilis*, the codification of Roman law undertaken by Justinian in the sixth century: "The word 'territory' means all the land included within the limits of any city. Some authorities hold that it is so called, because the magistrates have a right to inspire fear within its boundaries, that is to say, the right to remove the people" (*Digest*, L.xvi:239(8), quoted in Painter, 2010: 1102).

(a) classification: in particular, a sharp inside/outside distinction (e.g. "Not to be within the 300 block of E Hastings");

(b) communication: the space is intended to generate clear meanings to their subjects, such as Zora or Paul, or those charged with enforcing them, such as the police, even though, as we shall see, there may in fact be a great deal of ambiguity in the interpretation of the exact boundaries of such territories. We will also note later that such spatial restrictions are intended to send a message to businesses and local residents affected by criminal activity;

(c) enforcement and law-making: boundaries condition people's engagements with the state via embodied presence in relation to the in/out binary provided by the boundaries, such that physical presence serves as an indicator of legal conformity. In that sense, territorialization becomes potentially law-making. For instance, while occupying public space or consuming alcohol are not criminal offences, they become so within a designated space or during certain hours. Further, while police officers do not have the power to arrest and search someone for merely being in public spaces, they gain such powers within the red zone. In doing so, they create overlapping zones of regulation that can be triggered.

(d) displacement: the governance of territory, of course, entails the governance of the person. However, the effect of focusing on the former is to make the latter less overt. Power "is immanent to territory, and it is precisely this power that territory can obfuscate". (Clare et al., 2018: 4)

TIME AND TERRITORY

Conditions of release are clearly a spatial tactic. In what follows, we shall document the manner in which those who craft legal territories rely upon and imagine space in particular ways in the hope of fulfilling a range of legal objectives. Importantly, this process is embedded within a particular set of legal geographies, such as the enforcement priorities of the police, or the particular architecture of the courtroom. As seen in our opening cases, the territorialization of legal actors often collides with the lived geographies of the poor and dissenting with devastating effects. Spaces of imagined improvement can easily become carceral spaces (Moran, 2015).

Yet our analysis is incomplete if we fail to recognize the manner in which legal territories simultaneously seek to organize time. Conditions of release are time-specific (bail orders are in force pending trial, probation orders can last for a maximum of three years) or activated only at certain times (e.g. curfews).[3] They are also timely (used during strategic times, for instance, to neutralize protesters or to deal with a specific problem in an inner city neighbourhood such as the West End of Vancouver in the late 1970s or the Downtown Eastside afterwards (Ross, 2010). Designed to inculcate forms of behaviour, such as abstaining from drug use or political protest, conditions rely on the assumption that behaviour can change over time and thus requires repeated correction (Crawford, 2015). They are often forward oriented (rehabilitative and preventive – regulating offences that may not have happened) but can also be backward oriented (focusing on problematic areas or hot spots). In that sense, the temporality of the red zone produces and supposes judicial temporality.

Legal actors work on different temporalities that are reflected in their use of court orders. The police may work in a more immediate, present, conflict-solving temporality, whereas courts and prosecutors may be more concerned about long-term change (as expressed in recidivism rates, for instance). This is also true of criminal law institutions more generally. While bail has historically been understood as imposing temporary measures to ensure that someone appears in court, with increasing court delays, bail is now sometimes used to induce permanent change over time (from the perspective of judges and prosecutors) or to show that such change has indeed occurred and will endure (from the perspective of a defence lawyer). Bail is also used to shorten court delays and induce guilty pleas, giving greater importance (and thus, space) to pre-trial procedures over lengthy trials where the pace is different (faster).

It is necessary therefore to think of conditions of release in spatiotemporal terms. In so doing, we draw from a small but important set of arguments that seek to extend legal geography so as to include a simultaneous recognition of time, as well as space, to legal practice (Braverman et al., 2014). Time and space are, of course, closely intertwined. Yet, mostly for the sake of maintaining disciplinary boundaries, they have rarely been analyzed jointly in the literature (Valverde, 2015). Space and time are not just a backdrop against which socio-legal relations

---

[3] Interestingly, some of the earliest judicial recordation of area restrictions imposed in Vancouver were also time specific. See *R. v. Melnyk* (1974) 19 C.C.C. (2d) 311 (B.C.S.C.): "not to be found at any time during the night time, namely, after 6:00 p.m. or before 9:00 a.m. in the downtown area of Vancouver, namely the waterfront to the North, Stanley Park to the West, the extensions of False Creek to the South and Commercial Drive to the East"; and *R. v. Deuffoure*, BCSC (1979): "not to be found in an area bounded by Seymour Street, Robson Street, Thurlow Street and Burrard Inlet between the hours of 8:00 p.m. and 5:00 a.m." During the period 1975–1985, sex workers and marginalized populations were forcibly relocated from Vancouver West End to the Downtown Eastside (DTES) through by-law enforcement and red zoning (Ross, 2010).

are played out, but are produced by and productive of such practices and relations. Modern forms of social life and governance, for example, are reliant not only upon the organization of space, but also of time, such as the role of clock-time in disciplinary societies (Thompson, 1967; Foucault, 1977). Yet, like space, time under modernity is seen as objective and external to human experience (Adam, 1990; Lefebvre and Nicholson-Smith, 1991).

As such, we suggest that critical legal geography can no longer exclude the politics of time (Klinke, 2012; 2013) into its analysis of the law and power nexus. Here we can learn from a small but significant body of scholarship that recognizes the importance of time – more accurately, cultural conceptions of time, or "social time" (Greenhouse, 1989) – to legal practice. This includes the recognition that law produces and organizes multiple conceptions of time, in relation to and in tension with other non-legal temporalities (Mawani, 2015; French, 2001; Douzinas, 2006; Khan, 2009). The common law, for example, situates law within a temporality of antiquity, custom, and the immemorial. Greenhouse (1989) notes the centrality of linear time to Western legal practice, while also noting other temporalities at work as it also perpetually reclaims the past for the present through the use of precedent. The coding of time may also prove important in legal regulation, including its technicalities (Grabham 2016). Wiber (2014) explores the legal governance of the fishery, noting the presence of "multiple chronometers" operating at different tempos. She argues that controlling the tempo of regulatory change is as much a locus of struggle as the content of regulation. In reflecting on the lived experience of incarceration, Moran (2012) concludes that "timespace" is a useful tool for the "understanding of what incarceration is, which I would contend cannot adequately be achieved by focusing either on time, or on space, in isolation" (313).

However, the danger of such accounts, as Valverde (2015) points out, is that they can lead, unwittingly, to sustaining the binary divide between time and space. Rather than adding time to an already existing spatial analysis, we thus need to explore how different legal times create or shape legal spaces, and vice versa: how space "thickens" time, as Valverde (2015) puts it. This is useful in thinking of criminal law. Valverde (2015) notes the different ways in which local communities are imagined in crime fiction. Conventional police pro-cedurals often position a criminal event as a spatiotemporal shock, an unex-pected event disturbing an inherently safe and static space, that can be repaired by effective police intervention that will return to its natural state of peace and repose that is assumed to be inherent to this local community scale once the murderer is revealed, and removed. It is also instructive to think of the related semiotic work of the "breach" committed by those who violate conditions of release in violation of the maintenance of the "peace" in this light (Goodrich, 1990). As we shall suggest in Chapter 5, Lindsay Farmer also makes a compelling case for the need to think through "the neglected issues of the temporal and spatial logics that underlie the modern criminal law, and how the spatial and temporal boundaries set out in law help to construct social and political hierarchies" (2010: 336).

It is in these terms, perhaps, that we can begin to think of legal territories as simultaneously spatial and temporal. However, "little has been done to develop the temporal aspects of territoriality", notes Kärrholm (2017: 684), arguing that just as territory organizes space, it also defines times. In particular, territories, such as red zones, are created according to temporal periods and rhythms (Brighenti, 2006; Prior and Hubbard, 2017).

CUTTING AND JOINING AND THE BODIES OF LAW

To bring a spatiotemporal analysis to territory, it is useful to focus on how conditions of release, as a form of territorialization, work. In so doing, we consider territory "as an achievement, not a given; something that is actively produced and practised, relative rather than absolute, in its geometry" (Allen, 2011: 286), or as an act or event rather than a space. As such, it becomes crucial to ask how territory is constructed and experienced. If, as argued above, legal territories, such as the red zone and other conditions of release, are strategies or technologies, we can expect that they aim to organize, enforce, communicate, and legitimize a set of legal relations of power. Just as political action entails relational connection and disconnection, we argue that it may be useful to think of the work of territory as attempts at simultaneously *cutting* and *joining* socio-legal relations.

This rests on the argument that if all entities are embedded in a network of relations (Emirbayer, 1997), calculation and action depend on the provisional severance of such relations (Strathern, 1996). A network without distinctions and stops is unlimited: cuts in the network help organize relations and render them manageable. Certain relations are necessarily foregrounded, and made visible, while others are backgrounded. A frame, or bracket, establishes a boundary within which interactions "take place more or less independently of their surrounding context" (Callon, 1998b: 249), demarcating those relationships which are to be considered in any calculation, and those which are to be ignored.

Endemic to all social practice, bracketing takes on a particular importance within legal practice (Blomley, 2014a). The ability to disentangle from the "ever-tangled skein of human affairs" (Langdell 1871: vi) is endemic to legal practice. Messy urban conflicts involving homelessness, for example, that social justice activists insist be framed as entangled in poverty, ethics, social exclusion, and citizenship, may be tidily repackaged by judges as disputes over jurisdiction (Blomley, 2012). Spatial or temporal particularities may be erased in pursuit of a universal space of equality.

For legal actors, as we shall see, conditions of release are designed to construct boundaries that are both spatial and temporal, creating a space (inside/outside a red zone) and a time (before/after). Territorialization is here intended to cut a set of relations, embodied as physical presence and movement. Thus Paul is not to be physically present at any time on the 300 block of East Hastings Street while his bail order is in effect, and is to be in his residence at designated hours. The red zone constitutes legal space, designating permissions and prohibitions. Judges, as we shall see in Chapter 6, make such distinctions in order to physically remove alleged offenders from designated spaces at particular times, on the assumption that severance (from access to drugs, from the "temptations" that may induce theft, from legally identified people, from strategic sites of protests) will foster conformity or dispersal. In removing a person from a designated space, the red zone thus relies on a series of other conceptual cuts, "bracketing" those subject to them in an individualizing and often decontextualized manner. The multiple, overlapping relational connections – chemical, familial, communal – that tie people to places are often conceptually severed. Treated as singular moments, conditions of release often downplay or efface personal histories. Framed through the powerful bracket of "criminal law", other frames – poverty, colonialism, intergenerational trauma – are also marginalized.

In that sense, while a cut "puts the outside world in brackets ... it does not actually abolish all links with it" (Callon, 1998a: 249). Any bracket, Callon (1998a) notes, is necessarily subject to "overflowing". As Goffman (1974) notes, the performance of a play entails a careful set of frames (the suspension of disbelief, for example), but it would not work were it not for a set of prior expectations outside the cut: "Cutting is thus a corollary of connection and a condition for the existence of relations" (Myhre, 2013: 10). The red zone cuts and connects at the same time. The order banning Zora to have contact with designated persons only works to the extent that it is hooked up to a network of legal relations and obligations. Some of these are cultural – for example, the idea that the violation of a legal command is morally inappropriate – while others are institutional, such that presence in a designated space at a designated time, if observed, triggers a breach, with legal consequences.

Territory, as a form of legal infrastructure, thus has the effect of arranging spatiotemporal relations, cutting some in order to join others. A red zone seeks to remove a person from a space for a designated time, in order to remove them from a constellation of relations deemed legally problematic, or to allow other community relations to flourish by providing temporary relief to neighbouring residents. In so doing, it plugs that person into a network of legal relations, including future appearances, with the possibility of new cuts, including preventive detention for failure. One consequence, all too often, is that people become locked into repeated cycles of carceral control, a condition neatly captured by the spatiotemporal metaphor of the "revolving door". Already designated a legal subject, as an alleged or proven offender, conditions of release also have the effect of inserting a person into dense data infrastructures, available to legal actors such as the police and probation officers.

Cutting and joining are endemic to all social practice. However, not everyone gets to create legal territories that stick. Just as a legal trial is a struggle to impose a "principle of legitimized distribution" (Bourdieu, 1985: 729), so it is clear that only designated legal actors, by virtue of their social power, are able to mobilize territorial cuts and joins. But this entails hard, practical work. Brighenti (2006) suggests that territorial boundary-making poses a series of questions: (1) who is drawing the line; (2) how is it made; (3) what kind of drawing is performed; (4) why is the drawing made? Cuts and joins are made, not found. We thus trace the technical way in which legal actors cut and join, and the crucial spatiotemporal contexts within which they occur, including the negotiations between various actors (e.g. defence counsel and Crown prosecutors) and the assumptions that they make in cutting and joining (for example, that the conditions are reasonable and legible, or do not unduly "cut" alleged offenders from important resources, or that the entire enterprise is not to be "joined" to the domain of rights).

As a form of legal technology, conditions of release thus operate within a particular institutional envelope. They are calibrated to work within a particular economy. Put another way, they assume a type of society in which they would fit (Cloatre and Wright, 2012). They are expected to align to other forms of legal power. They rest on certain representations of urban spaces, associated with drug use and criminality, and are thus deemed bad and unhealthy (Moore, 2011). However, we shall suggest, the cuts and joins of the red zone – intentionally or otherwise – overflow their institutional bounds. As we shall see, such cuts, imagined by legal actors as surgical, are often catastrophic for those subject to them, removing them from valued relational networks of resources and support. The neat cartographic distinctions of the red zone, reliant on naive conceptions of rational actors moving through criminogenic landscapes, confronts dense lived geographies of addiction, poverty, and radically constrained choices. Joining people up to legal networks, imagined by legal actors as a form of beneficent regulation, can easily escape these parameters, placing already vulnerable bodies into situations of enhanced violence and risk.

The spatiotemporal conditions under which their conditions of release are produced, we note, also play an important role. The conditions factory is highly bureaucratic and routinized, we demonstrate, subject to austerity-driven underfunding and institutional pressures to speed up processing times. One consequence, however, is that it is easy to overlook the manner in which cutting and joining act upon bodies. Put another way, if red zones entail forms of legal governance that work through space and time, their primary locus is the body. While legal territory is discursive and ideological, it is most immediately corporeal, acting on bodies, containing, directing, or excluding them. Where and when certain bodies are, and what those bodies are doing at any time (having sex, consuming drugs, engaging in protests), is a central concern of the criminal law. Conditional orders are designed to position, remove, locate, or contain bodies that are engaged in objectionable legal acts. Judging by the legal actors, the goal is not to act upon the mind of the zoned, but to act upon their bodies (deemed objectionable or threatening to others). It thus becomes important to think through the corporeal dimensions of law's territoriality in relation to conditional orders.

As legal territory works on the body in multiple ways, including banning, bounding, containing, and making it legible, so conditional orders such as red zones are experienced by those subject to them in embodied ways. For many, they shatter a set of embodied associations and connections, or are simply an encumbrance to be negotiated in response to their own bodily dependencies and needs. If territory is one very specific attempt to control bodies in space/time, bodies are also governed by many other relations, desires, dependencies, and practices. Conditional orders thus often collide with these other spatiotemporalities. The red zone, to borrow from Massey (1991), is a form of "power topology" that structures people's ability to control their own movements through space and time: "some people are more in charge of it than others; some initiate flows and movements, others don't; some are more on the receiving end of it than others, some are effectively imprisoned by it" (26).

In this sense, we suggest, it is useful to think of conditions of release as a form of legal violence. Red zones are enforced: they act through law, and are plugged into other forms of enforcement and constraint. As such, they entail and mobilize forms of legal violence (Derrida, 1990; Sarat and Kearns, 1992). Space matters to violence, being "more than a passive template for the inscription of violence or an object to be manipulated to create political representations. Space [becomes] a power and an animated entity" (Feldman, 1991: 28). Legal violence acts upon bodies, confining, releasing, or moving them (Hyde, 1997). Violence is both implied or realized, enacted in formalized ways ("not to be present in this perimeter") and mobilized through networks of force (e.g. police threat, or overt violence). It may be sanctioned (detention), unintentional (drug withdrawal associated with detention), or unsanctioned (extra-legal police force). That alleged offenders appear to acquiesce to violence overlooks the realities of legal power. It is, Cover notes, grotesque to assume that the "civil façade" of a sentencing or bail order rests on the alleged offender's voluntary acceptance. It is "voluntary" only in the sense "that it represents the defendant's autonomous recognition of the overwhelming array of violence ranged against him [*sic*], and of the hopelessness of resistance or outcry" (1986: 1627).

However, legal violence is not easily seen as such for those who do not experience it. The violence endemic to conditions of release appears depersonalized, detached, disembodied, and depoliticized.[4] In part, this relates to the manner in which legal interpretation – the decision of the judge to impose an order – is detached from the practical enforcement of that order. Yet the order supposes a "pyramid of violence" as Cover puts it, via the "social cooperation of many others, who in their roles as lawyers, police, jailers, wardens, and magistrates perform the deeds which judicial words authorize" (1627). This relies on a form of organizational bracketing, in which violence appears removed from interpretation. As Cover puts it:

> We have done something strange in our system. We have rigidly separated the act of interpretation – of understanding what ought to be done – from the carrying out of this "ought to be done" through violence. At the same time we have, at least in the criminal law, rigidly linked the carrying out of judicial orders to the act of judicial interpretation by relatively inflexible hierarchies of judicial utterances and firm obligations on the part of penal officials to heed them. Judges are both separated from, and inextricably linked to, the acts they authorize.[5]

(1627)

---

4   It is ironic to note the centrality of "peace" in criminal law (via the preservation of "the peace"). According to Cover(1986: 1629), law "deal[s] pain and death" yet calls this violence "peace".
5   In this context it is important to ask how law, which is commonly understood in defining and enforcing responsibility, also organizes "irresponsibility" in its role in the generation of human suffering through disavowals and dispersals (Veitch, 2007).

The violence of the red zone, we suggest, extends beyond the direct exercise of force, such as the experience of detention, but also relates to the manner in which conditions of release shape "the very geographies of being: the existential resources that nourish and sustain, but also harm and violate" (Laurie and Shaw, 2018: 8). Red zones, we suggest, often produce "violent conditions" (Laurie and Shaw, 2018) that restrict the potential for life to flourish and actualize, advancing Galtung's definition of violence as the "cause of the difference between the potential and the actual, between what could have been and what is" (1969: 168). This divide – between what could have been and what is – is painfully evident in our research findings.

3

"Recognizances to Keep the Peace and Be of Good Behaviour": The Legal History of Red Zones and Conditions of Release

In *Beyond Brutal Passions*, Mary Anne Poutanen (2015) relates the story of Mary Ann Burns, Eliza Johnson, and Margaret Burns, arrested in 1834 for keeping a bawdy-house in Montreal, following the complaints of some of their neighbours. Knowing that the Court of Quarter Sessions only met four times a year and that sex workers needed to earn a living, the justice of the peace in charge released the women on a recognizance to keep the peace until the next meeting of the Court in October. Soon thereafter, however, seeing that both women resumed their activities, neighbours went back to the justice of the peace to lay another complaint. Burns and Johnson were then released following a renewed recognizance, in which they agreed, "not to return to the house where they had been arrested" (73). While Poutanen doesn't tell us precisely what happened next to these particular women, she shows that many keepers in similar situations in early nineteenth-century Montreal simply moved their operations to another location (73). We also know that three quarters of them were eventually released or found not guilty of the alleged offence: in fact, Poutanen reports, local elites and neighbours were more interested in using the pre-trial process to discipline women and their sexuality (252). Things were, however, quite different for prostitutes charged with streetwalking, idleness, or vagrancy, who were almost all found guilty and incarcerated for different lengths of time (272).

As this chapter will show, although conditions of release have not formally been part of the law of bail until the 1960s in Canada, the U.S.A., and the U.K., similar legal techniques have a long history, probably emerging along with the appointment of justices of the peace at the end of the twelfth century in England and the power conferred on them to bind undesirable individuals upon recognizance "to keep the peace and be of good behaviour" through peace bonds (De Haas, 1940; Meyer, 1972; Lermack, 1976). Similarly, probation in its modern form only appeared in the statutes in Canada, the U.S.A., Europe, and Australia between the 1870s and the 1920s, but it is also clear that the power to suspend sentences and to release a convicted person based on a pledge builds on ancient procedural mechanisms within the English common law (Chute, 1928; Gard, 2014). According to several scholars, the earliest forms of probation or suspended sentences might also directly go back to the use of recognizances to keep the peace and be of good behaviour (Grinnell, 1917; Timasheff, 1941; cf. Grunhut, 1958; Lermack, 1976; Vanstone, 2008; Gard, 2014).

This chapter explores the "antiquities of bail" (De Haas, 1940) and the origins of probation in order to contextualize and understand better the legal framework that governs them today, which will be presented in greater details in Chapter 4. In particular, we trace the history of judicially imposed conditions of release, trying to identify how and when they came to be included in bail and sentencing practices. We find that in order to trace the origins of conditions of release and their intricate connection with the regulation of the poor, one has to follow the history of another important instrument of law enforcement, namely recognizances to keep the peace and peace bonds. We hence trace the emergence of this legal instrument and its connection with the criminal process. In doing so, we are not suggesting that red zones and other conditions of release are in direct historical continuity with their predecessors or are merely the same legal technology. Instead, we suggest that these legal techniques rely on similar forms of territorialization with related effects.

In so doing, we shed light on the temporality of legal spaces by introducing the evolving social and legal arrangements on which the legal systems relied over time in different jurisdictions (Harvey, 1996: 261; Von Benda-Beckmann and Von Benda-Beckmann, 2014: 31). We show that institutions such as bail and suspended sentences or probation not only responded to changes in political authority and power relationships in earlier societies, but that they themselves created spatial and temporal arrangements that had an impact on the creation of those relationships. As such, we aim at showing how, throughout the history of English common law, legal actors used the criminal process and different forms of spatialization and temporalization to create and enforce territories, directly governing people's uses of spaces. Such regulatory tools were routinely directed at the poor and the criminalized.

In order to understand how conditions of release came to be used as spatiotemporal tools of governance, it is necessary to unpack the history of recognizances or peace bonds. We demonstrate, first, that recognizances did not historically apply to everyone in England; the governing class typically used them to control the poor and migrants who were coming into town. This is consistent with the functions assigned to justices of the peace, namely the regulation of the poor through the enforcement of the king's peace, and the resolution of minor offences (Langbein, 1974; Costello, 2014). Secondly, while many recognizances were generally constrained, requiring only that the person merely keep the peace, many also included other types of conditions, including not to be found in the presence of certain individuals, in specific places, and even the requirement to move out of town (Samaha, 1981). These strategies were followed in the U.S.A. (Lermack, 1976) and Canada (Poutanen, 2015). Scholars have also drawn parallels with English laws enacted in 1873 and 1875 introducing workhouses in England, which allowed for the confinement and supervision of beggars and vagabonds in certain spaces (Trought, 1927). As such, from very early on, conditions of release reflect local authorities' efforts to regulate the poor by creating mobilizing spatial and temporal techniques. As the opening vignette suggests, these recognizances attempted to produce clear spatial and temporal effects, preventing objectionable bodies from using private or public spaces in a certain manner and displacing them to other parts of town or into different territories, such as the prison, for specific periods of time. This was made possible because recognizances were extremely flexible and versatile legal instruments. They rarely appeared in law treatises or guide-books and relied instead on the discretionary powers of the justices of the peace. As we shall see in Chapter 5, these features also apply to a large extent to conditions of release in contemporary law.

The history of bail, which appears to go as far back as the Germanic system of compensation, and that of probation, which coincides with industrializa-tion, also show that evolving bail and sentencing practices have primarily developed to protect state interests and territories, instead of individual rights and liberties (Duker, 1977). While the rights against excessive bail and cruel and unusual punishments have been recognized as early as the enactment of the Magna Carta in 1215, reforms seem to have primarily responded to insti-tutional problems. Moreover, given their highly discretionary character, recog-nizances and other judicial tools did not entail any kinds of due process. Similarly, as we shall see in Chapter 6, modern conditions of release trigger multiple rights violations. Yet these arguments are rarely presented in courts.

Thirdly, we demonstrate that bail and probation have both historically developed against the backdrop of incarceration. As such, there are real corporeal dimensions to both institutions. This is of course also true of conditional sentence orders (CSO), which are jail sentences served in the community, and to which we will last turn in our historical survey. In Chapters 4 and 6, we will also suggest that the threat of incarceration plays a key role in structuring and legitimating legal practices around conditions of release.

BAIL: FROM COMPENSATION TO PRE-TRIAL RELEASE

While the first statutory regulation of bail was the Statute of Westminster I, enacted in 1275, legal historians believe that the institution goes back at least to pre-Norman England (De Haas, 1940; Meyer, 1972; Duker, 1977). "Bail" derives from an Old French word, "baillier" or "baillir", which meant to govern or take responsibility for someone, to hand over or lease. Starting in the seventh century, Anglo-Saxon families gradually attempted to eliminate blood feuds by establishing a system of compensation based on the payment of the *wergeld* (or tariff), which represented the value of a man's life in accordance to his social class or status in his family and community (De Haas, 1940). When a family initiated a complaint against a wrong done by the member of another, the defendant's family had to provide a pledge or a surety called a *werborh*, first to ensure the future payment of the *wergeld* were the defendant found responsible, but then later to ensure his presence before the court. If the defendant escaped, then his surety was responsible for paying the *wergeld*, which became a fine. As the kings gradually extended their peace to certain people and areas, they established their own tariffs and also required the payment of the *wergeld* for themselves in compensation for the injured parties under their protection (Meyer, 1972).

The surety system survived the Norman Conquest. While the Conqueror retained many Anglo-Saxon kings' laws, he replaced the payment of tariffed amends with the infliction of punishment. Normans also brought with them three key Franquist institutions, namely the jury, the king's court – a centralized entity combining administrative and adjudicative functions – and the royal *missi*, which represented the king and carried his Court throughout the country (Meyer, 1972: 1151). The *missi* conducted their own inquests and started initiating *ex officio* (without private accusers) prosecutions under the king's name. As a result of these transformations, the English surety system was no longer used to ensure the payment of the *wergeld*, but to take responsibility for the accused until he or she appeared at the duel or "until the coming of the [itinerant] justices" of the king's Court (De Haas, 1940: 32).

The Assize of Clarendon in 1166 is the first official enactment of the relationship between arrest and release on bail in the context of king's inquests, although in practice it surely started earlier following the Conquest. As opposed to private prosecutions, *ex officio* proceedings started with the arrest of an individual following the inquisition. At the time, the primary official responsible for arresting the accused and bringing them to justice was the sheriff, the guardian of the county's peace. This could prove rather burdensome given that the circuits of the itinerant justices were sometimes a matter of months or years. For instance, according to Langbein (1933), during Richard's reign (from 1189 to 1199) and in John's first years (from 1200 to 1216), "the eyres are already beginning to be spaced out at about four-year periods in any one county, and thereafter the intervals increase from an ideal seven-year period to lapses of sometimes as long as fifty years under the Edwards" (Langbein, 1933: 1333 n. 16), that is, from Edward I's reign starting in 1272 to the end of Edward III's reign in 1377. Moreover, prisons were not only costly but also largely unfit to keep the prisoners, who could easily escape (De Haas, 1940: 56). The bail system thus freed the sheriff from the personal burdens and costs of bringing the prisoners to court by shifting this responsibility to a surety who was responsible for the accused's custody (De Haas, 1940; Duker, 1977). Thus, from its inception, administrative priorities have played a crucial role in bail.

The Crown attempted to regulate bailing practices throughout the years. The first rules were established in the Statute of Westminster I in 1275, enumerating a list of bailable and non-bailable offences, the latter comprising four categories of offences, including those enacted by the special command of the king, offences punishable by death, perpetrated in the king's forest, or against the custom of England (Meyer, 1972), referring to Glanville, published between 1187 and 1189). Despite these regulations, however, the sheriffs' decisions to grant or deny bail remained highly discretionary, leading to multiple abuses, including demands for excessive fees, acceptance of bribes to grant bail in cases of non-bailable offences or the denial of bail in cases for which it should have been granted, and the creation of false indictments, also in order to secure money (De Haas, 1940; Desmond, 1952; Duker, 1977). These abuses persisted for years despite successive kings' creative solutions to limit the sheriffs' and other local officials' powers, including the imposition of maximum terms of detention and limitations to the amounts of bail, and the conferring of new powers onto keepers of the peace, who had been first appointed by King Richard I in 1195 in an effort to centralize criminal jurisdiction.

Keepers of the peace were knights appointed by the king to keep the peace in certain unruly areas. They progressively gained additional powers throughout the thirteenth and fourteenth centuries at the expense of sheriffs, when they became justices of the peace (JPs), including the power to try "all manner of felonies and trespasses" in the 1360–1361 Justices of the Peace Act (34 Edw 3 c. 1; Langbein, 1974), and the power to grant bail to those indicted before them in 1461 (Duker, 1977: 54). In 1483, Parliament finally gave justices of the peace the power and authority to arrest, imprison, or bail those suspected of felonies while prohibiting sheriffs from taking or seizing the goods of any arrested or imprisoned individual. As it happens, however, corruption and abuses did not end. Only four years later, Parliament had to adopt a new statute to curb the discretionary powers of JPs. The 1487 Statute provided that bail should only be granted if two JPs agreed to it and that the decision be certified at the next session of the Gaol Commission, and in 1554–1555, the Marian statute for the bailment of prisoners was enacted allowing the granting of bail only in open sessions, or following a series of strict conditions, including a certification taken in writing and the examination of the prisoner (Langbein, 1974).

In the sixteenth century, the decision to grant bail still displayed a wide range of judicial discretion, varying depending on the seriousness of the offence (including whether or not that offence was deemed bailable or not), the likelihood of the accused being found guilty, and the character and habits of the accused (him or her being of "good fame") (Samaha, 1981). Blackstone nonetheless tried to synthesize the law of bail in the eighteenth century in his *Commentaries*, distinguishing between a series of cases in which a justice of the peace could not grant bail (including treason, murder, manslaughter if the accused clearly appeared guilty, prison escape, arson, as well as persons caught committing a felony or outlawed) and those where he could use his discretion. For instance, bail had to be granted in the cases of misdemeanours. Two English statutes adopted in 1826 and 1848 further attempted to clarify the law, giving the justices of the peace discretion to grant or deny bail to any person charged with a felony or certain misdemeanours, except for treason. The Court of Queen's Bench in an 1854 ruling found that the main criterion for granting bail was whether or not the person will appear for trial, a decision which should be taken based on the gravity of the offence, the likelihood of the accused being convicted in light of the prosecution's evidence, and the severity of the punishment (Meyer, 1972).

THE RISE OF JUSTICES OF THE PEACE AND RECOGNIZANCES TO BE OF GOOD BEHAVIOUR

The transfer of powers from the sheriffs to the justices of the peace was consequential in the history of conditions of release. Prior to the fifteenth century, justices of the peace were only authorized to grant bail to all those who were not of "good fame" for future good behaviour, a power that was first conferred to them in an Act in 1360–1366, that empowered JPs to grant bail to

> them that be not of good Fame, where they shall be found, sufficient Surety and Mainprise [a particular form of surety] of their good Behaviour towards

the King and his People, and the other duly to punish; to the Intent that the People be not by such Rioters or Rebels troubled nor endamaged, nor the Peace blemished, nor Merchants nor other passing by the Highways of the Realm disturbed, nor put in the Peril which may happen of such Offenders.

That is not all that the Act did, however. It assigned both judicial and non-judicial duties to JPs, including what would now be considered a policing business (the duty to keep the peace: Lambarde, 1581), as well as jurisdiction over summary conviction offences, authorizing JPs to arrest, take, chastise, and imprison vagabonds or "all those that have been Pillors and Robbers in the Parts beyond the Sea, and be now come again, and go wandering, and will not Labour as they were wont in Times past for their Trespass or Offence" (Langbein, 1974: 5–6). Thus, in retrospect, the Justice of the Peace Act of 1360–1361 played a crucial role in the enactment of judicial territories by connecting three important duties assigned to judicial officials, namely the power to bail, the power to try minor offences, and the policing and regulation of the public poor.

The power conferred then on JPs to bind someone for future good behaviour was mostly used preventively against individuals who were thought to be likely to violate the peace, without laying criminal charges or securing conviction. Such recognizances, however, were also connected to appearance before trial in cases of both felonies and misdemeanours in which the accused could not secure bail (DeCicco, 1973; Note, 1966). Blackstone defined the recognizance as a very versatile legal instrument, being "an obligation of record, which a man enters into before some court of record or magistrate duly authorized, *with condition to do some particular act*, as to appear at the assizes, to keep the peace, to pay a debt, or the like" (our emphasis; Ehrlich, 1959). For Blackstone, these orders were intrinsically linked to preventive justice which consisted in "obliging those persons whom there is a probable ground to suspect of future misbehaviour to stipulate with and to give full assurance to the public that such offence as is apprehended shall not happen, by finding pledges or securities for keeping the peace, or for their good behavior" (Blackstone, *Commentaries on the Laws of England*, Book IV, chap. 18 – "Of the Means of Preventing Offences" (1753); see Ashworth and Zedner, 2014: 29).

This is confirmed by important historical analysis conducted by Joel Samaha (1981), who argues that during the Elizabethan era in England (1558–1603), recognizances or peace bonds played at least three functions. First, they were used as pre-trial instruments to bring an accused before justice in nearly all cases of misdemeanours and some felonies, as well as to secure the appearance of witnesses and prosecutors to testify in open court before a judge and jury in a felony case. Secondly, recognizances also aimed to prevent crime and appeared to have been important tools of conflict-resolution, even playing a more important role than criminal trials in law enforcement in sixteenth-century Colchester (198). Echoing their later use, then, they were preventive, and future-oriented, rather than simply responsive. Such recognizances, sometimes backed with one or two sureties, could be issued as peace bonds independently from the criminal process or used to ensure appearance. The recognizance sometimes directed someone to keep the peace generally, but often it was more specific: directing someone to keep the peace against another, only requiring that person to appear at the next meeting of the Quarter Sessions should he or she be found violating the peace bond or upon being called by a magistrate.

"Keeping the peace" was an all-encompassing and open-textured concept. It was clearly directed towards the prevention of any form of violence and serious threats to public order, in the past or in the future, but it was also more specifically aimed at certain targeted people, including robbers, rioters, suspicious persons, and vagrants (Lambarde, 1581; Samaha, 1981). While recognizances to keep the peace were used to prevent violence and serious threats to public order, recognizances of "good abearing" or to be of good behaviour, were most common in petty cases, such as vagrancy, and much broader in scope. They were meant to ensure "that a man demean himself well in his port and company, doing nothing that may be cause of the breach of the Peace, or of putting the people in fear, or trouble" (Samaha, 1981: 198, citing Lambarde, 1581: 124) Such recognizances were directed to "all them that not be of good fame", including "former convicted offenders who refused to work for a living and persons who had in the past breached the peace, rioted or barreted [engaged in strife and contention]", those who kept bawdy-houses, and others "who kept suspicious company" (Samaha, 1981: 199). Such individuals could be bound indefinitely ("for an indeterminate period" or "from henceforth"). Moreover, some of the conditions imposed were quite specific and directed at controlling behaviour in certain spaces, including not to be found frequenting the house of X, not playing any unlawful games, not selling specific games, etc.

This latter use of the recognizance brings Samaha to conclude that peace bonds were also used as instruments to control "undesirable and dangerous persons", aiming to control their presence in town enforce moral regulation, and get rid of vagrants, that "great scourge of the upper ranks of Elizabethan society" (202). He gives the example of Richard Patton, a Colchester tailor, "who was bound along with his wife and children not to become burdens to the town". According to Samaha, "Patton was allowed to remain in the town so long as he could support himself and his family. By means of recognizance, however, the town's governors retained the power to cast them out if they ever failed to be self-sufficient" (203). Others, like Robert Peartree and his wife, were even more explicitly banned, only allowed one month "to leave and not to inhabit within the town" of Colchester.

Recognizances to be of good behaviour, or peace bonds, thus clearly aimed at restricting entry and presence within certain spaces for specified or open-ended times. They involved creating and enforcing social and political relationships of exclusion and inclusion, inscribing them within bounded spaces (whether it was a bawdy-house or more generally the town itself), and allowing for the continued supervision over time of individuals who were considered unruly or dangerous: "it should be obvious that local officials had considerable flexibility in these cases – they could get rid of those who were considered risky immediately or keep them around long enough to find out if they were going to be burdens before they harried them out of the town" (Samaha, 1981: 203). This is not surprising when we consider the legal and spatial ramifications underlying the very notion of breach of the peace. According to Goodrich,

> in classical common law terms, a breach of the peace is a breach of the king's peace, a disruption *vi et armis* or by force or arms of the law of the land, of the custom of the realm … it is a breaking of the law, a breach of contract, a breach of promise, certainly, but it is also perhaps additionally a breach as in the breaching of a wall so as to invade a city, so as to end a siege, a manner of moving in, of invasion or intrusion, a breaking through. The breach itself is a wounded spot, a broken space, a disputed place, a gap or fissure in fortifications made by a battery. According to that broader lexical definition, the gap exists to be closed, something must be erected to fill the breach, to make the wall whole, to make the city secure, to reintroduce order.
>
> (1990: 242)

By the end of the seventeenth century, recognizances were at work in the North American colonies. In colonial Pennsylvania, for instance, peace bonds of a preventive nature were commonly used to resolve many petty conflicts among neighbours, including in cases of witchcraft, threats, or assaults independently of any criminal charges. Such peace bonds were in fact diversion measures used as alternatives to criminal prosecutions. Individuals were bound to keep the peace for a specific period of time under the supervision of sureties who possessed the power to bring them into custody should they be violating their bond.

But peace bonds also later accompanied criminal prosecutions. In these cases, people were placed under bonds to be of good behaviour and to appear at the next session of the Court of Quarter Sessions or Common Pleas (Lermack, 1976). Such bonds have also been used in colonial Massachusetts (Grinnell, 1917; Goebel and Naughton, 1944; Meyer, 1972). Interestingly, in that context, peace bonds have sometimes been used to "encourage undesirable persons to leave the province" (Goodrich, 1990: 182). In 1739, for instance, "two prisoners incarcerated for inability to pay fines were released and put under bond to leave the province immediately" (182).

As mentioned in the introductory vignette, there is also clear evidence that recognizances to keep the peace and be of good behaviour were used during the eighteenth century in Montreal for interim release while awaiting the next session of the Court of Quarter Sessions (Poutanen, 2015), but also more generally in Lower (Fyson, 2006) and Upper (Girard, Philips, and Brown, 2018) Canada. According to Fyson, who studied the "everyday criminal justice" in Quebec and Lower Canada following the British Conquest in 1763 to the Rebellions of the mid-eighteenth century, the "justices of the peace were the base of the criminal justice system" during that transition period and they had even more powers than they had in England at the same time (see also Girard, Philips, and Brown, 2018: 287 for Upper Canada). Specifically, JPs carried important legislative powers in matters that are now devolved to municipalities, such as the regulation of roads, markets, and public spaces, and made extensive local regulations, including the regulation of begging, vagrancy, and street vending (p. 32, referring to the 1817 Regulations for Montreal that contained some 180 pages). In addition, they combined peace-keeping (policing) functions, as well as ministerial or administrative (pre-trial decision-making) and adjudicative powers (Fyson, 2006: 33). In exercising their pre-trial functions in misdemeanour cases such as assaults, disturbing the peace, or prostitution, the justices commonly issued recognizances to keep the peace and be of good behaviour. In fact, Fyson found that defendants were only sent to custody and formal court in cases where the JPs considered the offence to be serious or where they lacked jurisdiction (235). These recognizances could be issued for a period of six to 12 months and included a bail bond with sureties.

In the U.S.A., recognizances and peace bonds seem to have fallen out of use after about 1780 as a pre-trial tool, only to be revived occasionally afterwards, including according to some authors against civil rights protesters in the American South in the 1960s (Goldfarb, 1965). Yet, as complaints about criminality rose in the eighteenth century followed by an increase in formal procedures, peace bonds were also imposed as additional punishments on individuals convicted of crimes. For instance, in the period 1754–1764, the Court of Quarter sessions imposed 41 peace bonds in addition to fines or whipping on people convicted of crimes, including 14 to people convicted of felonies (mostly, theft), 14 of assault, and three for running a disorderly house. The bond was set for a determined period of time, typically a year, but occasionally going on for longer terms (Lermack, 1976: 187). In these cases, peace bonds played the role of probation orders.

Indeed, both bail and probation seem to have strong historical ties to the use of recognizances for good behaviour or peace bonds. In an 1809 decision from the Pennsylvania State Supreme Court, *Commonwealth* v. *Duane* (1 Binney), Chief Justice Tilghman speaks about their joint origins:

> Surety for good behavior may be considered in two points of view. It is either required after conviction of some indictable offense, in which case it forms part of the judgment of the Court, and is founded on a power incident to courts of records by the common law, or it is demanded by judges or justices of the peace out of court, before the trial, in pursuance of authority derived from a Statute made in the 34th year of Edward 3.
>
> (p. 98, quoted in Grinnell, 1917)

Thus, in the early nineteenth century, recognizances also allowed justices of the peace, recorders, and magistrates to suspend, defer, or attenuate punishment for crime by releasing an offender in the hands of an officer in exchange of a promise of good behaviour (Gard, 2014: 16). Alternatively, and as further sign of the similarities between the two institutions, in some cases, defendants entered a guilty plea, no sentence was imposed, and they were then considered admitted to bail (Grinnell, 1917).

For Grinnell, suspending the sentence or sentencing someone to "good behaviour", was a "method of alleviating strict punishment for lesser crimes" that grew out of the court's equity jurisdiction (1917: 595 and 599). He even compared this remedy to other common expedients, such as the "benefit of the clergy", which initially allowed priests to escape the criminal process, then only the conviction, but was then extended by English Statutes to men who could read and even to those who could pretend to do so, and, later on, to women in some cases in order to escape the harsh punishments of the Bloody Code (Blackstone's Commentaries; Langbein, 1983). In a sense, Grinnell suggests, modern probation officers performed similar functions to those of bishops' clerks who advised the courts on the right to the benefit of the clergy (1917: 596). Thus, the courts arguably acted based on "tenderness and humanity", walking a fine line between terror and mercy (Hay, 1975), and responding to growing dissatisfaction with the use of incarceration in the cases of first and "unusually young" defendants (*Commonwealth* v. *Chase*, 1831, in Grinnell, 1917: 602).

At the same time, social and political concerns with the maintenance of social order in Britain and the U.S.A. also seemed to have been important contributing factors to the creation of probation. Such concerns specifically revolved around young and poor offenders. Gard (2014: 20) tells the story of a 26-year-old woman from Newcastle, Agnes Bevars, "who appeared for the 108th time for being drunk and disorderly" and was discharged in the hands of a police court missionary upon pledging to be of good behaviour, and that of a 13-year-old kitchen boy caught stealing a cheque of 21 pounds also released to the care of a missionary working for the London Police Court Mission following a promise to be of good behaviour and find alternative employment. In the U.S.A., one of the earliest judicial cases on the modern system of probation, *Commonwealth* v. *Chase* (1831), also refers to a defendant who was convicted for stealing in a dwelling house and whose sentence was suspended while she was released during good behaviour only to be caught again for larceny after which the court imposed a sentence for the initial offence, sending her to the house of corrections for six months (Grinnell, 1917: 603).

Probation in its modern form appeared in the statutes in North America, Europe, and Queensland between the 1870s and the 1920s, with the first probation law in Massachusetts in 1878, followed by other U.S. states such as Michigan in 1885, and other common law countries such as New Zealand and Queensland in 1886, Canada in 1889, and the U.K. in 1908 (Vanstone, 2008). This seems to have coincided with a period during which the courts appear more reluctant to rely on common law powers to impose punishment. For instance, in 1916, the United States Supreme Court held that the common law authority to suspend punishment and release a convicted defendant during good behaviour was ultra vires of the courts' jurisdiction without express statutory grounds (*Ex parte U.S. Petitioner 242 U.S. 27*). Suspended sentence, as a form of probation, was first introduced in Canadian law in the 1906 Criminal Code. In 1955, Parliament removed the necessity to have the Crown prosecutor's consent to impose probation.

Finally, although prevalent, recognizances were not the only "off the books" judicial instrument used to regulate the poor during the colonial period. For instance, Damon (2014) documents the history of "floating warrants" or "floaters" used along with vagrancy laws starting in mid-nineteenth-century Canada. At the time, justices of the peace or magistrates issued floating warrants against vagrants, loose or idle persons, temporarily withholding an order of committal issued against a convicted individual to allow them time to leave the community and escape imprisonment (Gordon, 2004).

Floating warrants lacked statutory authority, but were an efficient tool of spatiotemporal control, providing yet another example of how criminal procedure and discretion can be mobilized to remove undesirable people from certain areas or towns (Damon, 2014). They also directly responded to local authorities' interests in "moving the bums along" without having to incur the costs of incarceration and the subsequent charges related to poor houses and other forms of social welfare (Phillips, 2012: 145). While we do not know the exact number of floaters that were used, they appear to have been widespread. Phillips (2012), for instance, observed a sharp decline in incarceration time for vagrancy charges in nineteenth-century Halifax (between 1864 and 1890), which could "largely be attributed to a greatly increased tendency to remove vagrants from the area" (149). The courts also acknowledged their wide use, even into the twentieth century. According to Justice Dysart from the Manitoba's King Bench in *R. v. Litman* (1922), the practice of issuing floating warrants is "very general in its application" and "based upon wise public policy" that "affords the community all the benefits that would ensure from imprisonment without the burden of expense; it affords the offender the benefit of a restricted liberty but with the burden of supporting himself" (par. 14; quoted in Damon, 2014; see also *R. v. Pokitruski*, Alb. Sup. Ct., 1931). Further, according to Damon (2014), while in *R. v. Pokitruski* (Alberta Supreme Court 1931) and *R. v. Scott* (Manitoba's King Bench 1929), "higher courts found that the magistrates issuing floating warrants were operating outside their official purview", this did not lead to any substantial challenge or critique of this practice.

TWENTIETH-CENTURY BAIL: MOVING FROM COURT APPEARANCE TO CRIME PREVENTION

In Canada, England and Wales, and the U.S.A., conditional release first appeared as an official alternative to remand or bail in the 1960s (Wanger, 1987). There is clear historical convergence and mutual influence among these three jurisdictions. In England, the Criminal Justice Act of 1967 (c. 80) first provided for the imposition of special conditions on bail. Section 21(1) of the English 1967 Act reads: "The conditions on which any person is admitted to bail may include conditions appearing to the court to be likely to result in his appearance at the time and place required or to be necessary in the interests of justice or for the prevention of crime". The possibility of imposing conditions of release coincided historically with increasing concerns after the Second World War with the release of potentially dangerous offenders who went on to commit offences while on bail (Meyer, 1972). In the years that followed the adoption of the 1952 Magistrates' Courts Act (15 & 16 Geo. 6 & 1 Eliz. 2, c. 55), English courts made it clear that a justice of the peace could not only deny bail if an accused was unlikely to appear, but also if he or she might interfere with witnesses or impede the administration of justice or was likely to commit other offences while on bail. This was then explicitly included in the 1967 Act (s. 18).

Similar legislative changes have occurred in the U.S.A. both in response to concerns for dangerous offenders committing crime while on bail as well as for indigent offenders who were unfairly kept in custody because they were unable to post bail (U.S. Attorney General Committee on Poverty and the Administration of Federal Criminal Law, 1963, which promised to "render the poverty of the litigant an irrelevancy" (6)). The federal Bail Reform Act of 1966 (18 U.S.C. §3146) provided that the judicial officer could order release pending trial on the personal recognizance or an unsecured appearance bond. According to the Bail Reform Act, the federal officer could impose conditions upon pre-trial release, including "placing the person in the custody of a designated person or organization", "placing restrictions on the travel, association, or place of abode of the person during the period of release", or even imposing any other condition deemed reasonably necessary to assure appearance as required, including a condition requiring that the person return to custody after specified hours in addition to cash bail with or without surety and deposit. This disposition followed a successful experimental program called the Manhattan Bail Project launched in 1961, in which poor offenders who presented low risk of flight were released on a recognizance with conditions (Ares, Rankin, and Sturz, 1963; Bogomolny and Sonnenreich, 1969). The federal Bail Reform Act of 1966 has served as an important model for subsequent state reforms. Interestingly, in the discussions surrounding the legality and opportunity to resorting to preventive detention in the 1960s, scholars found historical support for doing so in peace bonds dating back from 1360–1361 in England (DeL, 1940: 331; Note, 1966: 1504).

The 1966 Act was replaced by the 1984 Bail Reform Act, which added a list of new potential conditions of release, including maintaining or seeking employment or an educational program, avoiding contacts with any victim of a witness, complying with a curfew, refraining from possessing any weapons, refraining from "excessive use of alcohol" or any drug and controlled substance, undergoing treatment, and "any other condition that is reasonably necessary to assure the appearance of the person as required *and to assure the safety of any person and the community*" (our emphasis). The 1984 Statute followed the passing two years earlier of the Pretrial Services Act of 1982 by the American Congress which required the establishment of a pre-trial services program in each federal judicial district to provide information about an individual charged with an offence, recommend certain release conditions, and monitor them.

The 1982 Pretrial Services Act was the first to address directly the issue of preventing criminal activity while being released on bail. In the past, courts considered that denying or setting bail based on the possibility of future offending might violate the defendant's right to due process. U.S. law has long been reluctant to ground bail decisions on the prevention of future criminal activity. The doctrine of preventive detention has met significant resistance in different American states (DeCicco, 1973). Scholars have argued that depriving an individual of their liberty on the basis that they may commit a crime in the future violates the due process of law. Thus, bail could only be denied if the defendant was likely to flee prior to trial.

Similarly, in Canada, the Bail Reform Act was adopted in 1971 (S.C. 1971, 19–20 Eliz. II, c. 37), amending the Criminal Code. It built on the important conclusions of the Canadian Committee on Corrections (Ouimet Committee, 1969) and an influential study conducted by Martin Friedland on criminal cases tried in the Toronto Magistrates' Courts (Friedland, 1965; 2012) who found that bail practices were highly "inefficient, inequitable and inconsistent" and that detention before trial was widespread. The new provisions of the Criminal Code gave new powers to the police to issue simple appearance notices instead of arresting an individual, as well as, for the first time, the power to release an arrested accused through an undertaking with conditions. More importantly, it established a clear and progressive release scheme by which the accused should be released on the least onerous grounds (an undertaking to appear without conditions). At the time of the passing of the Act, bail could only be denied if the accused was not likely to appear for trial or if there was a substantial likelihood that the accused, if released from custody, would commit an offence involving serious harm. This "liberal and enlightened system of pre-trial release" (Friedland, 2012: 320) did not last long. Two years later, in 1973, the Act was modified and the words "involving serious harm" were removed so that the accused could be denied bail if there was substantial likelihood that he or she would commit *any* criminal offence (Friedland, 2012: 320). A third ground was further added in the 1990s to "maintain the confidence in the administration of justice" (*R. v. St Cloud*, 2015 SCC 27). Moreover, reverse onuses were created for a limited number of offences, including, as we shall see, for failures to comply with bail orders.

CONCLUSIONS ON THE SPATIAL GOVERNANCE OF THE POOR

Although today's conditions of release bear some distinctive contemporary features (see Chapters 4 and 5), such legal techniques involve the mobilization of longstanding forms of legal territorialization. The use of the criminal process is particularly important in enforcing territoriality. This is based on highly discretionary powers and flexible procedural tools that remained unofficial. Indeed, in the sixteenth century, although they were widely used, peace bonds were rarely if at all mentioned in specialized legal treatises or guidebooks directed to justices of the peace or lawyers (Samaha, 1981). American legal historian Paul Lermack (1976) observed that the *Conductor Generalis*, a guide destined to justices of the peace and sheriffs, only noted that any justice of the peace could use them (176). An 1848 English statute (11 & 12 Vic., c. 42, s. 23) first acknowledged the possibility of releasing a person on bail based on a recognizance. It provided that a justice of the peace could admit an arrested person to bail "upon his procuring and producing such surety or sureties as in the opinion of the justice will be sufficient to ensure the appearance of such accused person at the time and place when and where he is to be tried for such offence; and that thereupon such justice shall take the recognizance of the said accused person and his surety" (Meyer, 1972), but it did not mention the possibility of issuing such a recognizance to control the behaviour of undesirable individuals or to move them around or outside of towns. At the time, the institution of bail was still formally focused solely on securing the accused's appearance in court and conditional release would only come to be recognized on the books in the 1960s in most common law jurisdictions. The same can be said of probation, which grew out of discretionary powers exercised by judges and was officially enacted by the end of the nineteenth century. Similarly, conditions of release appear pervasive in the contemporary criminal management of marginalized people.

Secondly, it is undeniable that these forms of territorialization have been central to the governance of specific groups of people throughout history, namely idle and disorderly persons, vagrants, and vagabonds (Blackstone's Commentaries; Foucault, 1977). Further, that bail was created to protect state interests rather than individual liberty seems clear. Individual rights were subordinated to the police power. Such an asymmetry continues to be evident, we note below. To be sure, the right not to be seized without due process and the right against "excessive bail" were respectively entrenched in the Magna Carta and the Statute of Westminster I as early as the thirteenth century, and thereafter included in the English Bill of

Rights in 1689 and in the U.S. Bill of Rights, Eighth Amendment, in 1791. This being said, there is strong historical evidence to suggest that releasing a prisoner was from very early on also very much in the interests of justice, from ensuring the stability and legitimacy of the emerging king's peace after the blood feuds and the Norman Conquest to mitigating the costs and hazards of detention and alleviating the burden of the sheriffs responsible for bringing the accused before the courts. Duker further implies that any concession based on rights also directly served to respond to bureaucratic problems. Whenever change occurred, it was incremental: "the steps toward personal liberty were small; each was meant only to correct the problem at hand" (1977: 58). To be sure, this does not mean that rights arguments have not been part of the discourse. In fact, they do permeate the statutes and case law. However, bail release practices seem to have evolved in response to pragmatic spatial and temporal constraints, such as finding an alternative to an inappropriate space, remand, in a context conducive to multiple abuses, while dealing with important judicial delays. For example, in a 1813 decision, the U.S. Supreme Court made it clear that the taking of a recognizance not only benefits the accused: "it is in the interest of the public as well as the accused that the latter should not be detained in custody prior to his trial".

Finally, bail and probation, and, in particular, conditions of release associated with both institutions, have developed against the backdrop of incarceration or as an alternative to harsher sanctions. While bail first took the form of a pledge of person and property made by a surety who could offer some guarantees that the accused would appear for payment should he be found responsible for the wrongdoing, in its origins, it grew from concerns for the body of the defendant whose physical custody was transferred from the family who claimed that it had suffered some wrong to the family presenting sureties. After the Norman Conquest, bail was granted if the sureties could bear responsibility for bringing the (body of the) accused to suffer punishment. Again, bail was secured as an alternative to holding the person in custody. In the sixteenth century, recognizances of good behaviour were also conceived as a lesser evil, as alternatives to the harsh sanctions associated with vagrancy, which included torture or even death by hanging. This made them both more acceptable and an effective tool to regulate the poor (Samaha, 1981).

This is also the case for probation. According to Vanstone (2008: 752), "Probation ... despite the resilience inherent in its complex and tenacious development and dispersion, was never to escape the shadow of the prison, whose temporary eclipse had been a strong and ubiquitous factor in its birth". Probation was meant to be a substitute to incarceration, growing out of concerns for prison conditions and its ability to treat and rehabilitate certain offenders, namely youth, first-time offenders, and the deserving poor. Yet, convicted individuals were sometimes transferred to other venues, including workhouses or voluntary homes, or handed over to the supervision of temperance societies and religious organizations pursing disciplinary and civilizing missions (Gard, 2014). As we shall see, spatiotemporal conditions of release continue to have a charged relationship to incarceration: while notionally detached, they are often experienced as a form of "carceral continuum".

PART II

Expansion

4

Territory Widening

The previous chapter revealed the longstanding use of conditional release in the common law world. As we demonstrate in this chapter, community supervision through bail or probation, and spatial restrictions in particular, play a continued and expanded role in contemporary criminal justice in Canada.

In later chapters, we draw from qualitative data to demonstrate the rationales and effects of spatial conditions. Here we explore recent quantitative court data from Montreal and Vancouver on bail and sentencing. Overall, these data comprise over one million conditions of release, roughly equally divided by each city. The data show that conditions of release have become increasingly pervasive, gaining in number and duration, that a significant proportion of the conditions imposed entail spatial restrictions, and that such conditions generate numerous offences against the administration of justice (namely, failures to comply with bail orders and breaches of probation).

In the following subsections, we first introduce our datasets and discuss some methodological issues, before making our central arguments. Echoing the concept of "net-widening" (Cohen, 1979; 1985), while also recognizing the importance of territorialization, we characterize spatial bail and sentencing conditions of release as a form of judicial territory widening. We first demonstrate that conditions of release are widely used, including at bail where they contravene the legal requirements that prescribe that they should only be used in exceptional cases. As we shall see, legal practices stand in stark contrast with formal legal requirements, as the vast majority of accused are released under some kind of conditions. Secondly, we show that geographical restrictions are among the most frequent at all stages of criminal proceedings, from bail to sentencing. Given the fact that many conditions comprise specific restrictions on the use of public spaces, they have the effect of expanding the role of the courts in the regulation and governance of public spaces. Thirdly, we show that such conditions generate an important number of offences against the administration of justice through breaches of court orders, and that geographical restrictions are generally responsible for a high number of such breaches. Given that spatial restrictions are associated with a high number of breaches, they also play an important role in the expansion of the criminal justice system. Finally, we show that bail, probation, and even conditional sentences, initially conceived as alternatives to incarceration, have in fact not become alternatives at all, but have increased the number of people, creating a pathway towards incarceration and long-term judicial surveillance through practically unavoidable breaches.

INTRODUCING THE DATASETS: METHODOLOGICAL CONSIDERATIONS

In Vancouver, we obtained quantitative data from the Justice Information System (JUSTIN)[1] administered by the Court Services Branch (CSB) of the Ministry of Justice of British Columbia through an application for access to court record information. The data comprised all adult criminal court cases either sentenced to probation or a conditional sentence, or cases not necessarily sentenced, but granted bail between 2005 and 2012 in the Vancouver Provincial Court (including the Drug Court) and Downtown Community Court.[2] The entire dataset contains 30,505 distinct accused individuals and 94,931 distinct court cases. Each court case may include one or more charges and some individuals have more than one case.

The dataset was then divided into three groups – "bail", "probation", and "conditional sentence". The first and largest group, "bail", includes 55,976 distinct court cases, the second "probation" group contains 31,915 distinct defined court cases, and the third "CSO" group contains 7,042 distinct cases. These groups are not, however, mutually exclusive: certain accused might have received bail and not probation, or bail and probation, or only probation,

---

[1] JUSTIN is a "computerized system used across B.C. for managing and administering the criminal justice process. It allows adult and youth criminal cases to be tracked and processed from initial police arrests and Crown counsel change assessments through to court judgment" (Office of the Auditor General of British Columbia, 2013: 9).

[2] The Downtown Community Court (DCC) is a provincial court that serves downtown Vancouver and has jurisdiction over all provincial offences, Criminal Code offences prosecuted by summary conviction, and drug offences within its geographical catchment: www2.gov.bc.ca/gov/content/justice/criminal-justice/vancouver-downtown-community-court/how-the-court-works/jurisdiction.

TABLE 4.1 *Summary statistics (Vancouver, 2005–2012)*

Order type	No. cases	Percentage	No. orders	Percentage	No. conditions	Percentage
Bail	55,976	59.0	74,408	73.6	326,388	61.8
Probation	31,915	33.6	22,814	22.6	157,435	29.8
CSO	7,042	7.4	3,930	3.9	44,493	8.4
Totals	94,933	100	101,152	100	528,316	100

and so on. Altogether, the dataset includes 101,152 court orders that generated 528,316 conditions during the period covered by our data.

Table 4.1 presents a summary of the Vancouver dataset. It shows that most of the cases (59%), orders (74%), and conditions (62%) were generated at bail. This is not surprising in the B.C. context. According to Malakieh (2018), there were a total of 42,943 bail orders issued to adults under correctional services in 2016–2017 (p. 10). Strikingly, the commencement of bail supervision was the most common point of initial entry into correctional services in that province in 2014–2015 (54%), followed by remand (17%) and probation (15%) (Reitano, 2017: Table 3).[3]

The Montreal dataset includes 89,898 decisions and 50,324 judgments rendered by the Municipal Court of Montreal in 88,911 cases associated with 146,988 offences (from a pre-established list of 18 Criminal Code offences)[4] between January 1, 2002 and May 20, 2014. The database refers to 40,975 distinct individuals (one individual can have more than one case, as a "case" include one or more charges based on information).

By contrast with its counterparts in other parts of the country, the Municipal Court of Montreal has a unique criminal jurisdiction (s. 2 (a.1) Cr. C).[5] It not

---

[3] Bail data are scarcer. The Canadian Center for Justice Statistics only started documenting bail orders in 2016–2017. Initial data were only available for two provinces during that year: British Columbia and Alberta.

[4] The list included offences against the administration of justice (interfering with a peace officer, failures to comply, and breaches of probation – ss. 129, 145, 733.1, 810–811), offences against the public order (unlawful assemblies and riots – s. 66), offences against public morals and disorderly conduct (causing disturbance and communicating for the purposes of prostitution – ss. 175 and 213), offences against rights of property (theft and fraud – ss. 334 and 342) and offences against the person (criminal harassment, assaults, assault against a peace officer – ss. 264, 264.1, 266, and 270) as well as conspiracy (s. 465). The offences were selected based on previous research on policing practices in Montreal against marginalized and homeless populations (Sylvestre et al., 2011).

[5] The Municipal Court of Montreal is one of two courthouses with criminal jurisdiction in Quebec, the other being the Municipal Court of Quebec City.

only has jurisdiction over the City of Montreal's by-laws and regulations – excluded from this study, but it is also a summary conviction court (s. 785 Cr. C.). It does not, however, have jurisdiction over drug offences, which are dealt with by the Quebec Provincial Court (criminal division).

The Montreal dataset differentiates between "decisions", primarily referring to bail decisions as well as other pre-trial decisions including changes to bail orders and stay of proceedings,[6] and "judgments", associated with sentencing. In particular, given our specific interest in conditions of release, "judgments" here refer to convicted individuals sentenced to one of two types of sentences: a form of probation (conditional discharge, probation, suspended sentence) or a conditional sentence (judgments imposing fines, incarceration, or other penalties that did not include conditions were expunged from the database). A case can include multiple decisions made as a criminal case proceeds, but only one "judgment" associated with a particular form of sentence. However, some judgments can include multiple sentences (overall, we have 52,821 sentences). Moreover, multiple conditions can be attached to one sentence.

Finally, there is one important limitation to the Montreal dataset: the database only provides detailed information about conditions associated with judgments (associated with sentencing) and not decisions (associated with bail or pre-trial). Thus, while we have obtained general statistics about the nature of the decisions taken by Municipal Court judges, we are unable to examine in detail the nature and number of bail conditions. Overall, we have analyzed 507,775 conditions imposed in different types of probation orders[7] and conditional sentence orders. The dataset (Table 4.2) predominantly comprises probation orders, accounting for 91.3% of all orders, as well as 8.5% comprising conditional sentence orders.

Young men are over-represented in both datasets. In Montreal (Table 4.3), the dataset comprises 81% men and 19% women (including 0.2% of the cases in which gender is not specified). On average, the accused individuals were 35 years old at their first appearance. Two-thirds of the men (66.5%) and the women (66%) were 40 years old and less, with half below 34 years old.

---

[6] Notes sent by Mr Sylvain Meloche from the Information Technologies Services of the City of Montreal (dated 23 May 2014).

[7] A reminder that there are three types of probation orders according to the Criminal Code: the sentencing judge can suspend the passing of sentence and direct that the offender be released on conditions (suspended sentence); secondly, the judge can impose a probation order in addition to a fine or a period or imprisonment not exceeding two years, and, finally, a judge can also make a probation order where it discharges an accused (conditional discharge). In the dataset, the Municipal Court also distinguishes probation orders that include restitution.

TABLE 4.2 *Sentences: summary statistics (Montreal, 2002–2014)*

Sentences	No.	Percentage
Probation (following incarceration)	30,220	57.2
Probation – suspended sentence	15,222	28.8
Probation with restitution	2,760	5.2
Probation – conditional discharge	40	0.1
Conditional sentence (CSO)	4,489	8.5
Other/Unknown	90	0.2
Totals	52,821	100

TABLE 4.3 *Age and gender (Montreal)*

Age group (years)	Men (80.9%)		Women (18.9%)	
	No.	Percentage	No.	Percentage
18–30	27,520	39.9	6,585	37.2
31–40	18,362	26.6	5,075	28.7
41–50	15,573	22.6	4,179	23.6
51–65	6,748	9.8	1,701	9.6
66 +	716	1	150	0.8
Totals	68,919	100	17,690	100

We find similar patterns in Vancouver, where 82% of all bail orders were issued to men and 18% to women. Slightly over half of all bail orders (51%) were issued to individuals of 40 years old or less, with 30% of them issued to individuals between 30 and 39 years old.

Neither dataset provides reliable information on the race or ethnicity of persons subject to conditions of release. While no information was available in Montreal, ethnicity is a self-reported field in the Vancouver database. According to the B.C. Court Services Branch, it is "notoriously inconsistent".[8] This being said, First Nations, Metis and Inuit, as well as Black Canadians are probably overrepresented in both datasets. For instance, according to Statistics Canada, in 2015–2016, Indigenous offenders accounted for 29% of admissions

---

[8] Shandley, 2013: 2. An accused may self-report using different ethnicities; the dataset comprised multiple examples of accused with inconsistent reporting throughout cases. Surname is also an unreliable indicator of ethnicity.

to provincial correctional services in B.C. (Reitano, 2017) Moreover, they make up one-third (34%) of the homeless population in Metro Vancouver despite representing only 2.5% of the population.[9]

The datasets were coded and analyzed using natural language processing (NLP). NLP draws from different fields of study, including artificial intelligence, linguistics, and computer science, and is designed to allow computers to process and analyze large amounts of natural language data (Chowdhury, 2003).

In light of their distinct characteristics, the two datasets are only comparable to some extent, and each of them has its limitations. For instance, the Vancouver dataset covers a slightly shorter period of time and does not allow us to account for the exact number of breaches associated with each case or individual. By contrast, the Montreal dataset provides extensive information on the evolution of cases over time, allowing us to follow the number of breaches, for instance, but is limited to probation and conditional sentences orders. Nevertheless, the datasets reveal some striking patterns, that replicate national trends, while allowing the opportunity for more detailed analysis.

CONDITIONS OF RELEASE ARE WIDESPREAD AT BAIL

Both datasets reveal the widespread use of conditions of release in bail and sentencing orders. This is noteworthy, as it raises questions concerning conformity with Canadian law, particularly in relation to bail. In Canadian law, accused persons are presumed innocent until proven guilty according to law. The right to presumption of innocence is protected by both s. 7 and 11(d) of the *Canadian Charter of Rights and Freedoms* (1982) as a fundamental principle of criminal law. This right also entails a constitutional right to bail, which is protected in section 11 (e) of the *Canadian Charter,* extending the effects of the presumption of innocence to the pre-trial phase.[10] According to the Supreme Court of Canada, s. 11(e) "contains two distinct elements, namely the right to 'reasonable bail' and the right not to be denied bail without 'just cause'".[11]

As a result, both the police and the courts have *the duty to release, to release at the earliest reasonable possibility, and on the least onerous grounds.*[12] Following an arrest, a peace officer shall release the individual unless it is

---

[9] Aboriginal Homelessness, 2017 Count in Metro Vancouver, Table 1 (September 2017): www.metrovancouver.org/services/regional-planning/homelessness/resources/Pages/default.aspx.
[10] *R. v. Pearson* (1992) 3 S.C.R. 665, pp. 688–689.
[11] *Ibid* at p. 689.
[12] *R. v. Antic* (2017) SCC 27, par. 67.

necessary to detain that individual in custody. The police officer may release that person unconditionally after issuing an appearance notice, or they may release him or her after requiring that he or she enters into an undertaking with conditions. According to the Criminal Code, conditions may include measures to ensure that the defendant will appear in court (e.g. remaining within the territorial jurisdiction, notifying the peace officer of any change of address or occupation, rendering one's passport, reporting on a regular basis), or "any other condition [. . .] necessary to ensure the safety and security of any victim or witness to the offence" (e.g. abstaining from communicating, possessing a firearm, consuming alcohol or drugs) (s. 503 (2.1) Cr. C.).

Alternatively, when the accused is held in custody, he or she may be released by a justice of the peace based on an agreement between the prosecutor and the defence in chamber, at the court of first appearance, or, in case of disagreement between the Crown and the defence, by a judge, after a bail hearing. The justice of the peace is to release the accused following the "ladder" principle: that is, *unconditional release is the default position* and the judge shall not make another order (conditional release or detention) unless the Crown shows why this is necessary and the other less restrictive rungs of the ladder have been rejected.[13] As a result, *there are no compulsory conditions of bail.* Unlike U.S. practice, recognizances with sureties or cash bails are considered extremely onerous forms of release, and are to be avoided, and if imposed should not be set so high that they amount to a detention order. Further, the justice has a positive obligation to inquire into the accused's ability to pay.[14]

In court, terms of release *shall only be imposed to address concerns related to one of three grounds*, namely (a) "to ensure attendance in court" (b) "to ensure the protection and safety of the public having regard to all the circumstances including the likelihood that the accused, if released from custody, will commit a criminal offence", or (c) "to maintain the public confidence in the administration of justice"[15] (s. 515(10) Cr. C.). In addition, conditions of release must not be imposed in an attempt to *change a person's behaviour* or to

---

[13] S. 515(3) Cr. C.; *Ibid* at par. 67 (c), (d), (e).

[14] *R.* v. *Antic, supra* note 12 at par. 67 (g), (h), (i).

[15] S. 515(10)(c) reads as follows: "[I]f the detention is necessary to maintain the public confidence in the administration of justice, having regard to all the circumstances, including (i) the apparent strength of the prosecution's case (ii) the gravity of the offence (iii) the circumstances surrounding the commission of the offence, including whether a firearm was used, and (iv) the fact that the accused is liable, on conviction, for a potentially length term of imprisonment or, in the case of an offence that involves a firearm, a minimum punishment of imprisonment for a term of three years or more".

punish. They should be *reasonable* and *not infringe on any constitutional rights.*

Despite these legal prescriptions, Canada-wide data reveal that unconditional release at bail is the *exception*, not the norm (Trotter, 2010; Sprott and Myers, 2011; Friedland, 2012; Myers and Dhillon, 2013; Myers, 2017). Nationally, there are currently more people held in remand centres then imprisoned after a finding of guilt: 61% of all adults in provincial and territorial correctional facilities in Canada are currently held in pre-trial detention, with Ontario (70%) and British Columbia (65%) having two of the highest rates in the country. By contrast, Quebec has slightly fewer remanded offenders than those sentenced in custody (45% in remand) (Malakieh, 2018). Regardless of these regional variations, however, while the rate at which Canadians are sentenced to custody has been steadily *declining* across the country, the rate at which people are held in remand has *increased* by 71% since 1998 (Burczycka and Munch, 2015; see also Webster, Doob, and Myers, 2009).

In addition, it is evident that when a person is released, the police and the courts almost automatically resort to (optional) conditions of release, instead of releasing individuals unconditionally, as the law and the Constitution stipulate. A 2013 government study made some striking findings in this regard, finding that, among the 1,729 accused for which data were available, 41.1% were detained in custody following arrest, while 58.9% were released. Among the 1,018 accused released by the police, at least 44.3% were released with conditions (through an undertaking or a recognizance), while in one of the three court locations this rate was as high as 76.4%.[16] Among all accused who were initially detained by police to appear in court, two-thirds were subsequently released at their bail hearing (65.9%) while 34.1% were remanded. However, it appears that not a single accused was released unconditionally at that stage of the proceedings (Beattie, Solecki, and Morton Bourgon, 2013: 14, 16, and 19; figure 4) (see also Sprott and Myers, 2011; Myers and Dhillon, 2013; Myers, 2017).

According to this study, the most common release type was an undertaking with conditions (54.7%), while 33.9% of the released accused signed their own recognizance with conditions and or sureties, 8% signed their own recognizance with conditions and deposit, and 3.3%, a recognizance with conditions, deposit, and surety (Beattie, Solecki, and Morton Bourgon, 2013). Therefore,

---

[16] The data used in the report were taken from the Justice Effectiveness Study (Beattie, Solecki, and Morton Bourgon, 2013) that collected data from Court and Crown files from five court locations in four provinces across Canada, including 3,093 unique criminal court cases. See Beattie, Solecki, and Morton Bourgon, 2013: 14 (Table 6).

TABLE 4.4 *Number of conditions per bail order (Vancouver)*

Number of conditions	Bail orders	Percentage	Cumulative percentage
0	2,326	3.1	3.1
1	7,754	10.4	13.5
2	12,245	16.5	30
3	12,415	16.7	46.7
4	11,541	15.5	62.2
5	8,050	10.8	73
6	6,619	8.9	81.9
7	4,640	6.2	88.1
8	2,997	4.0	92.1
9	1,662	2.2	94.3
10	1,056	1.4	95.7
11	923	1.2	96.9
12	1,440	1.9	98.8
13	358	0.5	99.4
14+	382	0.5	99.9
Totals	**74,408**	100	100

although the courts seem to adhere to the ladder principle when it comes to giving priority to the first rung of the ladder before the others are considered, they seem to forget that this principle first requires that "save for exceptions, an unconditional release on an undertaking is the default position when granting release: s. 515(1)" (*R.* v. *Antic*, par. 67).

Our own datasets also confirm these trends. As shown in Table 4.4, in Vancouver, 97% of all provincial court-imposed bail orders issued between 2005 and 2012 contained some kind of condition, nearly half (47%) of all bail orders had three conditions or less, while 41% contained between 4 and 7 conditions, with nearly 12% having 8 conditions or more.

Each bail order in the Vancouver dataset contained on average 4.4 conditions, while each bail case contained on average 5.8 conditions, all of them optional (Table 4.5). Overall, the 74,408 bail orders generated 326,388 conditions in the seven years, that is a total of 61.8% of all the conditions in the dataset (n = 528,316).

Furthermore, as we shall see in the next section, the number of "optional" conditions imposed at bail is actually higher than at probation (4.4 conditions on average per bail order as opposed to 3.9 optional conditions per

TABLE 4.5 *Average number of conditions per bail order (Vancouver)*

Order type	No. Orders	No. Conditions	Average number
Bail	74,408	326,388	4.4

TABLE 4.6 *Types of bail decisions (Montreal)*

Type of decisions (Cr. C.)	No.	Percentage
Undertaking with no condition: 515(1)	3,340	3.8
Undertaking with conditions: 515(2)(a)	39,088	44.8
Recognizance with no condition: 515 (2)(b)	730	0.8
Recognizance with conditions: 515 (2)(b)(c)	11,776	13.5
Recognizance without deposit or surety: 515(2)(b)	9,023	10.4
Recognizance with deposit or surety (cash bail): 515(2) (c) and (d)	4,130	4.7
Recognizance with/without surety (third party): 515(2)(e)	1,170	1.3
Change to court order – denied or granted	80	0.1
Undertaking – modified with conditions	17,801	20.4
Undertaking – modified with no condition	82	0.1
Totals	**87,220**	**100**

probation order). Interestingly, recent data from the Canadian Centre for Justice Statistics show that the number of conditions may have increased even further between 2012 and 2017. According to Malakieh (2018: 10), an average of seven conditions were imposed in each bail order issued in the province of British Columbia in 2016–2017.

We do not have the same detailed bail data for Montreal. Yet our analysis of aggregate data on the nature of the pre-trial decisions made by the Municipal Court of Montreal between 2002 and 2014 presented in Table 4.6 shows that the vast majority (95.3%) of all bail decisions included some kind of condition, including entering into a recognizance for a certain amount with or without sureties, leaving only 4,152 of those decisions (4.7%) without the imposition of conditions.[17]

---

[17] This includes 730 (0.8%) referring to an "accused released unconditionally upon him or her entering into a recognizance", 3,340 decisions (3.8%) referring to "accused released based on an undertaking with no condition", and 82 decisions (0.1%) referring to "undertakings, modified, with no condition".

PROBATION AND CSO GENERATE NUMEROUS
CONDITIONS OF RELEASE

The evidence suggests that bail is the major generator of conditions of release in general. Probation and conditional sentence orders (CSOs) are also noteworthy, however. Probation entails the release of a convicted offender in the community under supervision upon the promise of good behaviour. The offender is released subject to a series of additional conditions and under the supervision of a probation officer. There are three types of probation orders in Canadian law: the sentencing judge can suspend the passing of sentence and direct that the offender be released on conditions (suspended sentence); secondly, the judge can impose a probation order in addition to a fine or a period or imprisonment not exceeding two years, and, finally, a judge can also make a probation order when he or she discharges an accused (conditional discharge). Only the first and third types of probation orders are considered alternatives to incarceration, whereas the second type may be imposed in addition to incarceration and is better described as complementary. This second type of probation is distinct from parole.[18]

Canadian law limits the use of conditions in probation. During the period covered by our datasets, there were three compulsory conditions, including to keep the peace and be of good behaviour, to appear before the court when required to do so by the court, and to notify the court or the probation officer in advance of any change of address, employment, and occupation. In 2014, a fourth condition was added to "abstain from communicating, directly or indirectly, with any victim, witness or other person identified in the order" or that he or she "refrain from going to any place specified in the order". The sentencing judge may also prescribe optional conditions from a specific list or "any other reasonable conditions as the court considers desirable … for protecting society and for facilitating the offender's successful reintegration into the community" (s. 732.1 (3) (h) Cr. C.).

Probation orders impose certain restrictions on the freedom of an offender, but they have legally been understood as *rehabilitative* sentencing tools.[19] The sentencing judge may not impose conditions that would be contrary to

---

[18] By comparison, in the U.S.A., probation is imposed in lieu of incarceration and corresponds to that first type of probation orders, although in some jurisdictions incarceration itself can be imposed as a condition of probation. The second type of probation described here is sometimes referred to as "post-release supervision" following completed custodial sentences, or parole. See Klingele, 2013.

[19] *R. v. Proulx*, 2000 SCC 5, par. 32; *R. v. Shoker*, 2006 SCC 44, par. 10; *R. v. Goeujon* (2006) BCCA 261, par. 49.

provincial and federal laws or to the *Canadian Charter*. The conditions must also be *reasonable* and aim at protecting the society and facilitating the offender's reintegration. They cannot be primarily *punitive*,[20] and will generally be linked to the particular offence, but need not be.[21]

Finally, conditional sentences are jail sentences served in the community. First introduced in the Criminal Code in 1996 in response to the problem of overincarceration and critiques that imprisonment was costly and largely ineffective, conditional sentences have been consistently limited through subsequent modifications of the Code, first in 1997, then in 2007 and 2012, and are now rarely used in the criminal justice system.[22] They require that the court first decide to impose a sentence of imprisonment of less than two years before considering whether the sentence can be served in the community.[23] This being said, the sentencing judge need not impose a sentence of fixed duration during the first step of the process and there is no requirement that the duration of the conditional sentence be the equivalent of the jail term that would otherwise have been imposed (par. 104).

Like probation orders, CSOs include a series of compulsory and optional conditions, but they should include punitive conditions that are restrictive of the offender's liberty.[24] Until 2014, CSOs included five compulsory conditions.[25] In addition to the optional conditions available for probation, the court can also prescribe that the offender "comply with such other reasonable conditions as the court considers desirable, . . . for securing the good conduct of the offender and for preventing a repetition by the offender of the same offence or the commission of other offences" (s. 742.3(2)(f) Cr. C.).

In both Vancouver and Montreal, probation and CSOs generated many conditions beyond these compulsory requirements. In our Vancouver dataset, probation and CSO orders respectively generated on average 6.9 and 11.3 conditions (Table 4.7). Given that during the period covered by our study, there were, as noted, respectively three and five compulsory conditions attached to probation and CSOs in Canada's Criminal Code, these numbers

---

[20] *R. v. Shoker, supra* note 19 at par. 13–14; *R. v. Proulx, supra* note 19 at par. 33; *R. v. Ziatas* (1973) 13 CCC (2d) 287 (Ont. C.A.); *R. v. Traverse*, 2006 MBCA 7.

[21] *R. v. Shoker, supra* note 19 at par. 13–14; see also *R. v. Leschyshyn*, 2007 MBCA 41; *R. v. Etifier*, 2009 BCCA 292; *R. v. Timmins*, 2006 BCCA 354; *R. v. Baydal*, 2011 BCCA 211.

[22] In 2014–2015, conditional sentences were imposed in 4% of the cases across Canada and 7% in B.C. See www.statcan.gc.ca/tables-tableaux/sum-som/l01/cst01/legal22k-eng.htm.

[23] *R. v. Proulx, supra* note 19 at par. 29.

[24] *Ibid.*, at par 34 and 102.

[25] S. 742.3 (1.1). Cr. C.

TABLE 4.7 *Average number of conditions per sentencing order (Vancouver)*

Order type	No. Orders	No. Conditions	Average number (optional)
Probation	22,814	157,435	6.9 (3.9)
CSO	3,930	44,493	11.3 (6.3)

include an average of three mandatory and 3.9 optional conditions per probation order and five mandatory and 6.3 optional conditions per CSO.

Half (51%) of probation orders in Vancouver contained between 4 and 6 conditions and 44% of them included 7 conditions or more (Figure 4.1). By contrast, 34% of CSOs contained between 7 and 9 conditions and 46% of them included between 10 and 13 conditions. Furthermore, 60% of CSOs had 10 conditions or more whereas this was only the case in 10% of all probation orders.[26] Figure 4.1 presents the distribution of conditions per order type (adding bail for comparison purposes).

The number of conditions is slightly lower at the Montreal Courthouse (Table 4.8). On average, cases included 6.35 conditions with a median of 5 conditions. Nearly 80% of all sentences included between 4 and 7 conditions.

The number of conditions also vary considerably depending on the type of offences and sentencing order. As such, probation orders following incarceration and suspended sentences contained an average of 5.7 and 5.8 conditions as opposed to 6 conditions for conditional discharge and 10.3 for CSOs (Table 4.9).

Finally, the number of imposed conditions increases significantly as an individual accumulates cases at the Montreal Courthouse, ranging from an average of 5.9 conditions in the first case to 7.2 conditions for individuals who

---

[26] The high average number of optional conditions in CSOs is consistent with the fact that conditional sentence orders are by definition sentences of imprisonment and should generally include punitive conditions that are restrictive of the offender's liberty. However, in *R. v. Proulx supra* note 19, Chief Justice Lamer held that "conditions such as house arrest or strict curfews should be the norm, not the exception" (par. 36). He also insisted on imposing restrictive conditions, drawing the line between probation and CSOs: "[T]here must be a reason for failing to impose punitive conditions when a conditional sentence order is made. Sentencing judges should always be mindful of the fact that conditional sentences are only to be imposed on offenders who would otherwise have been sent to jail. If the judge is of the opinion that punitive conditions are unnecessary, then probation, rather than a conditional sentence, is most likely the appropriate disposition" (par. 37).

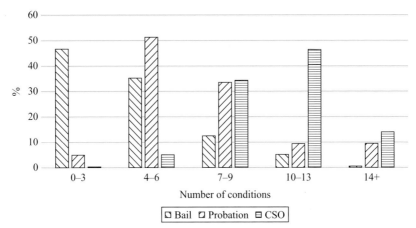

FIGURE 4.1 Percentage of conditions per type of order (Vancouver)

TABLE 4.8 *Number of conditions per case (probation and CSOs) (Montreal)*

Number of conditions, per case	No. of cases		
	No.	Percentage	Percentage (cumulative)
1	7	0	0
2	1	0	0
3	10	0	0
4	8,355	16.9	16.9
5	17,736	35.8	52.7
6	7,937	16.0	68.7
7	4,909	9.9	78.6
8	2,830	5.7	84.3
9	1,985	4.0	88.3
10	1,628	3.3	91.6
11	1,306	2.6	94.2
12	962	1.9	96.2
13	615	1.2	97.4
14	448	0.9	98.3
15 +	873	1.7	100

TABLE 4.9 *Average and median number of conditions by type of sentencing order (Montreal)*

Sentencing order	Average	Median
Probation – conditional discharge	6.0	6
Probation – following incarceration	5.7	5
Probation – suspended sentence	5.8	5
Conditional sentence	10.3	10
Conditional sentence + restitution	13	13
Totals	6.2	5

TABLE 4.10 *Number of conditions and accumulation of cases*

Case position	Average no. conditions per case
1st case	5.9
2nd case	6.2
3rd case	6.5
4th case	6.6
5th case	6.7
6th case	6.8
7th case +	7.2

are at their seventh case or more, suggesting the "revolving door" syndrome associated with conditional release (Table 4.10).[27]

DURATION

Not only are there multiple conditions in the Vancouver and Montreal database, but individuals remained subject to them for a long time period, increasing, as we shall see, the risk of breaches. It should be remembered that an undertaking issued by a police officer is effective immediately and even before the information relating to the charges is laid and an appearance notice confirmed (s. 145(5.1) Cr. C. and *R.* v. *Oliveira*, 2009 ONCA 219). Moreover, any form of release, including the powers of release conferred upon the police,

---

[27] These averages were obtained by removing the cases for which no condition was issued.

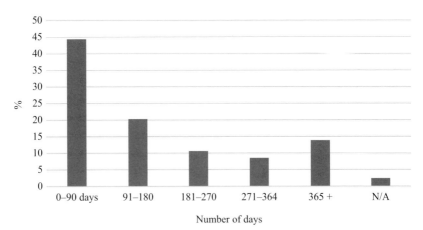

FIGURE 4.2 Number of days between bail release order and case conclusion (Vancouver)

TABLE 4.11 *Duration of probation orders (Montreal)*

	Number of days	
Number of cases	Average	Median
1	449.1	365
2	759.3	545
3	965.6	730
4	1207.1	869
5	1392.8	1,095
6	1467.7	1,161
7 +	2164.8	2,039

remains in effect until the end of the trial or until the accused is sentenced (unless reviewed or revoked).

In Vancouver, in almost two-thirds of the cases (64%), individuals stayed on bail for less than six months (44% of the cases were concluded in 90 days or fewer and 20% of the cases were concluded within 90 and 180 days). However, nearly 25% of the cases were concluded *after* six months, with 14% of them lasting over a year after the bail order is issued (see Figure 4.2).

Similarly, sentencing data from Montreal show that while a person with only one court case remained on probation for a little more than a year (a reminder that each probation order can span up to three years), those who accumulated seven cases or more can stay on probation for four years and a half with no interruption (Table 4.11).

GEOGRAPHICAL RESTRICTIONS ARE AMONG THE MOST
FREQUENT CONDITIONS IMPOSED

Judging by our datasets, conditions of release are widely used in both bail and probation, with multiple conditions attached to one order, in many cases, often operative for substantial periods of time. In what follows, we look at the nature of these conditions, noting the prevalence of geographical restrictions placed on release.

Overall, the most frequent condition imposed in Vancouver is the general condition to keep the peace and be of good behaviour (15% of all the conditions in the dataset). This is not surprising because it is a "compulsory" condition for probation and conditional sentence orders. Moreover, although optional at bail,[28] it is almost systematically imposed at that early stage as well: recent data from Malakieh (2018) shows that 74% of all bail orders in B.C. in 2016–2017 contained such a condition.

Yet, excluding all general and largely compulsory conditions, geographical restrictions occupy between 40% and 50% of all conditions imposed depending on the moment when they are imposed. In the entire Vancouver dataset, conditions that have a direct impact on people's spatial mobility and use of public and private spaces, namely no-go and no-contact orders, red zones, requirements to reside, and curfews (hereinafter referred to as "territorial conditions") represent 41% of all the conditions imposed. No-go conditions are the most prevalent within that category, representing 12.3% of all the conditions imposed, arriving in second place overall. No-contact conditions arrived in sixth position, with 8%, and area restrictions followed in seventh position, with 7.2% (Figure 4.3).

The frequency of conditions at bail is broadly similar to the overall pattern, with territorial conditions still representing 41.1% of all conditions imposed (no-go conditions represent 10.7%, while no-contact conditions and area restrictions come in fifth (10.3%) and sixth (10%) positions) (Figure 4.4).

[28] Although justices of the peace have the authority to impose it, this condition is discretionary insofar as the Crown is required to show cause that it is a reasonable condition to be imposed on a defendant at bail: *R. v. S.K.*, [1998] S.J. No. 863 (Sask. Prov. Ct), par. 25–27; *R. v. A.D.B.* 2009 SKPC 120: "Unfortunately there appears to be a belief among some counsel and justice officials that there are statutory conditions of release. I have been told on several occasions that the conditions to keep the peace and be of good behaviour and appear before the Court when required to do so are statutory. While these requirements are explicit in an undertaking or recognizance, they are not statutory conditions of judicial interim release. Nor should they be considered mandatory or usual conditions of release" (par. 11) "This is a practice which must not continue" (par. 22). See also *R. v. Doncaster*, 2013 NSSC 328 blaming the standard form used by prosecutors.

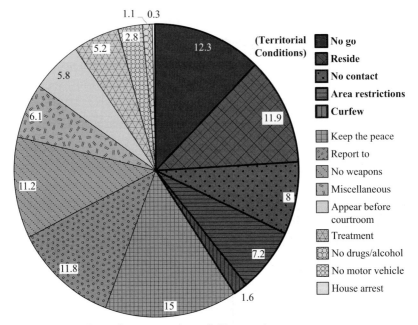

FIGURE 4.3 Specific conditions imposed overall (Vancouver)

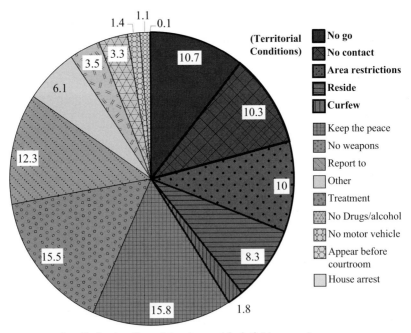

FIGURE 4.4 Specific "optional" conditions imposed for bail (Vancouver)

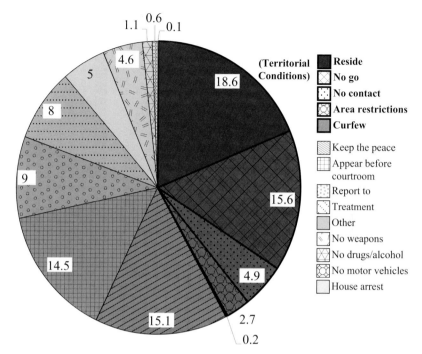

1.1 0.6 0.1

4.6
5
8
9
14.5
15.1
2.7
0.2
4.9
15.6
18.6

(Territorial
Conditions)

■ Reside
☐ No go
⋯ No contact
⊠ Area restrictions
■ Curfew

▨ Keep the peace
▦ Appear before
courtroom
Report to
Treatment
☐ Other
No weapons
⊠ No drugs/alcohol
⊠ No motor vehicles
☐ House arrest

FIGURE 4.5 Most common conditions (probation) (Vancouver)

The situation differs for probation orders where spatial conditions still represent 41.8% of all conditions imposed, but are distributed differently (Figure 4.5). The most frequent condition overall is to reside (18.6%) followed by no-go conditions (15.6%). Area restrictions arrive only in tenth position (2.7%).

Finally, territorial conditions account for 49% of all the conditions imposed in CSOs (Figure 4.6). This significant increase may be attributed to the fact that CSOs are jail sentences served in the community and thus require spatial fixity and strict mobility control. Conditions to reside and no-go orders are quite frequent (14.9% and 11.6%), while 5.5% of all conditions are curfews, with area restrictions and house arrest comprising 2% of the conditions.

The Montreal dataset also shows the great importance of geographical restrictions, particularly in probation orders. In the following tables, we focus on optional conditions of probation and CSOs,[29] distinguishing between those imposed for different types of sentencing orders.

---

[29] To conduct this analysis, we focused on 4,489 CSOs and 45,442 probation orders (including 30,220 probation orders following a period of incarceration, and 15,222 suspended sentences of

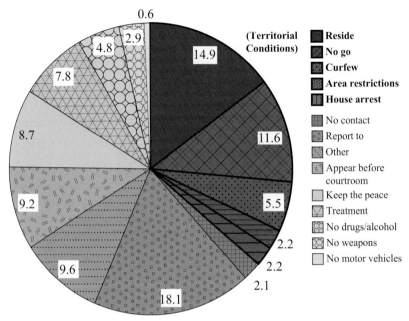

FIGURE 4.6 Specific "optional" conditions imposed for CSOs (Vancouver)

In Figure 4.7, we can see that territorial conditions are the most frequent type of non-compulsory conditions included in Montreal probation orders: 42% of probation orders issued after a period of incarceration and 25% of suspended sentences of probation contained at least one no-go condition, whereas abstinence clauses were the most frequent in CSOs, followed by conditions to reside (37.5%) and curfews (38%). Overall, 79.5% of probation orders following incarceration contained at least one spatial restriction of some kind. In comparison, conditions that are associated with changes in behaviour (such as abstinence clauses, therapies, and weapon carrying) were only present in 34% of such probation orders. By contrast, spatial conditions and conditions associated with desired changes in behaviour split half and half in CSOs (51% vs. 51%).

probation). We have excluded other types of sentences, including probation orders with an element of restitution. As a result, we only conducted our analysis on 383,932 conditions as opposed to a total of 507,775 in the overall database.

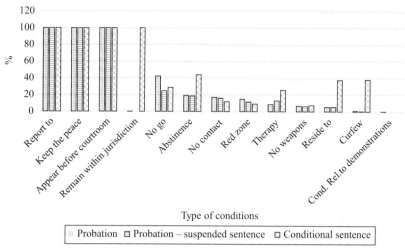

FIGURE 4.7 Percentage of court orders with at least one condition, per type (Montreal)

AREA RESTRICTIONS ARE PREDOMINANTLY APPLIED IN THE CASES OF DRUGS- AND PROSTITUTION-RELATED OFFENCES

Different types of conditions are imposed for different (alleged) offences. In Vancouver, put simply, drug offences mostly generate area restrictions, conditions to reside, and to report, whereas violent offences lead to area restrictions and no-contact conditions; and administrative offences are primarily associated with no-go conditions. Property offences attract all types of conditions (Table 4.12; Figure 4.8). Put another way, 53% of all bail orders issued in relation to alleged drug offences and 52% of all bail orders issued in offences against the person included an area restriction. Moreover, overall, 29% of all bail orders included a red zone (21,481 out of 74,064 bail orders)[30] (Table 4.13).

In Montreal, as the figures below illustrate, territorial conditions are heavily represented in every category of offence, although different kinds of offences attract different types of spatial conditions. Focusing only on optional conditions, no-go orders are the most prevalent territorial conditions in property offences (up to 66% of all sentencing orders contained a no-go condition)

---

[30] Interestingly, however, most recent data from Malakieh (2018) show that up to 58% of all bail orders issued in B.C. in 2016–2017 contained at least one area restriction, indicating that these numbers might be growing significantly.

TABLE 4.12 *Most common conditions by type of offence (Vancouver)*

	No-go (%)	Red zone (%)	No-contact (%)	Report to (%)	Reside (%)
Administrative	40.3	9.8	8.7	19.1	16.5
Drug	3.0	33.5	9.2	23.4	20.1
Property	45.3	20.7	15.0	36.2	41.8
Person	10.4	34.2	65.3	19.7	19.6
Other	0.9	1.8	1.7	1.7	1.9

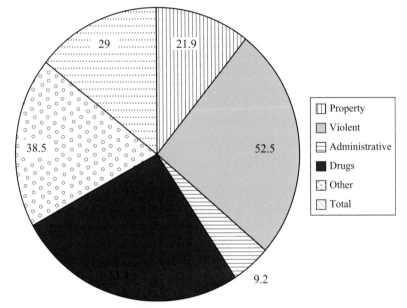

FIGURE 4.8 Number and percentage of bail orders with red zones (Vancouver)

(Figure 4.9), whereas no-contact and red zones are prevalent in offences against the person (61.3% contained a no-contact and 37.3% contained a red zone) (Figure 4.10). Red zones are also widely used in offences related to prostitution (referred to in Montreal as "public morals") (45.6%) (Figure 4.11). Not surprisingly, conditions related to participating in a public demonstration are the most prevalent condition for offences of illegal assembly and rioting (public order offences) (Figure 4.12). Finally, offences against the administration of justice tend to attract a more diversified set of conditions: they primarily include conditions related to changes in behaviour (22% and 11.5% of all orders respectively contain an abstinence clause and a condition to

TABLE 4.13 *Number and percentage of bail orders with red zones (Vancouver)*

	Property	Violent	Administrative	Drugs	Other	Totals
Cases with 1+ red zones	4,504	8,688	2,338	5,511	440	21,481
Total number of cases	20,547	16,537	25,511	10,326	1,143	74,064
Percentage w/red zones	21.9%	52.5%	9.2%	53.4%	38.5%	29%

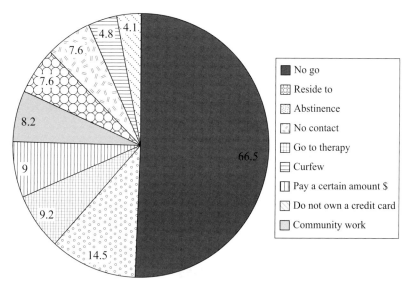

FIGURE 4.9 Property offences with at least one optional condition, excluding mandatory conditions, per type (Montreal)

attend therapy), but no-go orders are the most important type of spatial conditions (17%) (Figure 4.13).

It is clear, therefore, that conditions of release and particularly territorial conditions are widely used in both Vancouver and Montreal.

While this chapter focuses on the Canadian criminal justice system, comparative research shows that conditional orders also play an important role in the administration of justice in other common law jurisdictions, including the U.S.A. and the U.K. For instance, bail conditions are widely used in England and Wales, with up to half of defendants released on conditional bail and an important decrease of unconditional bail (Raine and Wilson, 1996; Hucklesby, 2001; 2002; 2009 – comparing bail in Australia,

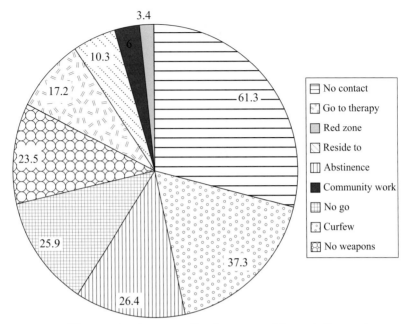

FIGURE 4.10 Offences against the person with at least one condition, excluding mandatory conditions, per type (Montreal)

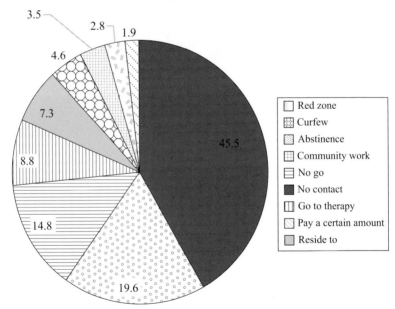

FIGURE 4.11 Offence against public morals (prostitution) with at least one optional condition, excluding mandatory conditions, per type (Montreal)

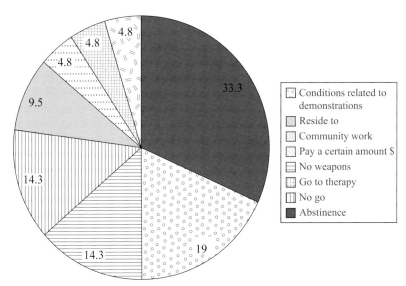

FIGURE 4.12 Offences against the public order (illegal assembly/rioting) with at least one optional condition, excluding mandatory conditions, per type (Montreal)

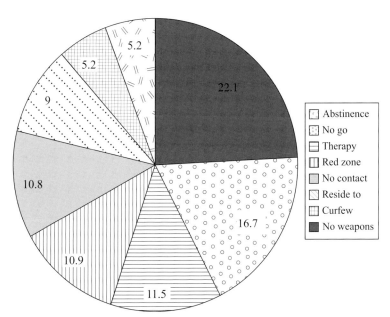

FIGURE 4.13 Offences against the administration of justice with at least one optional condition, excluding mandatory conditions, per type (Montreal)

the U.K., and Canada). English bail orders regularly include curfews, non-association, and exclusion requirements (Cape and Edwards, 2010; Turner, 2016). Moreover, police powers were recently extended in England by amendments to the Criminal Justice Act (2003) to include pre-charge (i.e. a person suspected, but not accused, of a criminal offence) release conditions prohibiting an individual from engaging in any protest activity, including the use of geographical exclusion zones (Lewis and Evans, 2009; Cape and Edwards, 2010; NETPOL, 2011). Finally, following amendments to the Criminal Justice Act (2003), exclusion requirements and curfews are also regularly imposed (sometimes with electronic monitoring) in the context of community orders as well as suspended sentence orders (see Sentencing Guidelines Council, 2004).

According to the most recent statistics from the Bureau of Justice Statistics of the United States, over 3.9 million Americans are on probation every year and 40% of them are found breaching their conditions (Carson, 2014). Geographical exclusion zones, including stay-out-of-drug-areas orders (SODAs), stay-out-of-areas-of-prostitution orders (SOAPs), as well as stay-away orders, are regularly used as probation conditions in the U.S.A. (Beckett and Herbert, 2010a; Hill, 2005). Moreover, recent studies have shown that U.S. attorneys systematically request pre-trial stay-away orders for defendants charged with a crime related to drugs or prostitution (Prince, 2006). Discussions regarding reform of the U.S. bail system may benefit from our findings, sounding a cautionary note regarding the use of community supervision as an alternative to incarceration, something which will become apparent in the following subsection (see Klingele, 2013).

CONDITIONAL ORDERS, INCLUDING AREA RESTRICTIONS, GENERATE NUMEROUS BREACHES

These pervasive and growing numbers of conditions, lasting for long periods of time and directly encroaching on people's spatial mobility and use of public space lead to an increasing number of breaches. In Canada, failure to comply with bail or probation orders are criminal offences of their own (s. 145(3)(5.1) and 733.1 Cr. C.), a subset of the broader category of offences against the administration of justice (AJO).[31]

---

[31] Administration of Justice Offences (AJO) are a suite of offences including failure to comply with a court order, breach of probation, failure to appear, being unlawfully at large, escaping or helping escape from unlawful custody, and other offences. See Department of Justice Canada, 2009: 4 (Table 1).

AJO violations may thus lead to arrest and additional charges for breaches, entrapping individuals in a spiral of criminalization and incarceration. As our vignettes in Chapter 1 pointed out and will be demonstrated in Chapter 7, marginalized individuals are frequently charged with a minor criminal offence, such as communication for the purposes of prostitution, drug possession, illegal assembly, small theft, or common assault. They are then released on bail with restrictive and often unrealistic conditions. Predictably, they often breach these conditions (Sprott and Myers, 2011; Myers and Dhillon, 2013). As a result, the police often arrest them and hold them in overnight custody before they appear before the judge. As an accused person found in violation of a bail order is subject to a reverse onus provision before he or she can be released again as per s. 515(6)c) Cr. C., they bear the legal burden of showing on the balance of probabilities that they do not present a risk of flight or a threat to the security of the public, including the risk of committing another offence, or that their release will not threaten the public confidence in the administration of justice. In many cases, individuals plead guilty at the first opportunity and are also released on probation with conditions, which they, in turn, may breach.

Finally, failure to comply with conditions issued in a CSO may include suspending the conditional sentence order and directing that the offender serve in custody a portion or the remainder of his or her sentence (s. 742.6(9) Cr. C). As a result, bail, probation, or CSOs which are all too often presented as alternatives to imprisonment come back full circle, bringing back individuals into custody and adding, in passing, yet another offence to their criminal record. Conditions of release are thus best described as complements to incarceration rather than substitutes.

This is not an exceptional phenomenon. A staggering *one in ten* of all police-reported Criminal Code offences Canada-wide is an offence against the administration of justice (Burczycka and Munch, 2015). Moreover, in 75% of the cases, administration of justice offences were *the* most serious offences involved in the incident. While the overall number of police reported offences against the administration of justice slightly decreased in Canada between 2004 and 2014, reports of the specific offence of failure to comply with conditions[32] increased by 8%. Failure to comply with conditions and breach

---

[32] The Uniform Crime Reporting Survey (UCR) code "failure to comply with conditions" 3410 includes the following Criminal Code sections: 145(3-5.1a), 145(3-5.1b), 810(3b), 810.01(4), 810.1(3.1), 810.2(4), 811(a), 811(b).

TABLE 4.14 *Breached cases (Vancouver)*

	No. of cases	Breach	Percentage	Additional breach cases	Averages
Bail	47,550	5,493	11.6	8,426	1.53
Probation	22,794	5,367	23.5	10,274	1.91
CSO	3,910	1,463	37.4	3,132	2.14
Totals	74,254	12,323	16.6	21,832	1.77

of probation[33] represented 79% of all police-reported AJOs committed in 2014, with failure to comply being *the* most common offence (57%) and breach of probation in second position (22%) (8; Chart 3).[34]

Failures to comply with a bail or probation orders have thus consistently been the top two most common offences in adult criminal courts for at least a decade in Canada, amounting to approximately 25% of all criminal cases. Further, in 2013/2014, in adult criminal courts across Canada, 40% of all completed cases included at least one administration of justice charge, an increase of 6% from 2005/2006 (13). Among those completed cases, 50% included a charge for failure to comply with conditions and 33% included a charge of breach of probation. While, as we shall see, the human cost is enormous, the financial cost in an already overburdened and under-resourced system is also noteworthy. In 2009 alone, it is estimated that administration of justice offences cost the Canadian justice system approximately $730 million (Department of Justice Canada, 2009: 14; Table 10).

Our quantitative data echo these findings. Conditional orders issued at bail and at sentencing are associated with an important number of failures to comply, or breaches, in both Vancouver and Montreal, clearly illustrating the revolving door in which individuals are caught. The Vancouver data (Table 4.14) reveal that of the 47,550 substantive cases of bail,[35] 5,493 were breached (11.6%). In turn, these breached cases generated 8,426 additional breaches, for an average of 1.53 additional breach per breached case. The number of breaches is even higher at sentencing. As such, 23.5%, or 5,357

---

[33] The UCR code "Breach of Probation Order" includes Criminal Code sections: 161(4a), 161(4b), 733.1(1a), 733.1(1b), 753.3(1).

[34] Other offences against the administration of justice include failures to appear, escape custody, prisoner unlawfully at large, and others.

[35] According to the memo from the Court Services Branch, substantive bail cases are "what breaches are measured against, i.e. how many substantive cases were breached". See Shandley, 2013: addendum.

cases of the 22,794 substantive probation cases, were breached, with the breached cases generating an additional 10,274 breaches, with an average of 1.91 breach per breached case. The actual breach of probation rates are likely to be higher because some of the substantive probation cases have breaching probation as their most serious offence. Finally, there were 3,910 substantive CSO cases, and, of those, 1,463 (or 37.4%) were breached. The breached cases generated on average 2.14 additional breaches for a total of 3,132 cases. The fact that breached orders led to between 1.5 or twice the numbers of charges strongly indicates that several individuals breached their orders multiple times.

While significant, recorded breach rates likely undercount actual rates, especially at bail, for at least four reasons. First, in many cases an accused may breach their conditions of bail but is never charged. In such cases the breaches will not be recorded in the JUSTIN database. This is confirmed by our interviews with legal actors who suggested that many people were brought to court for breach, and warned by the judge without being formally charged. Secondly, some of the substantive bail cases have breaching bail under s. 145 Cr. C. as their most serious charge, which indicates that the accused was already on bail for a previous offence. Thirdly, the data do not include police issued appearance notices or promises to appear. Cases charged under s. 145(5) Cr. C., which refers to failing to appear pursuant to a police-issued promise to appear, are not considered "breach" bail cases. Finally, some of the substantive cases have not had yet the opportunity to be breached given the cut-offs for the collection of the data.

While we are unable to follow the trajectories of distinct individuals in Vancouver due to database restrictions, in Montreal we found that roughly one in five (19.7%) of the persons who had three cases or more at the Municipal Court of Montreal accounted for more than half (55.8%) of the caseload of the Court, with those who have seven cases or more accounting for 30% of the caseload (Table 4.15), an indication that a group of individuals constantly cycle through the justice system.

Further, as shown in Table 4.16, 59% (55.3% + 3.7%) of those who had accumulated two cases or more had at least one offence against the administration of justice (AJO) on their record, and 55% of those who have accumulated four cases or more had a least 2 AJOs on their record. Finally, 99% of those who had 7 cases or more had at least one AJO. The vast majority of AJOs in the database are breaches (80%). In other words, breaches are directly associated with AJOs.

As a result, there is a strong correlation in the Montreal data between breaches and accumulation of cases (Pearson's r: 0.854). Furthermore, there was a greater correlation between the accumulation of cases and cases that

TABLE 4.15 *Accumulation of cases, per individual (Montreal)*

	Individual		Case	
No. of cases	No.	Percentage	No.	Percentage
1	26,572	64.8	26,572	29.9
2	6,344	15.5	12,688	14.3
3	2,749	6.7	8,247	9.3
4	1,511	3.7	6,044	6.8
5	949	2.3	4,745	5.3
6	667	2.3	4,002	4.5
7 +	2,183	5.3	26,613	29.9
Totals	40,975	100	88,911	100

contained at least one offence against the administration of justice than any other type of offences.

THERE IS A STATISTICAL ASSOCIATION BETWEEN BREACH RATES AND CERTAIN TERRITORIAL CONDITIONS OF RELEASE, INCLUDING RED ZONES

The data from Vancouver and Montreal reveal the widespread prevalence of conditions of release, including the common use of geographical restrictions, particularly in the case of drug- and sex-work-related charges. These, in turn, generate numerous breaches. By conducting regression analysis, we were able to identify whether certain types of conditions were statistically associated with a higher or lower likelihood of breach.

To do so, we followed William Damon's (2014) methodology, which in turn borrowed from Jane Sprott and Nicole Myers's 2011 analysis of bail conditions imposed in a Toronto Youth Bail Court. Sprott and Myers used a logistical regression model to show a correlation between an increased likelihood of breach, the time spent on bail, and the number of conditions imposed, controlling for a number of relevant demographic and legal variables.[36] While there are important differences between Damon's and our comparable dataset, and that of Sprott and Myers, which came from structured courtroom

---

[36] Logistical regression is similar to linear multiple regression, but it is more suitable for measuring the log odds of a dichotomous variable (in this case, breach: Y/N) rather than a continuous variable.

TABLE 4.16 *Number of offences against the administration of justice per number of cases (Montreal)*

No. of cases/AJO		0	1	2	3	4	5	6	7 +	Totals
1	N	24,978	1,594	0	0	0	0	0	0	26,572
	%	94.0	6.0	0	0	0	0	0	0	100
2	N	2,604	3,506	234	0	0	0	0	0	6,344
	%	41.0	55.3	3.7	0	0	0	0	0	100
3	N	492	1,538	672	47	0	0	0	0	2,749
	%	17.9	55.9	24.4	17.1	0	0	0	0	100
4	N	153	533	630	178	17	0	0	0	1,511
	%	10.13	35.3	41.7	11.8	1.1	0	0	0	100
5	N	58	185	392	249	59	6	0	0	949
	%	6.1	19.5	41.3	26.2	6.20	0.6	0	0	100
6	N	33	85	175	228	111	34	1	0	667
	%	4.9	12.7	26.2	34.2	16.6	5.1	0.1	0	100
7+	N	25	80	216	333	378	310	211	630	2,183
	%	1.1	3.7	9.9	15.3	17.3	14.2	9.7	28.9	100
Totals	N	28,343	7,521	2,319	1,035	565	350	212	630	40,975
	%	69.17	18.4	5.7	2.5	1.4	0.9	0.5	1.5	100

observation (2014), we reached similar conclusions in some regards. For instance, as we will see below, we found that there is a significant relationship between the number of bail conditions in a court order and the likelihood of breach.

Following Damon, the unit of analysis is an individual case. As a reminder, a case is defined as one accused person with one or more charges that have resulted in a first appearance in court. In cases in which the accused reoffends, one case could involve multiple bail orders each with unique conditions of release. The dependent variable considered in the following analysis is an allegation of breach. This variable was dummy coded (1 = Breach Yes). The statistical model used here begins by controlling for two demographic variables of the accused: age and gender. Age is an interval variable. Gender was dummy coded: 1 = Male; 0 = Female, as our data did not allow us to account for a broader gender spectrum. As the conditions are not normally distributed, they were split into four roughly equal categories (counts): 1 = 1 to 3; 2 = 4 to 6; 3 = 7 to 9; and 4 = 9+ conditions of release. The length of bail was dummy coded so that 0 = less than 190 days; 1 = 190 or more days. Finally, some types of conditions of release were added to the model as binary variables: red zones, residential treatment, curfew, and no weapons.

We conducted these regressions separately for the bail (Table 4.17), probation (Table 4.18), and CSO (Table 4.19) datasets. In each case, we ran four different models in order to assess the relationships between specific variables, deriving coefficients to assess the effect of the identified variable on the logarithmic likelihood of breach.

In the case of the Vancouver bail data, we found a significant relationship between the duration of the case, the number of bail conditions, and the likelihood of breach when we integrated information relating to the bail process in model 2, echoing the findings of Damon (2014) and Sprott and Myers (2011). In particular, those who breached had significantly more conditions than those who did not. There is a very strong relationship between having 4 to 6 conditions (25%) and 7 to 9 conditions (46%) and the likelihood of breach. In Table 4.8, we found that 35.2% of all bail orders had between 4 and 6 conditions whereas 12% of all bail orders had between 7 and 9 conditions. This means that almost half of the bail orders are either likely or very likely to be breached. This relationship ceases to exist, however, when the accused is released with 9 or more conditions (which only corresponds to approximately 5.5% of all bail orders). There are many possible explanations for these results. For instance, orders with 9 or more conditions may typically include a specific type of condition associated with a lower likelihood of breach, as we will see below.

TABLE 4.17 *Logistic regression: bail (Vancouver)*

Dependent variable:	Models			
	(1)	(2)	(3)	(4)
Age	−0.008***	−0.008***	−0.008***	−0.009***
	(0.001)	(0.001)	(0.001)	(0.001)
Gender (F)	0.814***	0.865***	0.855***	0.837***
	(0.238)	(0.239)	(0.239)	(0.239)
Gender (M)	0.831***	0.863***	0.850***	0.848***
	(0.237)	(0.238)	(0.238)	(0.238)
Count (4–6)		0.215***	0.255***	
		(0.033)	(0.033)	
Count (7–9)		0.456***	0.456***	
		(0.049)	(0.049)	
Count (9+)		−0.041	−0.040	
		(0.048)	(0.048)	
Bail Duration (190days)		0.389***	0.396***	0.396***
		(0.022)	(0.022)	(0.022)
Drug Related		0.194	0.187	0.151
		(0.219)	(0.219)	(0.219)
Red Zone Condition			−0.101	−0.140*
			(0.078)	(0.078)
Residential Treatment			−2.677***	−2.509***
			(0.451)	(0.450)
Curfew			−1.280*	−1.284*
			(0.725)	(0.725)
No Weapons			−0.078	−0.083
			(0.132)	(0.132)
Constant	−2.332***	−2.552***	−2.544***	−2.472***
	(0.240)	(0.241)	(0.242)	(0.242)
Observations	73,957	72,907	72,907	72,907
Log Likelihood	−29,443.420	−28,723.690	−28,672.910	−28,737.670
Akaike Inf. Crit.	58,894.850	57,465.390	57,371.820	57,495.350

Note: *p*<0.1; *p*<0.05; *p*<0.01

TABLE 4.18 *Logistic regression: probation (Vancouver)*

Dependent variable:	Models			
	logistic			
	(1)	(2)	(3)	(4)
Age	−0.017***	−0.013***	−0.013***	−0.017***
	(0.001)	(0.001)	(0.001)	(0.001)
Genderm	0.108***	0.033**	0.037**	0.107***
	(0.015)	(0.016)	(0.016)	(0.015)
Count 4–6		−0.057***	−0.064***	
		(0.021)	(0.021)	
Count 7–9		0.303***	0.313***	
		(0.017)	(0.017)	
Count 9+		1.288***	1.301***	
		(0.013)	(0.013)	
Drug-related		−0.154***	−0.177***	0.151***
		(0.053)	(0.053)	(0.051)
Red Zone Condition			0.157***	0.216***
			(0.034)	(0.033)
Residential Treatment			−0.110***	−0.036*
			(0.021)	(0.020)
Curfew			−0.100	0.289**
			(0.130)	(0.125)
No weapons			−0.286***	−0.042
			(0.028)	(0.026)
Constant	−0.511***	−0.919***	−0.905***	−0.513***
	(0.018)	(0.019)	(0.020)	(0.018)
Observations	156,456	156,456	156,456	156,456
Log Likelihood	−96,546.760	−91,433.130	−91,353.460	−96,515.050
Akaike Inf. Crit.	193,099.500	182,880.300	182,728.900	193,046.100

Note: $p<0.1$; $p<0.05$; $p<0.01$

TABLE 4.19 *Logistic regression (CSO) (Vancouver)*

Dependent variable:	Models			
	logistic			
	(1)	(2)	(3)	(4)
Age	−0.013***	−0.009***	−0.010***	−0.013***
	(0.001)	(0.001)	(0.001)	(0.001)
Genderm	−0.098***	−0.158***	−0.159***	−0.099***
	(0.027)	(0.028)	(0.028)	(0.027)
Count 4–6		−0.084	−0.108	
		(0.121)	(0.121)	
Count 7–9		−0.273***	−0.274***	
		(0.044)	(0.044)	
Count 9+		0.573***	0.579***	
		(0.026)	(0.026)	
Drug-related		−0.437***	−0.481***	−0.415***
		(0.047)	(0.048)	(0.047)
Red Zone Condition			0.044	0.093
			(0.067)	(0.066)
Residential Treatment			−0.033	−0.016
			(0.036)	(0.036)
Curfew			−0.594***	−0.587***
			(0.046)	(0.046)
No Weapons			−0.279***	−0.166***
			(0.059)	(0.058)
Constant	0.095***	−0.310***	−0.263***	0.160***
	(0.033)	(0.041)	(0.041)	(0.034)
Observations	44,096	44,096	44,096	44,096
Log Likelihood	−30,063.390	−29,579.680	−29,482.080	−29,937.540
Akaike Inf. Crit.	60,132.780	59,173.360	58,986.150	59,891.090

Note: $p<0.1$; $p<0.05$; $p<0.01$

We also found that those who breached had a significantly longer case-processing time. When the person is on bail for more than 190 days (a little over six months), it significantly increases the likelihood of breach. In the database, one-third of all cases (32.6%) had been on bail for more than 190 days (see Table 4.12). This means that these individuals are four times more likely to breach their bail order than those who are on bail for less than six months. The fact of being charged with a drug offence does not alter these relationships.

In Model 3, we assessed the statistical relationship between breach and particular conditions. We found that residential treatment and curfew conditions were significantly associated with a very significant decrease in the likelihood of breach. However, there was no significant relationship between having a red zone condition and the likelihood of breach at the bail stage. These results should be qualified. First, according to our predictive models, the type of condition does not appear to be the strongest predictor of breach when compared to other factors. The number of conditions (4+) and the case-processing time (190 days+) are the strongest predictors of breaches. This does not mean that red zone conditions are not likely to be breached or that having a red zone in a bail order does not contribute to breaching. In fact, our qualitative data – discussed in Chapters 7 and 8 – reveal that bail orders containing red zones are breached every day and that individuals subject to conditions are regularly caught in their red zones. Further investigation into the data may reveal a connection, particularly perhaps in relation to drug offences. However, this could reflect a reality expressed by legal actors – see Chapter 6 – according to which many individuals who are caught breaching their red zones are not formally charged, but only brought before the court at the bail stage. If the data were to confirm this practice, then this could mean that red zones are primarily used as surveillance and management tools to check on individuals. By contrast, residential treatment and curfew conditions have the effect of completely removing people from public spaces.

We found different predictive patterns in the case of the Vancouver probation data (Table 4.18).

Our results first show that the variable "number of conditions" has a slightly different influence on the likelihood of breach in the case of probation. Remember that at the time that the data was collected probation orders came with three compulsory conditions. Those who were imposed 4 to 6 conditions were less likely to breach, as the model shows a negative relationship between the number of conditions and the likelihood of breach at this level. Yet, the relationship is completely reversed as the number of conditions increases, so that those who have 9 conditions or more are much more likely to breach their probation order.

When we add the types of conditions to the model (3), we observe that those who have a red zone condition are significantly more likely to breach their probation order. This result differs from bail. At the stage of probation, curfews are also predictors of breaches. Similarly to the bail situation, however, there is a negative relationship between residential treatment conditions and the likelihood of breach. Therefore, those who are subject to residential treatment are significantly less likely to breach their probation orders.

There are several possible explanations for these results and further investigation is needed. One hypothesis is that those who were subject to few conditions of release already presented low risks of breach and of recidivism altogether. In their cases, it is also possible to suggest that conditions were superfluous. By contrast, the people subject to many conditions may be poor and vulnerable individuals living in such precarious conditions that it is very difficult for them to comply with the conditions imposed. In other words, by imposing conditions on them, we "set them up to fail" (Sprott and Myers, 2011; Canadian Civil Liberties Association and Education Trust, 2014).

Our results elsewhere also suggest that the nature of the conditions imposed can have a positive or negative influence on the likelihood of breach. Based on the results of our interviews with legal actors (see Chapter 6), we know that from their perspectives red zones are sometimes imposed to attempt to prevent crime by keeping an accused out of an area associated with criminal activity, whereas conditions imposing residential treatment are used to deal with drug addiction. The statistical analysis also shows that residential treatment conditions have a negative impact on the likelihood of breach whereas red zone conditions in the case of probation are more likely to be violated. Therefore, it seems to be easier for someone on probation to abide with a condition to follow a residential treatment than to comply with a geographical restriction. When legal actors are unclear about the objectives they pursue and simply add one condition on top of another the impact appears to be strongly felt and increases the possibility of breaching the court orders.

We finally conducted logistic regression for conditional sentence orders in Vancouver (Table 4.19).

The results show that the most significant predictor of future breach is still the high number of conditions. Those who have 9 or more conditions are more likely to breach their orders. In models 3 and 4, we also observe a

TABLE 4.20 *Predictive factors of breaches (Montreal)*
(age, gender, and number)

Breaches of conditions	
	Model
Predictive factors of breach	Signification
Constant	0.62
18–30 years old	0
31–40 years old	0
41–50 years old	0
51–65 years old	0
66 + years old	0
Men	0.51
Women	0.97
One condition only (or other)	0.32
Two conditions	0.36
Three conditions	0.22
Four conditions	0.38
Five conditions	0.37
Six conditions	0.47
Seven conditions	0.61
Eight conditions	0.72
Nine conditions	0.87
Ten conditions	0.97
Eleven conditions	0.96
Twelve conditions	0.87
Thirteen conditions	0.94
Fourteen conditions	0.90
Fifteen conditions	0.98
Sixteen conditions	0.44

negative relationship between curfew and no weapons conditions and the likelihood of breach. As a result, those imposed a curfew are less likely to breach than those who are not. Curfew conditions are commonly imposed in CSOs. Red zones and residential treatment conditions have the same impact on the likelihood of breach than they had in probation orders, although this relationship is not statistically significant in CSOs.

As repeatedly shown above, the number of conditions and the length of the orders are the most significant predictors of breaches whether it is at bail, probation, or in conditional sentence orders. As such, these results show that the cumulative imposition of numerous conditions fails to prevent breaches. On the contrary, it is statistically associated with a higher likelihood of breach. One likely consequence of increased breaches is heightened surveillance and attempts to control certain offenders within the criminal justice system.

We found similar results in Montreal with respect to probation and CSOs following Damon's methodology where the number of conditions was among the most significant predictive factors of breaches. A court case with a high number of conditions (between 8 and 15) is strongly correlated with breaches (between 0.72 and 0.99) (Table 4.20).

WHAT'S IN A BREACH CASE?

To fully measure the significance of these data, we pause and note that breaches and administration of justice offences are particular offences within the criminal law. First, the regulated behaviour subject to conditions of release are not criminal offences *per se*, but judicially created offences. In other words, going to a specific park, restaurant, or drug store, standing on the sidewalk of any random street, drinking alcohol, not abiding to the rules and regulations of a rooming house, or communicating with a relative, are not crimes in Canada, but become so if they are entrenched in a court order of release. Since the courts are defining the boundaries of what thus constitute a criminal offence, we can argue that they have created work for themselves. As the courts are "manufacturing crimes" (Murphy, 2009), the judicial machine enlarges itself, keeping certain offenders under constant judicial surveillance.

Secondly, being charged with an AJO is highly consequential. Studies show that prosecutors and judges consider an AJO more seriously than any other type of offences (Marinos, 2006). According to Canada's Department of Justice, a person charged with an AJO as the most serious offence is significantly more likely to be detained by police following arrest (66% as opposed to 41% for all offences), and to be held in remand following a judicial interim release hearing (39% as opposed to 34% for all offences) (Beattie, Solecki, and Morton Bourgon, 2013: 13 and 18). Such offences are also more likely to be prosecuted, to lead to a guilty verdict and to a jail sentence, than any other types of offences (see also Marinos, 2006; Reid,

TABLE 4.21 *Case resolution speed: number of days between first appearance and case conclusion, per offence type (Montreal)*

Offence type	No. of days	
	Average	Median
Offences against the administration of justice	412	260
Offences against public order (illegal assembly)	858	817
Offences against public morals (prostitution)	359	173
Offences against property	497	321
Offences against the person	456	308
Totals	453	294

2017). In 2014, 91% of all persons accused of an AJO were charged, as compared to those accused of other Criminal Code offences, for which only 49% were charged (Beattie, Solecki, and Morton Bourgon, 2013: 10). Moreover, 76% of the cases that included an AJO resulted in a guilty verdict, compared to 55% of the cases that did not include such an offence, and while only 35% of all criminal offences are punished with custody, incarceration is imposed in 56% of BOP (breach of probation) and 45% of FTC (failure to comply) offences.

Our Montreal data confirm that administration of justice offences tend to be dealt with expeditiously (Table 4.21), generating a high number of pleas (Table 4.22 and Figure 4.14) and more incarceration (Table 4.23).

Administration of justice offences also account for important increases in admissions to remand across the country. Remand, also referred to as preventive detention, is the court-ordered detention of an accused person while awaiting a bail hearing or trial. To reiterate: in Canada, there are currently *more* people held in remand centres then imprisoned after a finding of guilt: 62% of all adults in provincial and territorial correctional facilities are currently in pre-trial detention (Malakieh, 2018).

British Columbia has followed similar trends. According to the Cowper report, "the remand population used to account for one-third of inmates but is now half. In addition, the majority of inmates who receive a jail sentence are initially admitted through remand: this comprises about 75% of admissions to custody" (2012: 38). This use of remand is geographically concentrated in Vancouver (likely including many DTES-related charges included in our dataset). According to a snapshot from the B.C. Justice Dashboard in

Table 4.22 Type of judicial decisions, per offence type (Montreal)

Offence type	Number of offences	Acquittals	Stay of proceedings	Guilty plea or verdict	Other/In progress	Ratio guilty plea or verdict	Ratio guilty (w/out in progress)
Offences against the administration of justice	**151,363**	**10,345**	**3,217**	**99,539**	**38,262**	**65.8**	**88.0**
Failure to comply with bail order (s. 145)	42,859	4308	909	28,906	8,736	67.4	84.7
Breach of probation (s. 733)	78,602	4,047	1,728	61,519	11,308	78.3	91.4
Offences against public order	**639**	**166**	**128**	**66**	**279**	**10.3**	**18.3**
Illegal assembly (s. 66)	639	166	128	66	279	10.3	18.3
Offences against public morals (prostitution)	**8,481**	**322**	**219**	**7,201**	**739**	**84.9**	**93.0**
Offences related to prostitution (s. 213)	6,855	79	132	6,383	261	93.1	96.8
Property offences	**64,356**	**7,053**	**2,931**	**41,492**	**12,880**	**64.5**	**80.6**
Theft (s. 334)	44,501	2,914	1,929	32,536	7,122	73.1	87.0
Credit card theft/fraud (s. 342)	4,458	387	297	2,479	1,295	55.6	78.4
Mischief (s. 430)	14,428	3,663	556	6,091	4,118	42.2	59.1
Offences against the person	**68,943**	**30,764**	**1,957**	**14,817**	**21,405**	**20.6**	**31.2**
Criminal harassment, threats (s. 264; 264.1)	27,257	12,799	707	5,334	8,417	19.6	28.3
Assault (s.266)	34,105	16,635	869	6,023	10,578	17.7	25.6
Assault of police officer (s. 270)	7,581	1,330	381	3,460	2,410	45.6	66.9
Totals	**215,819**	**44,769**	**6,852**	**101,662**	**73,565**	**47.1**	**69.0**

TABLE 4.23 *Percentage of conditional sentences, per offence type (Montreal)*

Offence type	Conditional sentences	Total sentences	Ratio of CSOs (%)
Offences against the administration of justice	4,812	31,323	15.4
Offences against public order	1	21	4.8
Offences against public morals (prostitution)	148	3,050	4.9
Property offences	2,384	24,919	9.6
Offences against the person	627	10,220	6.1
Totals	**8,035**	**70,442**	**11.4**

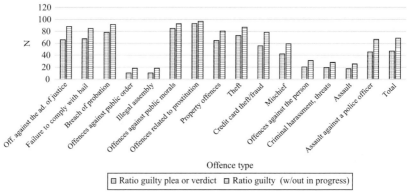

FIGURE 4.14 Ratio of guilty plea or verdict, per offence type (Montreal)

2011–2012, 62% of all provincial admissions to remand were in two pre-trial facilities in the greater Vancouver region.[37]

Finally, studies show that AJOs are directly linked to individuals being caught in the revolving door of the criminal justice system. Not only is there a clear association between AJOs and custody, data show that breaches of court orders are associated with short incarceration sentences (Ministère de la sécurité publique du Québec, 2013). Such offences have lighter median sentence lengths: 32 days for BOP and 20 days for FTC, compared to 118 days for all offences (Beattie, Solecki, and Morton Bourgon, 2013). In a study of short sentences of imprisonment in Canada between 1995–1996 and

---

[37] See B.C Corrections Dashboard (web resource): https://justicebcdashboard.bimeapp.com/players/beta/adult.

1999–2000, Marinos (2006) found that the greatest proportion of sentences of 30 days or less is for AJOs (46.8%; n=28,515), compared to all other types of offences (12.8%; n=66,204). This pattern of overrepresentation continued for sentences of up to 90 days; but for sentences of 91 days or more, the pattern reversed. As we will explain in Chapter 5, our own observations have shown that such short sentences are actually imposed when individuals appear in custody and, following a coerced guilty plea, are retroactively sentenced to the number of days already spent in detention prior to their appearance.

These patterns have not gone entirely unnoticed. Increases in the number of AJOs, and, in particular, breaches, have been an important source of concern for some policy-makers and law reformers in Canada in the last few years, although there seems to be uncertainty as to the reasons behind such anomalies. In B.C., Geoffrey Cowper's 2012 report paved the way, observing the significant amount of police, prosecutorial, and correctional resources that these offences now require. Cowper suggested that the treatment of these offences should be high on the reform agenda in B.C., pointing to the lack of consensus on the goals pursued by these offences and their outcomes: "What are we seeking to accomplish with these prosecutions, and are we succeeding?" he asked (Cowper, 2012).

The Fourth Year Anniversary update released in October 2016 noted that the increase in administrative offences "is an area which remains in need of a system-wide response that will necessarily include careful research, sound data and evidence" and called for a "rigorous consensus . . . common understanding, common goals and an over-all system approach" (8) to community supervision (Cowper, 2016). Finally, a review of the BC Prosecution Service conducted in 2016 by Former Ontario Attorney General Murray Segal also found that the Crown should review its policy with respect to these offences, urging the need for systematic analysis:

> One other area for Crown Counsel Policy review is the continued growth of administration of justice offences, particularly breach charges. There is no dispute that ignoring breaches may demonstrate a lack of respect for the justice system; however, there should be an informed discussion about what types of breaches warrant charging. At the current time, there is inadequate information about the type or nature of the breaches that have caused the number of charges to swell. The Cowper Report called for this study and discussion, and I would like to reinforce that it should continue to be a priority.
>
> (2016: 27)

---

[37] See B.C Corrections Dashboard (web resource): https://justicebcdashboard.bimeapp.com/players/beta/adult.

In Quebec, concerns with offences against the administration of justice recently arose in the context of what has been called the "Jordan crisis" that challenged the judicial system in the aftermath of the Supreme Court of Canada's decision in *R. v. Jordan* (2016). In that case, the SCC held that the accused's right to be tried within a reasonable time protected by s. 11(b) of the Canadian Charter required the application of presumptive ceilings beyond which delays were presumed unreasonable, save for exceptional circumstances. This decision paved the way for an important number of requests for stays of proceedings, some of which have been granted in cases of serious criminal allegations, including first-degree murder (e.g. *R. v. Thanabalasingham* (2017)). In the words of the majority of the Supreme Court, the Jordan decision aimed to confront "a culture of complacency" and "encourage all participants in the criminal justice system to cooperate in achieving reasonably prompt justice" (par. 4–5).

In the weeks following *Jordan*, the Quebec Department of Justice brought together different partners around a Justice roundtable and developed an intervention plan that included the creation of a monitoring committee to supervise the management of cases involving administration of justice offences (Table Justice-Québec, 2016).

In response to these concerns, a series of measures have been put in place by the provinces and the federal government. Most notably, in June 2019, the Canadian Parliament adopted Bill C-75 introducing some changes to the bail system, which included properly enacting a principle of restraint, adding the requirement that the circumstances of Indigenous accused and of accused from "vulnerable populations" are considered at bail, and introduced a new "judicial referral hearing", which allows the police or the prosecution to refrain from laying charges for breaches of bail orders that did not cause harm to victims or property damage or economic loss, but require instead that the accused appear before the court in order to review the conditions or revoke bail. We will come back to these changes in the conclusion, but it suffices for now to say that many experts believe that these changes are unlikely to reduce the number of breaches.

TERRITORY WIDENING

In "The Punitive City", Cohen (1979) alerted us to the growing phenomenon of "net widening", the increasingly expansive reach of the criminal justice system, warning that proposed "alternatives" to state intervention almost systematically end up supplementing the existing system, extending its reach to parts of the population that would have escaped its gaze in the first place. Similarly, Harcourt (2001) suggested that the popularity of the broken windows theory could be explained by its presentation as an alternative to incarceration, whereas it was in fact an addition.

When the Bail Reform Act passed into law in 1971, reformers hoped to "completely revolutionize" the bail system in Canada (Dumontier, 1972), emphasizing the right to bail and the duty to release, and creating an alternative to remand, namely conditional release, which ought to be used only exceptionally. Probation and conditional sentences were introduced much in the same way, the first in the late nineteenth century, and the other in 1996 following a major sentencing reform, in order to divert an important number of individuals away from custody. Most scholars and practitioners today agree that such reforms have not lived up to their expectations (Webster, Doob, and Myers, 2009; Friedland, 2012). As Cohen and others have convincingly shown, these "alternatives" too often focused on the "shallow end" offenders instead of the "deep end" offenders (1979: 347), and ended up increasing the number of individuals who were subject to state intervention in the first place, hence the net widening effect.

While in 2016–2017, the provinces of Ontario, British Columbia, and Quebec had some of the lowest adult incarceration rates in the country (standing respectively at 68, 70, and 75 per 100,000, below the Canadian rate of 136 per 100,000 (Malakieh, 2018)),[38] there were 9,710 adults held in sentenced custody in provincial or territorial facilities[39] in 2016–2017 and another 15,417 in remand, a vast majority (84,978) were supervised under probation orders (77.2%). Further, 43% of all guilty cases in adult criminal courts in 2015–2016 included a sentence of probation.

By imposing an increasing number of conditions of release over extensive periods of time, whether at bail where they are completely optional or in a probation order where they should be limited, and thus increasing the risks of breaches, the courts have not only been involved in "manufacturing crimes"

---

[38] The adult incarceration rate has been consistently decreasing since 2012–2013 in Canada, with the noticeable exception of Indigenous and Black inmates, the number of which have continued to skyrocket. For instance, Indigenous people accounted for 28% of overall admissions into provincial and territorial correctional services and 27% in federal services in 2017.

[39] In Canada, correctional responsibility is shared between provinces and the federal government. The federal government is responsible for all offenders sentenced to a prison sentence of two years or longer.

(Murphy, 2009), but they have directly contributed to the expansion of the criminal justice system itself. Contemporary "net widening", we suggest, has entailed particular forms of territorialization, through the pervasive adoption of spatial conditions of release.

This, however, is only the beginning of the transformation, as we shall show in Chapter 5.

5

The Shifting and Expanding Terrain of Criminal Justice Management

INTRODUCTION

It is Monday morning in courtroom 301, part of the sprawling 1950s era provincial courthouse at 222 Main Street, in the heart of Vancouver's Downtown Eastside. The justice is sitting on her dais, in front of the Arms of Her Majesty in Right of Canada, and she is presiding over arraignments and bail hearings. A Crown counsel and a defence lawyer stand before her. A clerk quietly types. To one side sprawls the court sheriff, busy with a crossword puzzle. A large wall-mounted digital clock counts down hours, minutes, seconds. Beside the prosecutor is a stack of files. A list of names is marked up on a white board to one side. As the cases progress, the sheriff periodically ticks off the names of those before the court.

The atmosphere is a curious mix of theatre and the mundane. The majesty of the Crown and the colourful red sash of "Your Honour" combine with a highly bureaucratic and routinized process. The cases are dealt with quickly, often taking only a few minutes to process. The assembly line of the criminal justice system rolls forward, with only the occasional moment of confusion and hesitancy (do they have video conferencing in Surrey? Who should we deal with next?). It does not appear to trade in "rights" as such. Rather, the language is a technical one of "show cause", failure to appear, CSOs, "breach", and "time served".

The only variation is that of the alleged offenders who are brought, one by one, before the court, some in person, and others via video feed from a suburban remand centre. Most of them are charged with petty offences (stealing $159 worth of meat and cheese from a Safeway store, assault, using a fake I.D., failing to report to a bail supervisor), with contextual and extenuating circumstances noted quickly by the defence lawyer (grew up in Nova Scotia, a history of abuse, a heroin addiction, a background of mental illness, and so on). Standing in a glassed-in prisoners' box, they wear bright red, loose-fitting tracksuits, and trainers. All are reserved and respectful. Some look worried, others simply confused, perhaps going through withdrawal. They say little, if anything, but appear as bit players in a much larger performance. The judge periodically addresses the accused person, not unkindly, explaining the process, making sure they understand the bail orders. This is not an overtly punitive discourse, but often one of therapy and help, albeit sternly framed. Each case trails more or less data, as counsel notes criminal records and, in particular, failures to appear in court and breaches of previous court orders. As they depart, they generate more data.

In the cases where the defendants appear for trial and choose to plead not guilty, the court generally grants bail. Bail hearings are often unnecessary because the defence and the prosecution have agreed on the release conditions beforehand, perhaps tweaking them a little in the moment. In many cases, however, the accused plead guilty upon first or second appearance and are readily sentenced. But whether they are released on bail or sentenced after a guilty plea, offenders are often released with a set of conditions related (or not) to the alleged offence or the background of the offender. These typically include conditions that they "keep the peace and be of good behaviour", that they report to a probation officer at times stated in the order, and that they notify the court of any change of address. Several also receive red zones or no-go orders, stipulating that they stay away from designated sites, like the home of the complainant, subject to an alleged assault. But these can be broader, requiring persons not to access any named supermarket or payday loan outlet in the province of British Columbia, not to enter into a five-block area in the Downtown Eastside, or even not to be found in the city of Surrey or West Vancouver. Some orders contain additional restrictions with spatial consequences, including the requirement to comply with a curfew, a requirement to reside in a treatment facility and comply with the rules and regulations thereby, or to abstain from communicating with certain people. In a strikingly high number of cases, people are before the court because they have breached one of these requirements. In many cases, they are released again under similar or identical conditions, adding a line to their criminal record. But in other cases, they are simply issued a warning and mandated to comply with their previous order before being discharged. Many, if not all, of such cases are uncontested: the offender is eager to accept the conditions and get out of remand.

* * *

Previously in this book we have shown that bail and sentencing conditions of release with spatial dimensions have become increasingly pervasive in Canada and contributed to the expansion of the criminal justice system (Chapter 4).

Drawing from ancient common law instruments such as recognizances to keep the peace or peace bonds (Chapter 3), these release orders have progressively gained in scope, number, and duration. They have become powerful tools of spatiotemporal governance. In Vancouver, for instance, 97% of all provincial court-imposed bail orders issued between 2005 and 2012 contained some kind of conditions and 21% included a prohibition to be found in a specific area ("red zone") or location ("no-go" order). More specifically, 53% of all bail orders issued in drug offences included a red zone. Further, 92% of all the red zones related to drug offences were concentrated in the Downtown Eastside of Vancouver (Damon, 2014). Similarly, in Montreal, over 60% of all probation orders issued at the Municipal Court of Montreal between 2002 and 2014 included a red zone or no-go order. The Court imposed a red zone in 46% of all prostitution-related cases and a prohibition to demonstrate in over 35% of all cases of unlawful assembly or rioting.

In Chapter 3, we noted the historical origins of such orders, and their longstanding use as flexible, spatiotemporal instruments of regulation and governance, driven by administrative criteria. In this chapter, we suggest that the contemporary uptake of red zones and other conditions of release are also revealing of important trends in criminal justice management, as illustrated in our opening vignette. Specifically, they contribute to the development of a self-perpetuating disposition model of criminal justice administration (Feeley, 1992 [1979]) with managerial and preventive characteristics and overtones (Ashworth and Zedner, 2014; Kohler-Hausmann, 2018).

Through a particular strategy of territorialization, that is by imposing stringent and unrealistic conditions of release against the backdrop of incarceration to marginalized people who then repeatedly breach them, the criminal justice system has created a self-generating cycle of surveillance and institutional recidivism. The resultant model, we suggest, displays and relies on a specific spatiality and temporality that departs from more traditional expectations of justice. For instance, justice and power are shifted to the streets, with judges and lawyers shifting authority to justices of the peace and police officers with often-unchecked discretionary powers. The pace of criminal justice administration is also particular, characterized by both speedy interactions in courts and long-time supervision. Finally, the process becomes more circular than linear as individuals are brought back to the courts for continuously breaching their conditions. The same can be said about punishment, which is often administered at the pre-trial stage in a bail order without being labelled or recognized as such, only to be extended in a probation order. These changes directly impact marginalized people's rights and their possibilities to resist legal violence.

In the last decades, criminal justice scholars and practitioners have documented the presence of three distinctive models of criminal justice administration: the adjudicative, plea-bargaining, and pre-trial or managerial models. The first model, alternatively referred to as the "legal" (Dubber, 2005), "adjudicative" (Langbein, 1979; Kohler-Hausmann, 2014), or "due process" (Packer, 1964; Feeley, 1992 [1979]) model, is presented, and still widely taught in law schools, as paradigmatic. This model relies on fundamental assumptions about crime (as an actual legal transgression) and responsibility (mostly, individualized) (Feeley and Simon, 1994). The model follows a particular *process*, namely the trial, and displays a particular *logic*, focusing on the adjudication of guilt, based on the presentation of evidence and respect for individual rights, as well as the imposition of a fair punishment (Feeley, 1992 [1979]; Kohler-Hausmann, 2014, both referring to Fuller, 1963; 1978).

Starting in the 1960s, scholars critiqued the centrality of the adjudicative model in criminal law, showing it was not an accurate description of what actually occurred in criminal courts, but rather the exception (e.g. Langbein, 1979), suggesting instead the dominance of the "plea-bargaining" model. Instead, most defendants see their cases being decided administratively based on plea bargaining and prosecutorial discretion (Lynch, 1998). While this model still adheres to individual responsibility, it is based on a non-trial procedure (although it may include other truth-testing forums: Feeley, 1992 [1979]), and is centred on imposing punishment irrespective of guilt findings and respect for most procedural guarantees. As a matter of fact, law's impact on plea bargaining is relatively limited: parties do not negotiate in the "shadow of law", but rather in relation to "prosecutor's preferences" (Stuntz, 2004; see also Lynch, 1998).

The third model, alternatively referred to as the "pre-trial" or "managerial" model, first appears in the literature in the 1970s, but has arguably a much older history in the Western world (Dubber, 2005; Ashworth and Zedner, 2014), echoing many of the logics we described in Chapter 3. Sometimes understood as a mode of governance, the pre-trial model is connected to Feeley and Simon's description of the "new penology" (1994) and Dubber's (2005) police power. While it is applied on the individual, this form of justice relies on the conflation of individuals with certain "dangerous classes", such as the homeless, sex workers, or drug users, who are imagined to present particular threats to the community or the State (Feeley and Simon, 1994; Neocleous, 2000). It is less concerned with producing punitive responses to crime than with establishing preventive measures to control nuisances based on insecurity and fear, or, more recently, actuarial and risk assessments (O'Malley, 2006; Maurutto and Hannah-Moffat, 2006; Harcourt, 2007; Blomley, 2012). Like the plea-bargaining model, the pre-trial model is highly discretionary and flexible, yet it is more concerned with control, obedience, and the ordering and disposal of bodies, than their actual punishment and conflict-resolution. Fault is largely circumvented (Natapoff, 2013), or at best considered irrelevant, as threats alone suffice (Lacey, 2001; Dubber, 2005). Unlike the other two models, however, punishment in the form of a sentence may or may not be imposed, and, if so, it is coerced rather than negotiated (as in the second model). Rights and due process are not central considerations.

In the American context, Feeley (1992 [1979]) was among the first to document this particular form of criminal justice administration, widely evident in lower courts, contrasting it with the adjudicative and plea-bargaining models: "In the lower courts, trials are rare events, and even protracted plea bargaining is an exception" (3). Instead, in the "pre-trial" model, the "locus of sanctioning shifts away from adjudication, plea bargaining and sentencing to the earlier pre-trial stages", or onto the process itself (15, 30).

Building on Feeley's work, Issa Kohler-Hausmann conducted a study of misdemeanour justice in New York some 30 years later (2013; 2014; 2018). She describes what she refers to as a managerial model, which diverges from the adjudicative model in that social control operates irrespective of guilt or conviction (2013). Interested in the relationship between the outcomes of misdemeanour justice and social regulation, she focuses on two particular outcomes of misdemeanour arrests, including adjournments in contemplation of dismissal (ACD) and speedy trial dismissals ("30.30 dismissals", referring to the New York Criminal Procedure Law). ACD consists in adjourning a case for a specific time period ranging from six months to a year, after which the charges will be dismissed, and the prosecution nullified. In the meantime, the court may set conditions including "staying out of trouble" or, more specifically, enjoining defendants to follow educational or therapy programs or community service. In using this procedure, Kohler-Hausmann suggests, the courts and legal actors rely on three techniques or tools of social control, including *marking,* or the imposition of traceable marks of previous encounters with the criminal justice system in individual records in order for the courts to determine the level of social control (2018: 145); *procedural hassle,* referring to the "costs and burdensome experiences" of case processing that prevent defendants from invoking their rights but also create opportunities for disciplining and reforming offenders' behaviour (2018: 183); and *performance,* requiring defendants to abide by certain conditions during the adjournment period, including coming back to courts (2013; 2018).

Our empirical findings on the regulation and governance of marginalized populations in the Canadian criminal justice system reflect many of the characteristics described by Feeley and others in that third model of criminal justice administration. Specifically, conditions of release are integral parts of a self-perpetuating *disposition* system concerned with the surveillance and ordering of at-risk populations (Ericson and Doyle, 2003; O'Malley, 2006; Harcourt, 2007; 2001). This system follows managerial logics and rationalities, including, for instance, marking offenders who have had previous encounters with the police or the criminal justice system, and it primarily applies "coercive" or "punitive" preventive measures (Harcourt, 2013; Ashworth and Zedner, 2014: 1). Furthermore, the process through which conditions of release are imposed is highly discretionary, and conditions are often subject to interpretation and abuse. The police play a central role.

However, our findings also highlight some distinctive features. While the locus of the criminal process and punishment often shifts to the pre-trial stages, in several cases it also extends to the sentencing stage, where probation orders either duplicate and extend bail conditions, or are conditioned by the success or failure of earlier forms of surveillance. This disposition model is also singularly characterized by its circularity and, in particular, by its capacity for self-generation and perpetuation through breaches of court orders. As explained in Chapter 4, this is made possible because legal actors conceive of conditions of release as alternatives to incarceration, whereas such conditions effectively initiate a never-ending cycle that starts in the streets, is channelled through the courts and comes back full circle in remand centres.

Finally, this system relies heavily on forms of spatialization and temporalization that reinforce these features. In what follows, we insist on the spatiality and temporality of the disposition system in which conditions of release are embedded and suggest that we might be able to perceive better their impact on marginalized people's rights and on their ability to resist such punitive practices when we focus our attention on these two dimensions.

Space and time are central features of criminal law in general, yet often overlooked. Farmer (2010) has drawn our attention to "the neglected issues of the temporal and spatial logics that underlie the modern criminal law, and how the spatial and temporal boundaries set out in law help to construct social and political hierarchies" (336). Most immediately, criminal law needs to secure spatially defined territories so as to exercise jurisdiction: "in order to establish criminal liability, the law must establish that the conduct was criminal under the law of the place where the action occurred, that it took place within the jurisdiction of that legal system – normally within the territory of the sovereign state – and that the accused person is a proper subject of the criminal law" (Farmer, 2014: 400). Too often, Farmer notes, conceptions of criminal wrongdoing are thought of within criminal law in abstract terms, such as the autonomy of the subject. However, he argues:

> such judgments are always mediated through practices that institutionalize certain ways of distributing responsibility or irresponsibility, or shape the ideas of harm and wrong. More than this, the logic of criminalization suggests a pattern in which certain spaces, material or symbolic, are demarcated in law to protect against forms of deviance, and that particular temporal logics underlie the definition of crime. This requires us to take seriously the idea that space and time are *fundamental* to criminal law and criminalization.
>
> (353; our emphasis)

The practice of criminal law thus rests on some foundational conceptions of time and space. These can be observed in the sites of law, such as the architecture of the courtroom (Mulcahy, 2010), and spread to other substantive areas of law, including the assessment of criminal liability itself. For instance, minimum standards of conduct claim to apply universally to all persons at all times, regardless of social space or status (Sylvestre, 2010b; Valverde, 2014), and criminal offences, in many jurisdictions, have no statutory time limitations. Critical legal scholar Mark Kelman (1981) also notes the particular way in which legal actors and interpreters use broad or narrow time frames as "interpretive constructs" to resolve complex legal questions such as criminal liability without having to deal with any fundamental political and ethical problem. According to Kelman, legal doctrine developed at the hands of judges and lawyers allow them to choose either narrow or broad time frames to analyze factual events that have led to the perpetration of an offence in order to distinguish between purely volitional acts (and thus emphasizing free choice and intentionalism), typically requiring narrow time frames, or those deriving from a preceding chain of events (and, thus, emphasizing causal determinism), generally corresponding to broader time frames.

Similarly, in this chapter, we want to argue that the spatiotemporal framings of the criminal process do matter, in particular with respect to the ability to challenge and resist important restrictions on people's lives and rights. We thus suggest that each of the models previously described displays particular spatial and temporal characteristics that influence the administration of justice, the role of legal actors, and the nature of punishment. While scholars and advocates have primarily focused on the objectives, logic, and principles behind the different models of criminal justice administration, we suggest that they are also spatially and temporally constructed in a particular manner.

Specifically, we argue that the system of criminal justice management in which conditions of release are embedded, structure time and space in ways that stand in stark contrast with the adjudicative and plea-bargaining models. As we shall see, the particular spatiotemporality of that system has the effect of reducing resistance and rights-based challenges.

(1) *Shifting Spaces and Time of Criminal Justice Administration*

(a) Places of (In)Justice: From the Courts to the Streets

Feeley's pre-trial model rests on several important spatial shifts. First, the locus of criminal justice administration is relocated from familiar sites of criminalization, adjudication, and punishment, such as the courtroom or sentencing hearings, to administrative or managerial sites of criminalization. As locations of justice diversify, so do the actors involved. In the pre-trial model, the process shifts from being controlled by judges (in the adjudicative model) and lawyers (in the plea-bargaining model) to being centred on prosecutors, justices of the peace, and, most importantly, the police.

Similarly, here, in many bail cases, defendants are released by the police following their arrest. In a study conducted in three Canadian provinces and four jurisdictions, one-half of arrested individuals in four different sites were released by police, with at least half of those released on conditions (Beattie, Solecki, and Morton Bourgon, 2013).[1] Defendants are also released by a justice of the peace sitting in chamber or in a court of first appearances. A few respondents in Vancouver and Ottawa also suggested that the police informally red zoned them from specific areas (i.e. not through a police-issued undertaking with conditions). As a result, only a minor proportion of those arrested end up having the "benefit" of a proper bail hearing held in front of a judge. This greatly affects power dynamics, neutralizing judges and, in many cases, defence lawyers. Further, at the appearance stage, the justice of the peace rarely intervenes, our informants pointed out: "You've been to hearings, you see how it goes: the Crown says here are the conditions … and, to be frank, if the defence counsel doesn't point out a problem … we won't intervene", noted one Montreal judge to us. "Justices have no discretionary power at appearances", suggested a Montreal defence lawyer. "Whether we oppose release or not is at the discretion of the Crown. During the bail hearing, it's different". This is only accentuated by the fact that in some

---

[1] Researchers found, however, considerable variation in the forms of release depending on the sites, ranging from 11% to 76% of those released who were released with conditions.

Canadian jurisdictions, such as Ontario and British Columbia, justices of the peace are not required to have any legal training.

Criminal justice administration thus too often starts and ends in the streets, cycling through the hands of police officers. According to Feeley (1992 [1979]), in the pre-trial model,

> arrest is typically viewed as the first stage of the criminal justice process, as the beginning of an effort to resolve a dispute and render a verdict. But for police, arrest is often a convenient way of avoiding or ending trouble. [...] In such instances, adjudication is little more than a book-keeping ritual, a formality necessary to terminate a problem which for all practical purposes has already been resolved.
>
> (24)

This is particularly true given that an (actual) undertaking issued by a police officer is effective immediately and may or may not be followed by actual charges.[2] Similarly, many conditions of release are first issued in the streets, where they are not subject to negotiations. Perhaps reliant on sharply territorial logics of control (Herbert, 1996), police often opt for spatialized undertakings, removing bodies from designated areas. This is certainly the experience of marginalized individuals living in the Downtown Eastside of Vancouver or in the inner cities of Montreal and Ottawa, who report being shoved from one location to the next depending on law enforcement priorities. Sophie, a Montreal-based sex worker, explained how she had to move east of the downtown area in order to comply with the conditions of her red zone, and then even further east when she got caught a few days later. Clyde, in Vancouver, also explained how a police red zone "was basically thrown at" him right in the heart of the Downtown Eastside.

In the case of protesters, conditions of release are widely imposed during political events as a measure of surveillance and neutralization, and, as such, they generally lack the level of individualization associated with judicial adjudication (Esmonde, 2002; Sylvestre et al., 2018). In 2001, Commissioner Ted Hughes, who investigated the conduct of the Royal Canadian Mounted Police (RCMP), Canada's federal police, in the context of the Asia-Pacific Economic Cooperation (APEC) Summit held in Vancouver, condemned the fact that the RCMP had planned to arrest political activists and release them under a pre-established set of conditions consigned in undertakings or bail

---

[2]   S. 145(5.1) Cr. C. and *R. v. Oliveira*, 2009 ONCA 219. However, if as of the first appearance date no criminal proceeding has been commenced or no information sworn, the undertaking is no longer of any force or effect: *R. v. Killaly*, BCPC 138.

orders to prevent them from participating in the demonstrations (Pue, 2000; Commission for Public Complaints against the RCMP, 2001).

These were also used in the context of the meeting of the G20 in Toronto and of the Winter Olympic Games in Vancouver, both held in 2010. For instance, in the days preceding the opening of the Vancouver Olympics, the police arrested a great number of protesters and released them on bail using the same pre-written template – the police carried pre-filled form pads – preventing arrestees from "being within 100 m of a security fence surrounding Olympic Winter Games Competition and Non-Competition Venue, Training Venue, Athletes Village, UBC University Endowment Lands and the District of West Vancouver, the Resort Municipality of Whistler and the Integrated Security Unit Office, between now and March 23, 2010" (on file with authors).

When the police do not directly impose the conditions in the streets – for instance, when someone appears in custody – they may still initiate the process by making suggestions in their reports. In particular, as we demonstrate in Chapter 6, the police are important in communicating "territories" and key "hot spots" within the city to court actors that are then likely to be targeted for area restrictions. In doing so, the police often react to public pressure, relaying the voices of certain residents (Sylvestre, 2010a). For instance, a prosecutor in Vancouver discussed the adoption of area restrictions in Oppenheimer Park, an important community space and site of resistance for street residents of the Downtown Eastside (Lupick, 2017b). The prosecutor described it as "a particular park in our city, that is known for drug use, so there are really no pro-social activities that happen in this park, it really is just drug use and drug dealing", noting that

> the business association and citizens that live around that park have petitioned the police on numerous occasions to say, "You have to clean up this park, it is terrible, we have kids living here". Because of that public pressure from the citizens that live around that and through the police to the Crown, that is one example where we would seek an area restriction to that park, even if that person wasn't arrested in that park. Currently nothing happens in that park except drugs, so just keep them out of there, in part because the local area wants to clean up the park.

Conditions are then conveyed to the prosecutor and to the court in a bureaucratic decision-making cycle:

> It is usually the police who suggest them to us [the red zones]. When the person appears in custody, it is not uncommon for them to say: "If the person is released, these are the conditions we suggest to the Court". It's to guide the prosecutor, to guide the Court. So, in the case of red zones, they generally will tell us, because we don't always know all the problem areas, so generally

it is they who will suggest the red zone, without knowing the specific situation for each accused.

(Prosecutor, Montreal)

The parties suggest together and by mutual agreement, and we follow because, in fact, you know, in criminal matters, the judge intervenes if the proposal appears unreasonable, but if it is not unreasonable, then we ratify it.

(Judge, Montreal)

The same goes for the choice of probation conditions. Legal actors mostly go along with the police report whenever they start negotiating probation.[3]

In the streets, police often have discretionary powers to enforce and monitor orders (whether they first imposed them or whether the courts approved them), which are themselves often subject to interpretation. There is ambiguity inherent in, for example, directing the accused to avoid a "four block radius of the intersection of Hastings" or "300 m from any college or university on the island of Montreal" (Does the first radius refer to an area of four blocks surrounding an intersection? An area delimited by a radius of four street blocks? Where is the edge of the zone – the centre of the street? Should we consider all university-owned buildings, including administration, maintenance, student housing, and so on, or only the main campus?)

This ambiguity is combined with discretionary police-enforcement practices. For instance, protesters typically get instructed not to take part in a demonstration "that is declared illegal and becomes non-peaceful". Determining when a protest becomes "non-peaceful" grants considerable discretionary powers to the police. As a Montreal judge explained to us: "It's hard when [people subject to a demonstration order] come and tell us, 'Yes but it was peaceful, or at least it wasn't illegal, or the police shouted it out [that it was illegal], but personally I didn't hear them'".

Finally, many respondents told us that the police did not hesitate to abuse their powers or to play on the ambiguity and complexity inherent to legal proceedings and court orders to create "informal red zones". For instance, Martin from Vancouver was once arrested and the police seized his drugs before verbally "red zoning" him:

M: So [the police] took my dope away and they turned around and verbally said that I was not allowed back in the area.

Q: Which area?

---

[3]   The process whereby files come through the courts has changed in the B.C. context. One Vancouver Federal Prosecutor noted that when she started, two decades ago, almost every file came into the office on an in-custody basis (i.e. a person has been arrested and remains in detention until the Crown determines bail conditions), whereas, now, the police submit a report on an out-of-custody basis, with conditions of release specified by the police.

M: The 200 block of Hastings. They gave me a condition for four blocks.
     From Abbott straight to Main Street.
Q: Did they give you a paper that said that?
M: Nope, just verbally

Secondly, and most importantly, our findings confirm a movement away from
the trial, from the courtroom and the adjudicative process. This is reminiscent
of what happens through plea bargaining, except that here conditions are only
rarely negotiated. At the bail stage, many defence lawyers report being unable
to challenge the conditions because they are negotiating in the shadow of
another space, the carceral territory of the remand centre. As one Montreal
defence lawyer complained: "Some prosecutors abuse bail hearings, with their
abusive conditions. They know that the accused will say 'yes', that you may tell
them anything and they will still say 'yes'". Aware of their powerful position,
prosecutors claim to exercise self-restraint. Yet, as one prosecutor reported,
candidly:

> You know, there's no point hiding it, someone who wants to be released is
> willing to make a lot of compromises. When we see them, they are often
> ready to go to therapy, to go to rehab, when they have been drinking and
> having problems for 20 years. [T]hey are in there, they're in custody ...
> they're willing to do anything. So it can be negotiated. But I wouldn't say that
> we have the big end of the stick, it's not that, but it's a little bit like that. At the
> same time we have to keep in mind that it's not a question of power, it's a
> question of ensuring their presence in court, avoiding reoffending, protecting
> the victim, protecting society.

This is also true of probation as it is often the only viable alternative to
incarceration in sentencing. While conditional sentences, or suspended sentences of imprisonment as they are referred to in the United Kingdom,[4] can be
imposed since 1996 under Canadian law, they are rarely used in the criminal
justice system.[5]

This significantly modifies the nature of what is going on in the courtroom
as well as legal actors' roles. While we lack statistics on the number of bail
hearings held compared to other forms of release, our findings reveal that most
hearings are circumvented or speeded up through a "consensual" process in

---

[4]   Recently reformed in the Criminal Justice Act 2003 (UK).
[5]   In 2014–2015, conditional sentences were imposed in 4% of the cases across Canada and 7% in
      B.C. See www.statcan.gc.ca/tables-tableaux/sum-som/l01/cst01/legal22k-eng.htm. Introduced in
      1996, CSOs have been consistently limited through subsequent modifications of the Code, first
      in 1997, then in 2007 and 2012.

which the accused agrees to comply with conditions of release or pleads guilty only to be sentenced to a few days in jail followed by a probation order. Further, the judge's role (and power) differs: during the bail hearing, the judge is only rarely an adjudicator. Instead, he or she is more accurately described as a trainer or parental figure. Indeed, the judge will either make sure that the accused brought before the court understands and agrees with the conditions that have been read by the Crown prosecutor, emphasizing that a potential breach will be considered a sign of contempt of the court's authority (Murphy, 2009), and is likely to lead to detention, or the judge will remind the accused who has already breached (and was brought before the court only to be properly warned and reminded of his or her obligations before having the breach charge withdrawn) that, next time, he or she will most likely be kept in custody and properly charged. The power to structure the event lies in the hands of law enforcement and prosecutors: temporarily removing the accused from one space (the streets), confining him or her in another (remand centre), checking in on them, adding on to their record or marking them (Kohler-Hausmann, 2015), perhaps securing a guilty plea, and disposing of their bodies for a few weeks, until their next appearance.

(b) The Pace of Criminal Justice Administration

The disposition system in which conditions of release are embedded also differentiates itself from the adjudicative model in terms of their temporal pacing. Here, individuals and their files are disposed of speedily, as the clock on the wall in our opening vignette illustrates. Most court appearances only last a few minutes. But it sometimes takes a few days to get there, not to mention to get a bail hearing, depending on court backlog (and jurisdictions: Ontario, for instance, is notorious for delayed appearances and bail hearings). Meanwhile, if the defendant wasn't released upon arrest, he or she is held in custody.

At the Montreal Courthouse, for instance, prosecutors indicate on a sheet of paper whether they will object to the release, or request conditions. They have many files to deal with. Defence counsel often have only one hour to make their way in and talk to their many clients; thus, they often have only a vague idea of the case:

> [the client] arrives at the Courthouse around 1:00 p.m., in a small detention bus. Court appearances are at 2:30 and the visitation rooms close at 2:10. There are so many lawyers downstairs, you may not even be able to see him [the detainee] at all. If you do see him, you will talk to him, but the Crown

prosecutor arrives in the courtroom at 2:30 and he doesn't want to know anything about you.

(Defence lawyer, Montreal)

Further, if the prosecution objects to their release when their "number" is called, the case is pushed back to the following day, or three days later, for the bail hearing. Otherwise, the accused is called upon to stand up and the prosecution reads the conditions imposed upon him or her.

Such an expedited process does not provide much space or time to discuss the conditions. "At the appearance stage, when conditions are suggested, because of the number of clients we have, we go ahead with the appearance, it is these conditions, and if we disagree for whatever reasons, we postpone to the next day at the release hearing" (judge, Montreal). Thus, as one of our participants told us: "It's take it or leave it" (Mary, Montreal student). The time frame is particularly prejudicial to defendants who use drugs, whether they are still incapacitated at the time of their appearance or whether they are going through withdrawal and are extremely sick.

> In general, these people have a history, they're showing up in court, coming down from a night of drinking or drugs; they're not all there, they don't understand anything, they have a [expletive] headache; they're in a rush, some of them didn't get their methadone, they're going crazy, most of them are at that stage, and all they want to do is get out.
>
> (Defence lawyer, Montreal)

Further, if the parties do not agree on conditions of release, bail hearings are sometimes held only a few days later while the defendant stays in custody:

> Discussions on conditions at appearance are not common. There's no debate because they agree, because people who commit offences often do not want to take the time needed for the bail hearing, because during the bail hearing, you are remanded, and it is set for the next day or within three days, but often it is the next day. And that is just for the conditions. They don't want to spend a night in there just for that, which makes it clear that *there's pressure from the system itself to accept conditions. Not by the system, rather by the time needed for the procedure.* Because they are remanded until conditions are imposed.
>
> (Judge, Montreal; our emphasis)

In most cases, remand centres are overcrowded, and defendants want (or need) to get out as soon as possible. As such, the court's pace is not only at odds with that of the defendants and court delays are not only costly in terms of time and energy (Feeley, 1992 [1979]), but they can also be life-threatening in many different ways, as one of our informants made clear:

It is only for a couple hours, but it's mental anguish that really hurts the most, because you are in there with a whole bunch of drug addicts and people that are looking at long sentences that don't have anything to care for. Anything is possible. Your life could be threatened … Yeah, they are withdrawing, they're jonesing [craving], they're dope-sick; they're shitting and puking everywhere. I'm here for what, an area restriction violation? These guys are waiting to be put in jail. I'm waiting to be released.

(Adam, Vancouver)

Even in the context of the bail hearing, the decision to remand or impose conditions on a person is made in an extremely short period of time. If the courts are running out of time, when a person must finally be released, their case is often settled within minutes. Although these decisions are not made lightly and are subject *a posteriori* to justification by the actors, they are also made rapidly and are part of a judicial routine.

It goes very, very fast, so you have to make your mind up very quickly. At times, if it's complex, you may need to take a step back when you think it's necessary… but at the same time the bail hearing is an urgent procedure and it requires a quick decision. As for the principles, well, we have that under control.

(Judge, Montreal)

The pressure is high for the accused trying to keep track. In this context, other considerations such as whether the conditions imposed are in direct violation of some fundamental rights, including the right to the presumption of innocence, the right to life, liberty and security of the person, the right to freedom of expression or association, appear secondary.

Rights discussions about conditions happen very rarely. There is no discussion because they agree. And they agree because people actually want to get out. If the lawyer says they're going to challenge, the client will say: "And I'm going to stay in custody in the meantime?" He's going to say, "Hey, you idiot, stop! Negotiate, settle it, or I'll change lawyer, I'm certainly not going to be the one to pay for your fight".

(Judge, Montreal)

At first sight, this appears to stand in contrast with the slow pace of the adjudicative model where rights are directly activated and full assessment of guilt, including the possibility of presenting defences, is central. But this has not always been the case. Legal historians have convincingly shown that the form and duration of the criminal justice process is inversely proportional to the extent of available legal representation and procedural guarantees. Historically, the courts' concerns (indeed obsession) with reducing delays and caseload were not only a question of efficiency and good administration. Instead, speedy case resolution often meant circumventing robust adversarial trials and their associated legal guarantees, including the right to full defence and answer and the right to the presumption of innocence. As such, Langbein and Feeley, among others, have observed that the practice of plea bargaining emerged in the middle of the eighteenth century following the professionalization of the criminal process and the rise of adversarial procedure and the law of evidence (Langbein, 1979; Feeley, 1997). Before that period, "the jury trial was a summary proceeding", trying between 12 and 20 felonies per day (Langbein, 1979: 262). Thus, it may very well be that criminal justice administration in the era of conditions of release is just today's new expedient, both in terms of achieving high efficiency and reduced complexity, and circumventing rights and due process.

(c) Court Management over Time

While on the one hand time is compressed, on the other, it can be expansive or open-ended. For instance, the accused may never know how long he or she will be on bail, as it depends on court delays (Pelvin, 2017). In the meantime, any form of release, including the powers of release conferred upon the police, remains in effect until the end of the trial or until the accused is sentenced (unless reviewed or revoked).

As shown in Chapter 4, in Vancouver, we found that in almost two-thirds of the cases (64%), individuals stayed on bail for less than six months (44% of the cases were concluded in 90 days or less and 20% of the cases were concluded within 90 and 180 days). However, nearly 25% of the cases were concluded *after* six months, with 14% of them lasting over a year after the bail order is issued (see Table 5.1, reproduced here for the sake of convenience). This explains the uncertainty some of our respondents noted as to whether they were still subject to conditions.

The length of time someone will actually spend on bail will also vary greatly depending on the type of offences committed. For instance, criminal proceedings for offences against public order, which are more likely to be used against demonstrators, can span several months or years. In Montreal, demonstrators arrested during the students' strike in 2012 were subject to bail orders for an average of 21 months, including the case of Marius who remained on bail for 27 months. Marius was subsequently subject to a probation order for another 36 months and thus remained under some kind of community supervision for over five years. At some point, he was simultaneously subject to 25 conditions of release. Furthermore, in the cases of protesters, it is not unusual for arrested individuals to be released under restrictive bail conditions for lengthy periods,

TABLE 5.1 *Days between bail release order and case conclusion (Vancouver)*

No. of days	No. of cases	Percentage
0–90	33,051	44.4
91–180	15,114	20.3
181–270	7,857	10.6
271–364	6,285	8.5
365 +	10,334	13.9
N/A	1,749	2.4
Totals	74,408	100

only to be found not guilty for lack of evidence years later (on this, see Balbus, 1973; Starr and Fernandez, 2009; see also *R. v. Aubin*, 2008, *R. v. Singh*, 2004).

For instance, a group of 30 political demonstrators were arrested in October 2000 in the context of a meeting of the Finance Ministers of the G20 held at the Sheraton Centre in Montreal for unlawful assembly, rioting, mischief, and obstruction of a police officer in duty. The accused had a joint trial which lasted no fewer than 30 days between June 2002 and September 2003 at the Municipal Court of Montreal and they were found guilty in a judgment released in February 2004, some three and a half years after the events; but their convictions were not overturned by the Court of Appeal until 2009 (*R. v. Bédard*, 2009). In *R. v. Aubin*, (2008) the proceedings against more than 300 individuals arrested in the context of a demonstration against police brutality lasted more than six years. In various cases, the proceedings were stayed for unreasonable delays, charges were withdrawn, or the accused were found not guilty for lack of evidence.

Probation orders can only be imposed for up to three years (and the median length of probation is one year: Maxwell, 2017). However, since an important number of people will breach their court orders and accumulate offences and court cases, they are likely to stay under judicial surveillance for years, extending time indefinitely.

Data from Montreal also show that while a person with only one court case remained on probation for a little more than a year, those who accumulated seven cases or more can stay on probation for four and a half years with no interruption (Table 5.2).

Conditions of release, for many people, are thus not singular temporal events, but overlapping. Consequently, many individuals are transformed into "institutional recidivists" as they shuttle back and forth from bail to probation,

TABLE 5.2 *Duration of probation orders (Montreal)*

	No. of days	
No. of cases	Average	Median
1	449.1	365
2	759.3	545
3	965.6	730
4	1207.1	869
5	1392.8	1,095
6	1467.7	1,161
7 +	2164.8	2,039

sometimes for having committed only one or two substantive offences, repeatedly breaching their conditions. Paul, for instance, whom we met in the introduction, had multiple encounters with the criminal justice system for most of his adult life, spreading over the course of 20 years. In each case, he was charged for minor offences (for a total of 54 offences), including several breaches, and sentenced to short periods of incarceration followed by probation until he was caught breaching again. Similarly, Martine's trajectory lasted at least eight years during which she committed only two substantive offences, but was convicted for seven counts of breaches. Anne, from Vancouver, also explained how she "used to get arrested and put in jail for 3 to 4 days at a time, every couple of weeks, because of [red zones] and other charges". While she has never been sentenced to more than three months in custody for any given offence, she accumulated offences over three years of custody, cycling through remand centres and alternating between breaching bail and probation and drug possession.

Thus, for many people, the criminal justice system does not operate as a linear process, from prosecution to trial and sentencing, but as a circular self-perpetuating one, due in large part to the spatialized conditions of release in which they become entangled. While they may be only held in detention for specific periods, their experience may amount to a carceral continuum. Gill et al. (2016) reject the "popular impression of prisons as impervious, closed-in on themselves and cut-off from the wider world" (2). This echoes Moran's (2015) observation: "rather than being the primary loci of punishment and rehabilitation, prisons are now just some of the many nodes on the carceral continuum, in the context of a punitive state which operates in places far beyond the prison, through pervasive and pernicious policies which incarcerate and confine without actually imprisoning" (110). As such, the boundary that

TABLE 5.3 *Breached cases (Vancouver)*

	No. of cases	Breach	Percentage	Additional breach cases	Averages
Bail	47,550	5,493	11.6	8,426	1.53
Probation	22,794	5,367	23.5	10,274	1.91
CSO	3,910	1,463	37.4	3,132	2.14
Totals	74,254	12,323	16.6	21,832	1.77

divides the prison from other forms of carcerality becomes hard to identify (Moran, 2013; Beckett and Evans, 2015; Turner, 2016).

The carceral continuum is also highly dependent on the work performed in another important space – the streets – where the police walk their beat and routinely engage in numerous street checks for violations of city by-laws, which in turn allow them to run individuals' records and find out about outstanding warrants and bail or probation conditions. The imposition of stringent court conditions thus relies heavily on law enforcement. Moreover, such by-laws regulate public spaces, such as parks, subway stations, and sidewalks, construct physical and geographical barriers, and create spaces of exclusion for the poor and the homeless, creating the infrastructure where policing and law enforcement of court orders are possible (see Chapter 7 for more interactions between by-laws and breaches).

On a systemic level, data first introduced in Chapter 4 on breaches show that a significant number of people are caught in the revolving door of the criminal justice system. As a reminder, in Vancouver, the data revealed that there were 74,254 substantive cases between 2005 and 2012 and that 12,323 of them were breached (16.6%). More importantly, these breaches generated 21,832 additional breach cases, with an average of 1.77 breaches per breached case, as reproduced in Table 5.3.

Further, in Montreal, 59% (55.3% + 3.7%) of those who have accumulated two cases or more have at least one offence against the administration of justice (AJO) on their record and 55% of those who have accumulated four cases or more had a least 2 AJOs on their record. Finally, 99% of those who had seven cases or more had at least one AJO. The vast majority of AJOs in the database are breaches of conditions (80%) (see Chapter 4; Table 4.16).

The frequency of breaches of conditions of release, not surprisingly, is observed by legal actors. Yet some seem strikingly oblivious to the manner in which the courts are actively generating crime. In the words of a defence lawyer from Vancouver:

> I have seen most stuff coming through these courts these days being failing to comply and breaches, and I don't understand. *Where did all the real criminals go?* Why isn't everybody charged with new offences? Because most of what we see on a day to day basis anymore are failures to comply and breaches.
>
> (our emphasis)

While legal actors generally justified their use of conditions of release based on legal grounds, some spoke explicitly about how conditions of release are a form of case management and a tactic of control exercised over marginalized individuals, as they are systematically brought back before courts and in custody.[6]

> We're imposing conditions on him, and if he doesn't want to help himself with that condition, it'll give the police a lever to stop him and bring him back here, you know? And if he remains detained while awaiting his trial, for 12 days, 14 days, he may well understand, and then perhaps he will help himself afterwards. Prison helps to make people realize that you can't do this in a society; public interest should take precedence over self-interest.
>
> (Defence lawyer, Montreal)

One prosecutor even spoke of a "harm reduction" strategy, believing that she was disciplining chronic offenders who would otherwise have committed more serious offences. Breaches, from this perspective, are a marker of success:

> I have a theory about this. It's that they stop committing substantive Criminal Code offences and they begin to breach . . . The only criminal offence they're committing is a breach. I consider that a huge success, even though breach of court orders is very serious of course, but that's my harm reduction model. So curfew breach, well it's not actually illegal to be out after 10 o'clock. It's only because the order stipulates that it's a crime. There's no victim, no one is being hurt. I think that's a success. If the person isn't committing any other substantive offences, that's a huge success in my view. I have several chronic offenders who are in that situation.
>
> (Prosecutor, Vancouver)

---

[6] This is not unique to Canada. In the U.S. context, Bisharat, 2014 explains how defendants who are arrested for felony charges in California are held in custody while awaiting their preliminary hearing and are pressed to plead guilty and accept probationary sentences with multiple terms and conditions to get out of custody. Conditions typically include not violating the law and surrendering their rights to be free of a search. According to Bisharat, given that prosecutors know that defendants are very likely to come back a few weeks later on a new charge of breach, probation conditions become part of case management.

(2) *The Shifting Locus and Timing of Punishment*

In our system, we first administer the major part of the punishment and then enquire whether the accused is guilty.

(Puttkammer, 1953: 69)

In the adjudicative model, criminal law rules propose to inflict pain after a certain process has taken place, namely the trial ("the paradigmatic sequence of prosecution-trial-conviction-punishment": Zedner, 2016). By contrast, in the plea-bargaining model, punishment is anticipated or, as most critiques of plea-bargaining suggested, it is merged with concerns about guilt (Feeley, 1997).

Here, the nature, place, and timing of punishment change. In many cases, the pre-trial process effectively becomes the punishment as the punitive effects are displaced to the front end (as opposed to the "intentional" infliction of pain traditionally associated with punishment: Ashworth and Zedner, 2014). In others, it extends to sentencing where pre-trial conditions of release are determinant. Considerations of guilt become superfluous.

"THE PROCESS IS THE PUNISHMENT", REVISITED

In his seminal book, *The Process is the Punishment*, Feeley (1992 [1979]) suggested that "the time, effort, money and opportunities lost as a direct result of being caught up in the system ['the costs'] can quickly come to outweigh the penalty that issues from adjudication and sentence" (30–31). The costs of the pre-trial process include the consequences of pre-trial detention as well as the costs of securing pre-trial release, the costs of securing an attorney (including the time/money wasted in unproductive meetings with defence attorneys who are very busy, miss appointments, and often need to reschedule), and the costs of courts continuances and delays. In this context, the costs of exercising due process rights are very high and the incentives to plead guilty and waive procedural rights often heavier. Consequently, the process can become the punishment (199 ff.).

Such conditions still apply. Our argument here, however, is slightly different. We suggest that bail release conditions themselves – not merely the process through which we impose them – are a form of punishment, and, in some cases, they are the only punishment that the person will ever endure. Yet their hybrid nature and the fact that they are not legally recognized or characterized as "punishment" *per se* means that they do not come with the safeguards and protections associated with formally punitive measures imposed after an adjudicative process, or even a negotiated plea.

First, the fact that bail is a form of punishment is sometimes unofficially acknowledged. For instance, prosecutors and judges often systematically include some of the compulsory conditions of probation (a punitive measure) into optional bail orders (where the presumption of innocence applies). This is particularly true of the conditions to "keep the peace and be of good behaviour" or "to report to the Court when required to do so", which are among the most common conditions in undertakings.[7] Moreover, at the sentencing stage, the judge will often turn to bail conditions to fix the appropriate level of punishment. When the individual has spent considerable time on bail, the judge will rely on the conditions imposed in that context as a benchmark for probation. If the defendant performed well on bail – meaning if he or she complied with the conditions – he or she is likely to receive a more lenient sentence or more lenient conditions.

This is so not only because the judge will determine that the defendant has made progress or shown an ability to follow court orders, but more importantly because in many cases the court is convinced that the accused has actually suffered substantial hardship,[8] or has in fact already started serving his or her sentence. For instance, in *R. v. Downes*, the Court of Appeal for Ontario makes it clear that bail conditions are effectively part of the sentence: "Stringent bail conditions, especially house arrest, represent infringement on liberty and are in violation of the presumption of innocence. House arrest is a form of punishment, albeit of a different character than actual incarceration".[9]

More recently, in *R. v. Lacasse*, the Supreme Court of Canada held that we should consider the length of a driving prohibition imposed at the pre-trial stage, emphasizing the connection between bail and sentencing:

> In the instant case, the driving prohibition has the same effect regardless of whether it was imposed before or after the respondent was sentenced. In *R. v. Sharma*, [1992] 1 S.C.R. 814, Lamer C.J., dissenting, explained that the accused had in fact begun serving his sentence, given that the driving prohibition would have been imposed as part of his sentence had he been tried and found guilty within a reasonable time. In short, where a driving prohibition is

---

[7] See Chapter 4, fn 28.

[8] *R. v. Irvine* (2008) MBCA 34. The Court refused to take bail conditions as a mitigating factor because "there is a virtual absence of evidence as to what substantial hardship, if any, the accused actually suffered" (par. 29).

[9] *R. v. Downes* (2006) CanLII 3957 (Ont. C.A.), par. 29. See also *R. v. Lindsay* (2009) ONCA 532; *R. v. Junkert* (2010) ONCA 549 ; *R. v. Belcourt* (2012) BCSC 404.

not only one of the release conditions imposed on an accused but also part of the sentence imposed upon his or her conviction, the length of the presentence driving prohibition must be subtracted from the prohibition imposed in the context of the sentence.[10]

As a result, contrary to the pre-trial model exposed by Feeley, the locus of the criminal process and punishment also extends to the sentencing stage where probation orders either duplicate and extend bail conditions or are conditioned by the success or failure of earlier forms of surveillance. The fact that defendants can barely tell the difference between a bail or probation order speaks to that point. But it also illustrates the circularity that now characterizes punishment.

Yet, the fact that bail is not officially a form of punishment also means that bail orders will get less consideration and may even be harsher than sentences would be, despite the fact that they are actually imposed on individuals who are presumed innocent (Myers, 2017). In our interviews, legal actors appeared to be more sensitive to the severity of the conditions imposed at the sentencing stage because they have a better sense of its duration. While the actors perceived bail release as temporary and urgent, sentencing decisions are more long-term by nature. This time factor has a significant impact on the number and nature of conditions: "Because probation is longer, when it comes to imposing something that we know will be there for two years, for example; it's not the same as waiting for the case to proceed" (Prosecutor). Thus, while some actors recognize in the abstract that a person may be subject to bail conditions for a long period of time because of judicial delays, they do not give bail orders the same character and consideration, even being oblivious to what is at stake (namely the presumption of innocence).

As a result, in some cases, bail conditions will actually be imposed for a longer period of time than would have been the case had the accused been sentenced right away. In *Burdon*, the Court of Appeal of Alberta stressed that the accused had been under house arrest for three years as part of his bail conditions when he finally got sentenced. For him, bail conditions were as onerous as some imposed for conditional sentences and lasted well beyond the maximum term of conditional sentences (the maximum term for a CSO is two years). As a result, the Court observed that this accused

---

[10] R. v. *Lacasse* (2015) SCC 64, par. 113.

would in fact have been under judicial surveillance for six years at the end of his probation.[11]

Secondly, the process becomes the punishment in a more egregious manner. As noted, in many cases, bail conditions pave the way for harsher forms of punishments as individuals accumulate practically unavoidable breaches. For Rob from Vancouver, for instance, breaches build up over time, leading to an escalation of punitive consequences:

> For your first breach they will be lenient, give you a slap on the wrist, then kick you out the door. The second time they might do that or they will just hold you over, so the more breaches that you accumulate on your record, the punishment gets more severe. Next time you get two weeks, maybe the next time you get 30 days, next time 3 months. It just goes higher and higher and higher.

As such, breaches will bring detention much faster, one defence attorney explained, because the person will appear in custody and, following a coerced guilty plea, will often be sentenced to the number of days already spent in detention. Worse, this first period of custody will inevitably lead to further custody as a result of the application of the principle of gradation of the severity of the sentence:

> Let's say that you are arrested on Friday late into the night. You won't appear in Court until Monday, so you are going to be detained for four days. The best, well, not really the best, but the fastest way to release this person is for them to plead guilty and spend four days in jail. But want to or not, it's still four days of detention in their file for a breach, and the next time the person is arrested, we start from four days. While if the person had not appeared in custody, he or she could have received a suspended sentence on the breach or a fine or something like that, but we will often consider that the person has already paid for their crime with their four days of detention.
>
> (Defence lawyer, Montreal)

Thirdly, and more fundamentally, conditions of release themselves may become "punishment", since individuals subject to conditions often experience bail conditions as harsher than their actual sentence given the manner in which they "cut" them from their everyday lives, professional activities, and political activism, as revealed at length in Chapter 7. Conditions "felt like a big punishment, that's for sure, and for nothing", noted Chad in Vancouver.

---

[11] *R. v. Burdon* (2010) ABCA 171: "The bail conditions imposed on the respondent were as onerous as some imposed for conditional sentences and lasted well beyond the maximum term of a conditional sentence" (par. 8).

At the very least, from the perspective of those subject to the orders, the differences between bail and probation are hard to discern: as one judge noted to us: "often the guys don't know what [order] they are on, when they are in jail. Are you on bail, are you on probation, are you on a CSO? They don't know which one they are on, they just know they're been arrested and are supposed to be seeing somebody".

Of course, in strictly legal terms, bail conditions are not meant to be primarily punitive. They also are not typically included in the definition of "punishment" according to Canadian *Charter* jurisprudence.[12] Instead, they may be deemed preventive in nature, referring to future risks of flight or recidivism (see Ashworth and Zedner, 2014).

But in other cases, as we shall see in Chapter 6, bail orders pursue therapeutic, rehabilitative, or "benevolent" objectives (Moore, 2011; Hannah-Moffat and Maurutto, 2012) that are more appropriate for sentencing.[13]

In that sense, conditions of release do not amount to the intentional infliction of pain (Zedner, 2016). They may be more accurately described as "coercive preventive measures" (Ashworth and Zedner, 2014: 20). Nonetheless, they clearly have important punitive effects. As we will explain later in Chapters 7 and 8, the spatiotemporal effects of conditions can be particularly punitive, acting on already vulnerable bodies as forms of legal violence. This is particularly so when orders prevent individuals from accessing life-saving resources such as food, shelter, health services, or social assistance. Patrick noted, for example, that he could only access his welfare cheque by conforming to the court's requirements:

> Every time, it's like a leash around your neck. You don't show up, you don't get it. You have an appointment two weeks before and you missed it and you show up to get your check, you ain't getting it. They'll issue a breach. And they'll arrest you right there. It happens all the time. Not just me, there is a lot of people that get their welfare through the community court.

Demonstrators in both Montreal and Toronto also echoed these sentiments. Nico, a student who was arrested during the students' strikes in Montreal in 2012, was quick to conclude that his conditions were "more of a punishment than [his] actual sentence ... than [his] trial". For Marius, his extremely restrictive bail conditions (that included a prohibition to be found within

---

[12] *R. v. K.R.J.* (2016) SCC, insisting that "punishment" should necessarily follow proper conviction for an offence.
[13] Conversely, when probation orders immediately follow the arrest and a guilty plea, they may include pre-trial concerns with securing certain spaces and protecting the public.

300 m of any learning institution, a red zone covering most of Downtown Montreal, a curfew and a prohibition to demonstrate) amounted to being condemned without having had a trial: "When I was released on bail, I was convinced that I had been issued a guilty verdict. I was held in custody in my own house as a result of my conditions, so yeah, it was like if I had already been declared guilty". Similarly, Zora, whom we met in the introduction, reported that her bail conditions amounted to a severe form of punishment. She even suggested, as noted earlier, that had she had "less trauma response" while being held on remand, and more time to think about it when she appeared in court, she would have chosen to do "more jail time to gain less restrictive conditions".

Importantly in Zora's case, and many others on bail, conditions were the *only* form of punishment, given that she was ultimately released free of criminal charges some 14 months after her arrest when the Attorney General of Ontario concluded an agreement with the defence. Zora's case is not unique. In June 2010, 1,118 people were arrested in Toronto at the demonstrations protesting the G20 Summit, in the largest mass arrest in Canadian peacetime history (Toronto Police Service, 2011). However, less than a third of those arrested (330 individuals; 29.5%) appeared before the court, while 207 of those 330 individuals had their matters stayed by the Crown, withdrawn, or dismissed, 40 low-risk offenders were dealt with through direct accountability outside of the criminal justice system, 9 were listed by error, and 12 were released with a peace bond (again not charged with a criminal offence). Only 5% (55) of those arrested pled guilty or were found guilty after a trial (Ministry of the Attorney General of Ontario, 2014).

For many protesters, this "pre-punishment" is not only key to neutralizing political dissent, but also acts as a deterrent – both important sentencing objectives:

> if they had never convicted us, if we had never done jail time, they still would have got two years of a whole bunch of people not being able to really do anything political. So, it's the pre-punishment that is the most benefit to them. But I think the bail conditions make people nervous even more than the possibility of going to jail. Yah, so I think they use bail conditions as a deterrent and as a restriction on protest.
>
> (Emma)

Moreover, one can even argue that in the case of protesters, the arrest constitutes the punishment (Fortin, 2018). Indeed, the very fact of being arrested and physically removed from certain places not only prevents citizens from exercising their democratic rights, but it also has a direct impact on the political movement and the message that such movement is trying to convey. As the work of Tim Zick (2009) shows, "message placement is often inextricably intertwined with message content". As such, protesters carefully and deliberately choose the places where demonstrations will take place either for their proximity to a certain audience, their symbolic status, or their high visibility. Although arrests, including mass arrests, get their own type of visibility, they also directly stigmatize the protesters and often negatively affect their message.

In addition to being displaced to the pre-trial phase, the punitive effects of conditions of release extend through time, as many individuals are unclear about the legal boundaries and exact duration of their court orders. In Montreal, for instance, at least two participants reported still being subject to red zone conditions while they had long expired. Maya, for instance, was convinced that she was subject to a red zone for the last 12 years: "my lawyer told me I was still red zoned. I think it will remain in place for the rest of my life. The judge told me this was a life condition. I need to ask for it to be removed because otherwise they will keep me on it". Another was also unaware that his probation had ended a year ago when we met him for an interview.

Thus, the place, timing, certainty (as revealed in the abovementioned ambiguities), and very nature of punishment change, yet it is often not recognized as such. This raises important issues with respect to the safeguards and protections that should follow (Ashworth and Zedner, 2014).

CONCLUSION

In this chapter, we suggested that an emphasis on the spatial and temporal characteristics and movements inherent to criminal justice administration allow us to see the shifting nature of criminal law and punishment. The spatiotemporal configuration of the disposition model we described (moving away from the trial, to the streets, centred on the process as a form of anticipated punishment, and over both speedy and extended periods of time) has the effect of deflecting and neutralizing rights claims and resistance.

Taking our spatial and temporal analysis of the systemic models at another level, however, may also allow us to perceive the manner in which the models, including our findings, are in fact interacting with each other, co-existing and reinforcing each other, at different times, in different spaces (streets vs. courtroom and remand centres, but also involving different normative systems), creating an extensive web of regulation and punitive sanctions.

For instance, criminal justice administration in the era of conditions of release first reinforces and supports the plea-bargaining model: holding individuals in pre-trial custody or under strict conditions of release goes a long way towards inducing guilty pleas (Kellough and Wortley, 2002). In particular, the prospect of breaching and adding to their clients' criminal record appears to have created an incentive for defence lawyers to deal with the case at once:

> We've developed a flair. You know right away that some people won't be there by the next date. We're still trying, we explain it to them, but you know that not only they won't show up at the next Court date, but that the next time, there will also be a new charge of not going down to the police station or not abiding by their court order and we'll have to deal with three cases. So *sometimes, it's worth pleading guilty on day one, we close the case, that's it.* We really must avoid over-multiplying conditions.
>
> (Defence lawyer, Montreal; our emphasis)

Further, this complementarity may not be limited to the criminal justice system. In fact, criminal law may be borrowing from other normative regimes through a process of legal hybridity. In the last decades, scholars have documented the growth of less "prominent locations of punishment" (Galanter, 1991) such as civil law (e.g. punitive damages) or administrative law, including immigration law. While Steiker (1998) has alerted us to the rise of the preventive state, others refer to the expanding "shadow carceral state" (Beckett and Murakawa, 2012) to include the proliferation of civil preventive measures backed with the threat of criminal sanctions.

For some, criminal law is simply expanding its logics and practices, contaminating other normative systems as in the "crimmigration" literature (Stumpf, 2006; Beckett and Evans, 2015). Along the same lines, in their ground-breaking study of banishment in Seattle, Beckett, and Herbert (2010a) suggested that the combination of criminal, administrative, and civil law has the effect of expanding the scope of the criminal justice system (2010a; b).[14] Yet, for others, we should not be too quick at imposing crime-related categories on different fields of law, and instead insist on the concurrence and interactions of different normative systems with distinctive logics and practices that may have reinforcing effects (Vieira Velloso, 2013).

Our findings show, in fact, that it is not only that we are turning to administrative regimes and non-criminal normative systems (such as immigration law), but that criminal law itself has undergone a process of hybridization, incorporating administrative law logics and *dispositifs* (Garland, 2014).

---

[14] In the policing field, the combination of criminal law, constitutional law, and state/police surveillance is sometimes referred to as surveillance law. See Lippert and Sleiman, 2012.

Criminal law is dangerously becoming much like administrative law, incorporating many features which have traditionally characterized this area of law, including discretion, preventive goals, and lack of adjudicative procedures (Lynch, 1998). But "the legally hybrid nature of these tools and the weak rights protections they offer make it difficult for defendants and their attorneys to contest them" (Beckett and Herbert, 2010a: 101).

PART III

Territorialization and Its Consequences

6

Territorializing: How Legal Territory Is
Made and Justified

"If they don't comply, it's not the fault of the Court ...
It's he or she that breached those conditions".
(*Judge, Montreal*)

The previous chapters provided some macro-level insights into the particular spatiotemporality of criminal justice administration, with its shift away from the courts, and into more discretionary spaces of legal regulation, and a temporal pattern that combines fast, individualized processing and longer repeating loops of charge–release–breach. This chapter provides a more detailed perspective on the work conducted by legal actors. Drawing from 18 interviews with defence counsel, prosecutors,[1] justices of the peace, and judges in Montreal (12) and Vancouver (6), we focus on the manner in which territorialized conditions of release are crafted by legal actors and the rationale they put forward to justify them. In so doing, we consider the manner in which these conditions rely on forms of legal territorialization, structuring relations through forms of bounded classification, communication, and enforcement, organizing space and time through practical forms of "cutting" and "joining".

In the first section of this chapter, we present the routinized character of condition-making in the words of those who craft them. Specifically, as explained in Chapter 5, prosecutors and judges design conditions of release based on internalized culturally induced practices and a decision-making chain initiated by the police who have identified problematic places. Legal actors show limited consciousness of the spatial ramifications of the orders for those who are subject to them, often including extremely broad areas, such as downtown cores or entire neighbourhoods.

---

[1] In this chapter, the term 'prosecutors' refers to Federal prosecutors in Vancouver and Municipal Court prosecutors in Montreal. See the methodology section in chapter 1.

We then analyze the objectives they pursue, focusing on bail where most of those conditions are imposed. Specifically, we suggest that legal actors follow a series of rationales, primarily but not exclusively coming from the bail provisions of the Criminal Code of Canada, ranging from crime prevention, particularly in certain "hot spots" in the inner city, to therapy. Further, they build these territories in the shadow of other legal spaces. For instance, judges see conditions of release as a lesser evil given that they are concerned with preserving the defendants' liberty and offering an alternative to another important territory, remand centre, or jail, but they also rely on the fact that the territories so designed are already occupied and, more specifically, policed. In the last sections of this chapter, we explore the questions of reasonableness and effectiveness of such court orders, from legal actors' perspectives.

Two qualifiers are necessary, however. First, while we discern consistent patterns between Montreal and Vancouver, there is evidence that conditions of release are deployed differently across jurisdictions. There is considerable anecdotal evidence, for example, of their informal use in many smaller communities across Canada, as well as in many suburban contexts (Pasternak, 2017: 237, 239; Pivot Legal Society, 2018). Some jurisdictions have developed standardized red zones applied to targeted repeat offenders, as opposed to the supposedly personalized restrictions adopted elsewhere.[2] There is some evidence that certain jurisdictions may rely more heavily on conditions imposed by police officers, as suggested by our informants in Ottawa.[3] Red zones are also differently bounded. In Vancouver, for example, designated street blocks are specified, while in Montreal, radial distances from designated locations are used.

Secondly, while focusing on bail, we also refer to sentencing orders. While bail and probation share some common characteristics when it comes to imposing conditions of release, they remain distinct legal institutions and are guided by different philosophies and pursued different legal and penological objectives. As mentioned in Chapter 3, while rehabilitation, treatment, and guided supervision were at the heart of the penal reforms that introduced probation, bail itself, apart from the use of recognizance in the Middle Ages and into the colonial period, did not overtly pursue other goals than securing the accused's appearance until much later in the twentieth century when conditions of release were introduced, and, in some cases, with significant resistance. It is now clear, however, that at least in Canada, crime prevention

[2]   See www.cbc.ca/news/canada/british-columbia/rcmp-want-red-zone-in-maple-ridge-1.3812342. See also Chapter 1.
[3]   See also Beattie, Solecki, and Morton Bourgon, 2013 showing important disparities among sites.

and protection of the public have become the primary purpose and concern of legal actors at bail. Moreover, as problem-solving courts and specialized tribunals grew in importance across the country, rehabilitation and therapeutic interventions have slowly but surely been introduced, to a point at which one can observe the mutual influence and indeed merging of pre-trial and post-trial strategies (see Chapter 5, and the discussion of the process as the punishment). In fact, as we have seen, decisions made today at one stage of criminal proceedings, whether bail or probation, are likely to have a direct influence on the other stage.

"IT'S LIKE CUTTING [A] SANDWICH ...": RED ZONES AS ROUTINIZED PRACTICES OF THE COURT

As mentioned earlier in Chapter 5, most conditions of release are imposed without a bail hearing, but are rather suggested by prosecutors or negotiated with the defence with the consent of the accused person who is often held in custody and wants to be released at all costs. As such, while conditional orders are personalized, they are also highly routinized.

Given the bureaucratic and time-sensitive nature of the bail court, and the work conducted by defence counsel and Crown prosecutors behind the scenes, it is not surprising that the practical work entailed in making conditions of release appears highly doxic, to borrow from Bourdieu (1977). As described by its practitioners, it relied on behaviour that was self-evident and transparently normal. A judge described it as akin to a form of muscle memory, in which the cutting of the sandwich echoed the cuts of conditional release:

> It's very difficult to answer your questions because it seems like a second nature. When you're a Crown attorney and you have a lot of files to approve and then to make decisions on conditions, you don't spend half an hour questioning yourself... *[I]t's like cutting your sandwich in four instead of two, by force of habit, by practice, by being immersed in the situation.* That's how it works.
>
> (Judge, Montreal, also a former prosecutor; our emphasis)

For example, unwritten standards or institutionalized templates structure the definition of an area restriction in cases of spousal violence, as observed by a prosecutor and another judge:

> It's a bit of an *automatic procedure*, I would say. When we talk about a residence, it's 100 m to 300 m; when we talk about a physical person, we put 10 m, 15 m, 20 m or 25 m.
>
> (Prosecutor, Montreal; our emphasis)

> I can't explain the logic behind it except that *there is a rule based on a number*. You're going to hear about 30 metres from a person, and when it's a

place, like a workplace, a school, a home, well, you're going to hear 100 metres or 300 metres. It's like it's established.

(Judge, Montreal; our emphasis)

Standardized red zones are also created in relation to certain problematic areas in Vancouver or Montreal, the boundaries of which are learned on the job.

It's relatively the same areas. Let's say they want to remove prostitution in Ahuntsic [a Montreal district], on Lajeunesse Street. They will identify something like a zone, meaning the person cannot go on Lajeunesse Street between Henri-Bourassa and, I don't know, like maybe Crémazie Street, something like that. And if it happens in Hochelaga-Maisonneuve, they will probably do a different red zone.

(Judge, Montreal)

Spatial conditions of release, therefore, often rely on a routinized legal geography, in which legal actors discern particular spaces as problematic. This is particularly evident in highly criminalized spaces, such as Vancouver's Downtown (DTES). A visible and demonized space, characterized in the dominant discourse as a site of drugs, criminality, and ill-health (Liu and Blomley, 2013), the DTES is intensely regulated and policed. For instance, data compiled by the Vancouver Area Network of Drug Users (VANDU) and the Downtown Neighbourhood Council (DNC) indicate that VPD District 2 (which includes the DTES) is the location of five times as many drug charges than other districts, significantly more "street checks", and other signs of elevated police attention, including an overwhelming majority of tickets issued pursuant to city by-laws.[4] Strikingly, this also reveals that conditional release is used to facilitate the surveillance and apprehension of marginalized people, thereby facilitating the work of police and prosecutors. In this case, the imposition of red zones must be understood as part of a broader attempt to control this particular neighbourhood.[5]

It is not surprising, therefore, that the DTES is saturated with individualized red zones. Indeed, until recently, a laminated map of the neighbourhood was posted in Vancouver Criminal Court, for ease of reference (Damon, 2014: 1). As one Vancouver prosecutor reported:

Area restrictions have always been imposed, and from the very beginning I learned the standard Downtown Eastside area restriction: Gore Avenue to the East, Abbot Street to the West, Pender Street to the South, and Cordova

---

[4] According to data obtained by Pivot and VANDU, this includes 76% of jaywalking tickets, 31% of panhandling tickets, and 95% of street vending tickets. See King, 2013b.

[5] King, 2013b.

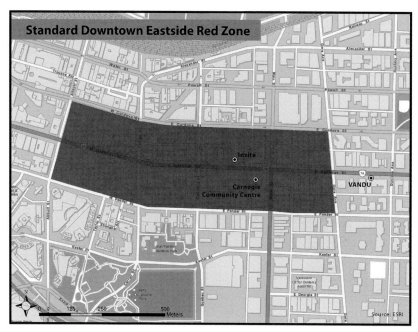

MAP 6.1 The "standard" Downtown Eastside red zone (Vancouver).
Sources: Esri, HERE, Garmin, USGS, Intermap, INCREMENT P, NRCan, Esri Japan, METI, Esri China (Hong Kong), Esri Korea, Esri (Thailand), NGCC, © OpenStreetMap contributors, and the GIS User Community

Street to the North. Those [were] sort of ingrained in my head from the very beginning.

> (Prosecutor, Vancouver; see Map 6.1)

To illustrate the effects of territorialization on a systemic level, William Damon, an MA student associated with the project, analyzed a sample of the Vancouver dataset of conditions of release for the month of January 2011. He found that 37% of all area restrictions were centred in the Downtown Eastside of Vancouver. In particular, the DTES accounted for 92% of area restrictions related to drug offences (Map 6.2) (Damon, 2014: chap. 6).

Legal actors thus spoke specifically of using area restrictions to prevent people from entering the DTES, especially those they identified as being non-addicted drug traffickers, the goal being to "stop the influx of people in this area who are sort of higher up in the trade" (Prosecutor, Vancouver).

There is such a pervasive drug culture here in the DTES that it is our hope that if somebody is awaiting trial or I guess even on probation conditions that the hope is that if they are removed from this war zone, the DTES, that it reduces the likelihood that they will sell again, because that is where most of

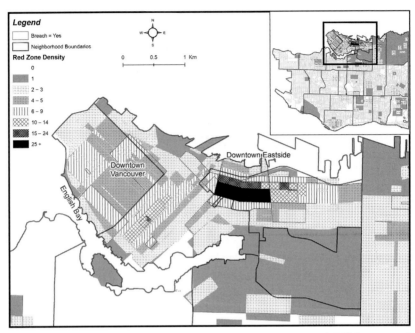

MAP 6.2 Density of sample of Vancouver red zones issued in January 2011. © Will Damon, used with permission

the users are, they are in the DTES, so we are trying to remove the supply away from the demand.

(Prosecutor, Vancouver)

While the DTES is a permanent space of abjection and criminalization, other spaces "come and go" (Von Benda-Beckmann and Von Benda-Beckmann, 2014) in the legal atlas. Episodic sites of protest, notably, become red zoned. For instance, during the 2012 Quebec students' strike, that led to over 3,500 arrests over the course of seven months, the courts became well attuned to the location of students' meeting places:

For student demonstrations, Parc Émilie Gamelin was the gathering place, where everything started. We all know that some colleges are like powder kegs … Some CEGEPs were constantly involved in these situations. Those were gathering spaces, places of more direct demonstrations, places of overflows, or where there were acts of repeated vandalism.

(Judge, Montreal)

Similarly, in the days preceding the opening of the Vancouver Olympics in 2010, the police arrested a great number of protesters and released them on bail using standardized pre-written forms, red zoning protestors from areas proximate to the Games (Sylvestre, Bernier, and Bellot, 2015; Sylvestre et al., 2018). Conditions of release were thus used to support law enforcement and secure certain spaces during highly publicized international events.

In the case of both bail and probation orders, the regularity and familiarity with which legal actors impose restrictive conditions is only strengthened by the fact that court actors work with a pre-established form which contains a list of typical, yet optional, release conditions next to discrete boxes that can be easily checked (Vanhamme, 2016; Sylvestre, Bellot, and Blomley, 2017). In British Columbia (B.C.), this bureaucratic form, which represents the technicality *par excellence* (Sylvestre et al., 2015), is supplemented by various picklists that include standardized wording used to craft conditions of release (Pivot Legal Society, 2018: 89). Interestingly, in the red zone sections of the bail and probation picklists, the authors of the document warn justices that "this condition should be used sparingly. It is rarely appropriate for the court to foist one community's problem onto another. Banishment can sometimes remove the accused from his only support network, creating bigger problems then it was intended to solve".[6]

INTERPRETING LEGAL RATIONALES: RED ZONES AS
CREATIVE LEGAL PRACTICES

While often routinized, spatial conditions of release are governed by a series of often overlapping legal rationalities. Formally, as noted in Chapter 4, legal actors are to follow a series of legal rules when crafting conditions of release. In the case of bail, these purported goals derive primarily from the provisions of the Canadian Criminal Code. As a reminder, section 515 of the *Code* specifies that conditions of release should only be exceptionally imposed – although we showed in Chapter 4 that the practice is otherwise – and must be justified on one of three grounds: ensuring attendance in court, maintaining the protection and safety of the public (including the "substantial likelihood" that the accused will, if released from custody, commit a criminal offence or interfere with the administration of justice), and maintaining confidence in the administration of justice.

Despite these legal prescriptions, the interviews reveal a more flexible interpretation of these grounds, with the addition of more practical regulatory concerns, as well as the presence of other criteria that have no basis in law, such as a desire to reduce crime on its own terms, to monitor and regulate certain populations and assist policing, or to provide "therapeutic"

---

[6] E.g. Provincial Court of British Columbia, 2017 May 1, 2017, online: http://www.provincialcourt
.bc.ca/types-of-cases/criminal-and-youth/links#Q7 (see also Probation Picklist).

interventions for the wayward. This becomes clearly evident in the territorializing work of legal actors, as they craft spatial conditions of release, in an attempt at structuring socio-legal relations through the configuration of space and time. As discussed in Chapter 2, this can be thought of as a form of territorialization, reliant upon simultaneous spatiotemporal "cuts" and "joins". While necessarily connected, we treat cutting and joining separately, for ease of presentation.

(a) Cutting

The function of spatial conditions of release as a means of cutting individuals from specific territories at designated times was clearly on legal actors' minds when imposing red zones and other spatial conditions. Red zones were seen as discrete, surgical cuts that served to detach offenders or accused persons from a set of spatiotemporal conditions deemed problematic. Speaking of area restrictions, one Vancouver Prosecutor observed that the offence is "very much geographical, it is a problem that is geographically contained [...] So it is really hard to separate the offence from where it happened. And that is why the area restriction is so often imposed". In that sense, the red zone is less oriented to individual acts of criminal behaviour than exclusion from a place within which an offence has (allegedly) occurred: it is hard to "separate the offence from where it happened", in other words (Prosecutor, Montreal). "For someone who committed a theft", noted a Montreal judge, "we will go with the specific place where the theft happened". Similarly, added another judge, "when it comes to drugs, we know that it's a territorial activity, so the street corner is going to represent the territory of a group, so we're going to impose that street corner".

While notionally individualized, there are no biographies or lived geographies recognized in these cuts. They produce managerial or actuarial spaces that act, largely, on the placement of largely interchangeable bodies. Red zones remove risky bodies from risky spaces. For one Vancouver defence lawyer, the purpose of the red zone "is to keep the person out of an area that is going to draw them back into criminal activity, or allow them to continue in criminal activity".

Drug dealers, for example, are seen as tied to specific locations: "they've got their territory to be selling the drugs out of, they've got their corner or block. So usually when we ask for an area restriction, we are trying to keep people out of those blocks" (Prosecutor, Vancouver), or, in the words of a Montreal judge:

> When it comes to narcotics, preventing them from being on the same street corner and continuing to sell their drugs, and in the case of a demonstration, it is to *prevent them from finding themselves in the same context where reoffending will be almost inevitable*.
>
> (our emphasis)

By removing people from certain spaces, legal actors thus assume that red zones will regulate the future. For one Montreal Prosecutor, the objective is preventive: "Yeah, it's to prevent reoffending. We think that if the conditions are met, in principle there should never be any recurrence. *We avoid putting them in the red zone where there is trouble*" (our emphasis).

POLICE CUTS

Designed as individualized, personally crafted conditions of release, legal actors who are confined to the courtroom do not always have the detailed geographical knowledge required to identify problematic spaces, particularly if they change. Illustrating the decentralization of legal decision-making associated with criminal justice administration described in Chapter 5, the police play a crucial role in identifying conditions, given their assumed expertise in identifying the spatial and temporal patterns of criminality. A Montreal Prosecutor noted that for red zones the police "generally will tell us, because we don't always know all the problem areas, so generally it is they who will suggest the red zone". While some legal actors were clear that the courts were institutionally distinct from the police, they also noted that often they would take some direction from them: "Often the police will make bail requests . . . I don't always follow them but usually . . . I'll request what the police have asked for. When I don't follow them, it is because I think they are maybe a little too draconian" (Prosecutor, Vancouver). This chain of decision-making thus moves from the police, to the prosecutors, and then the judges.

The symbiosis between police and court actors is intensified in relation to the appearance of "problem areas" or "hot spots" – spatially and temporally moments of legal problematization, from which alleged offenders are to be excised. Police sweeps of such hot spots will be buttressed by red zones. Legal actors appear well aware of these dynamics: "In Montreal, the police received complaints from residents who live nearby, and to the extent that the offence is related to the park or the place, it's a measure intended to try and reduce the number of people coming and going to this place which encourages the alleged offences" (Judge, Montreal). This is also confirmed by our analysis of the case law.[7]

---

[7] For instance, in *R. v. Deuffoure*, BCSC (1979), the Supreme Court of British Columbia found that the imposition of an area restriction in a bail order was justified in the case of a sex worker given that "[t]here was evidence of the prostitution problem in the downtown area and, particularly, in the areas adjacent to the corner of Georgia Street and Hornby Street. The problem is so notorious as to not need evidence. Since the decision of the Supreme Court in *R. v. Hutt*, [1978] 2 S.C.R. 476, prostitutes feel free to ply their trade with impunity. Nightly, they congregate in the area mentioned and accost any and all males. The police receive numerous complaints from the public and from the management of hotels and businesses in

Such territorial exclusions are deemed to be justifiable in that they reduce problems in some areas, even if it is acknowledged that the solution is only temporary, and public disorder will likely only be displaced. Spatial conditions of release are thus imagined not as a spatiotemporal fix but a respite, beneficial mostly to localized publics rather than the person subject to conditions. "In the case of an individual, it has little impact", agreed another Montreal prosecutor, "but if that individual were to reduce the quality of life . . . if that person is no longer there, one can think that the citizens will feel better in their home".

In the Montreal case, interestingly, the pragmatic concerns of police affairs in responding to complaints or seeking to manage "hot spots" was systematically translated into juridical terms by legal actors. Frequently, legal actors justified conditions of release in order to "protect the public", to "avoid reoffending", and in direct connection with the offence and the objectives set in the Criminal Code, rather than more practical policing considerations, such as the governance of specific public spaces. For one judge in Montreal, a red zone was not designed "to protect the public space, it's to protect citizens against offences: the angle is the offences, it's not the public space. . .". Further, as another pointed out, public safety should be distinguished from governance issues encountered by the police:

> A police officer will describe the problem and the problem will lead us to consider the restriction in terms of public safety and public interest, so once the police have explained that to us, it will be justified, but it will be justified for those considerations, not for considerations of governance. If a station commander comes in and says "We have a problem, it creates a dangerous situation for the public and all that, and would you forbid this individual to go into the red zone to help us in terms of public safety", it's going to be a consideration that I'm going to evaluate with a lot of thought. But if he tells me that it causes him problems, that it creates administrative problems for him, and that he has a governance problem, and an overtime problem, and administrative problems, in that case, it's no. . .

"POLICE" LOGIC

As illustrated here, it was common for legal actors to refer to the need to protect the public. While this may entail structuring conditions of release, such as no-go

the area whose patrons have been bothered. Ladies, other than prostitutes, are accosted by men interested in engaging the services of a prostitute. The police have had to helplessly stand by. It is in that light that one has to consider that matter" (par. 5). See also *R.* v. *Pedersen* (1986) 31 C.C.C. (3d) 574 (B.C. Co. Ct), speaking of a "notorious area" and *R.* v. *Williamson* (1992) O.J. No. 1958 (Ont. Ct. J. Gen. Div.), speaking of a "known drug trafficking area".

orders or no-contact orders, so as to protect victims of crime, particularly in the case of domestic violence, it was also clearly articulated as the desire to prevent reoffending. The link between public protection and the prevention of reoffending was so strong that in many cases the focus of judicial actors was primarily on crime prevention or the risk of reoffending *per se* regardless of its consequences, without even mentioning the issue of public safety,[8] or that of the victims or the witnesses, or the degree of danger this person represented.[9]

Rather than a direct relationship between an alleged offender and the public, the connection is thus often more diffuse. Public "protection" and "safety" morph into a more generalized "public interest". Thus, a prosecutor in Vancouver rationalized red zones for those engaged in drug offences on the principle that "there are legitimate ... businesses that are operating that are affected by the drug trafficking trade. There are schools ... and children that use the community centre, day cares, there are all kinds of public facilities where the public is impacted by the drug trade that happens". The "impacts" of the drug trade, she noted, are more than proximity to people consuming drugs, but entail a "sort of a ripple effect ... that effects people running their lives, and so that is what I mean by considering the public interest". As here, this can entail localized "publics" in particular areas who must be protected from "crime". But it also appears to be extended to a more generalized logic whereby crime in general is to be controlled through conditions of release so as to protect a wider public. Strikingly, another Vancouver Prosecutor described the use of red zones in relation to drug trafficking as "a harm reduction type of approach" on the principle that "we are trying to reduce the likelihood that they will reoffend, and thus protect the public".

At work here, surely, is a police logic of criminal law, reliant on "the regulation of the internal life of a community to promote general welfare and the condition of good order" (Neocleous, 2000: 1; Blomley, 2012). To promote the "general welfare", law must prevent the commission of offences, even those that have not yet occurred, or have been legally proven. It is in these terms that we can understand the widespread justification of conditions of release, even in the case of bail orders, where the offence is only alleged.

[8] To be sure, it should be noted that s. 515 (10)(b) Cr. C. does not link the protection of the public, victims, or witnesses to the presence of a real or imminent threat to their safety. This section was amended shortly after the new Part XIV of the Criminal Code came into force in the 1970s to remove the reference to "serious harm", thereby allowing the Court to consider the strong possibility that the accused would commit any type of offence if released.

[9] Vanhamme (2014) came to a similar conclusion, stating that by assessing "the concept of public protection or public safety, [the judges] do indeed include events involving violence, but also other less serious events", including the protection of citizens' material assets.

Q: What would be the reasons underlying the presence of conditions?
A: It's always the same reason! These are always the reasons provided for in the Code, to prevent the continuation of an offence, or to prevent them from committing other offences in the future. (Judge, Montreal)

For a Vancouver judge, the purpose of a red zone is to "prevent crime. That's the rationale. It's not as a punishment; it's to prevent crime". The mutually entangled objective of protecting victims and society is defined as a time-out, given the temporal immediacy of the offence. The goal is "to protect society, to protect the victims. When someone appears in court, often the crime has just happened, you have to find a way to stop and then see what you should do next" (Judge, Montreal).

As such, the concept of "public interest" seemed fluid, and capable of a number of meanings. On occasion, it seemed to be defined in terms of the financial cost of dealing with excess breaches, in the case, for example, of a person with limited mental capacity. Finally, for one prosecutor in Vancouver, it related to the third "ground", which she defined as the "public's perception of the administration of justice". She noted that this might be compromised by the situation when an alleged offender – perhaps charged with dealing drugs outside a particular business – is released without conditions, and returns to the same spot.

THERAPEUTIC CUTS

If our findings reveal a very broad-textured reading of the legal grounds for conditions of release, it is also important to note that legal actors are pursuing objectives through conditions that are not recognized in the Criminal Code. For example, release is frequently used therapeutically to implement social support and rehabilitation despite the clear injunction that such ends are not to be applied in cases of bail [R. v. *Antic* (2017); see Chapter 4]. While judges and prosecutors are aware that conditions imposed at this stage of the proceedings should not be imposed in this manner, in practice, conditions often seek this end. In many cases, this preventive concern is combined with alleged therapeutic goals (Moore et al., 2011). Speaking about the usefulness of a red zone for an offender, a Montreal judge noted how the protection of the public, reoffending, and rehabilitation end up merging, particularly when the temporality of the criminal justice system is factored in:

> The judicial process being what it is, it takes a certain amount of time. Often when the case ends after two years, the individual hasn't gone to his red zone

in two years . . . Time and the procedure have been used to get him out of a certain environment in many cases. Not in all the cases, but in many cases . . . In terms of protecting the public, in terms of rehabilitation, he must not go back. Of course, in terms of bail, it's the protection of the public that guides us, rather than rehabilitation, but it's clear that rehabilitation is not excluded. I mean, we're going to do it, when people are sent to rehab during bail. It's clear that in the long term, we're aiming for rehabilitation.

Yet, as one Vancouver Prosecutor noted, bail should not be used to facilitate rehabilitation, such as requirements that people attend a drug treatment facility:

> the purpose of bail is to address these three concerns, attendance in court, public safety, and the confidence in the administration of justice, having regard to the various factors in the code. The place for measures aimed at deterrence, rehabilitation, denunciation, you know, all those types of things, is sentencing. So, they should differ.

Regardless, a Vancouver judge frankly noted that, for him at least within the Downtown Eastside drug market, red zones are to be rehabilitative. Thus, a red zone that serves to keep people away from areas of the Downtown Eastside "when they're coming down and getting into the drug scene, is rehabilitative in the sense that you're keeping them away from where the influences are, the negative influences on them". Red zones are deemed useful in temporarily removing people from areas deemed problematic not only in order to prevent them from reoffending, but with a view to supporting them.

> I think it's simply to try and *stop* this problem and to a certain extent, it may sound silly, but to *help* the person as well, because if he or she is still in this problematic area and he or she is still living in that environment, it's a bit difficult to get out of it after a while. I would say that often, it's people who have a similar background, there is really a problem and the purpose of ordering a red zone is to try to get the person to . . . to help him or her get out of it or to say, at some point, that's enough. They are arrested every second week for that. At some point there has to be a *time-out*.
>
> (Prosecutor, Montreal; our emphasis)

(b) *Joining*

Such rehabilitative "cuts" are also connective. While attempting to fencing them off from certain areas, legal actors also hope to connect individuals with social and health services through enforced conditions. For conditions of release, of course, are conditional. Territory must be enforced. The force of the condition only works by hooking up the alleged offender to a legal web of obligations, controls, and constraints. If conditions of release are valuable in severing bodies from spaces, they are also deemed useful in hooking bodies up to subsequent legal consequences. Conditions are issued in order to keep a person in continued relation with the courtroom, which of course has its own spatiality (sometimes, located far away from where people live) and its own temporality (namely court delays and the impossibility to deal with all cases at once).[10] For a Vancouver Prosecutor, area restrictions serve as a powerful enforcement tool: "there is a *certain force* in enforcing that condition, telling the accused that if you are in possession of drugs, you are going to be arrested not just for the substantive offence, but also breach, if you are not supposed to possess it" (our emphasis).

The territorial "force" of enforcement includes the legal power of detention. Importantly, detention, rather than unconditional release (as legally required) is the default position, leading to the blunt calculus: (1) Accept the conditions, come what may, or remain in detention; or (2) breach the conditions, and return to jail:

> if the conditions I am about to hand someone are justified and justifiable, and I know that the individual will not respect them, then unfortunately his place may be in detention. So the problem is not to say we shouldn't give him conditions, it's rather should he be released? (Judge, Montreal)

Yet, ironically, legal actors also justify conditions of release as a tool that keeps accused individuals out of spaces of incarceration, such as remand centres. As such, from the legal actors' perspectives, conditions of release are understood as an alternative to custody, not, as we suggest, as an adjunct to it. So, at a rhetorical level at least, release is an important concern of judges.[11] This is a mistake, we argue, in legal terms. Conditions of release should be justified against the backdrop of unconditional release, rather than the imminent

---

[10] This is in line with the first ground in s. 515(10), namely ensuring appearance in court, but also goes beyond that because conditions of release also ensure their constant re-appearance before the tribunal.

[11] However, judges and prosecutors are fundamentally risk averse and they worry that the person will not show up again or commit crime while on bail, so they need guarantees and feel reassured by imposing (too many) conditions, leading to breach and detention. Several prosecutors noted the heavy responsibility they felt at the release stage: "It's a really big responsibility; it's very subtle, it's clear that tragedies happened when people were on conditions. But if we had a crystal ball … [T]here may be people who stayed in jail because the judge had too many fears about other offences, and maybe he would have respected them in the end. It is hard to be 100% sure, but we are tied to the Criminal Code criteria" (Prosecutor, Montreal).

threat of incarceration. Yet in this distorted logic, conditions of release are often perceived as the offender's last chance to avoid incarceration.

> We're imposing conditions on him, and if he doesn't want to help himself with that condition, it'll give the police a lever to stop him and bring him back here, you know? And if he remains in custody while awaiting his trial, for 12 days, 14 days, he may well understand, and then perhaps he will help himself afterwards. Prison helps to make people realize that you can't do this in a society; public interest must take precedence over self-interest.
>
> (Defence lawyer, Montreal)

Yet, precisely because conditions of release hook people up to legally enforceable obligations, they are seen as valuable pragmatic tools. So, for example, the first rationale set out in Section 515 (10) – presence in Court – also appears to be applied for people who are homeless. Because they do not have an address, and thus cannot easily be traced, detention may be necessary, noted one Montreal prosecutor.[12]

Strikingly, our interviews also reveal that detention and conditional release are used to facilitate the surveillance and apprehension of marginalized people outside detention, thereby facilitating the work of police and prosecutors. Territorialized conditions of release hook people up not only to remand, but also to the police, who are the everyday enforcers of these territories. The existence of spatialized conditions of release, because of their geographical visibility, make police work easier. When a police officer finds a person in their red zone, he or she does not need to have other reasonable grounds for intercepting, searching, and detaining the person. Simply by virtue of their visible noncompliance with a red zone, the police have grounds for arrest. Territorializing law renders it visible, and thus more easily communicated and enforced (Sack, 1983).

This was made clear by one Vancouver Prosecutor, who noted that red zones are "easy for the police to spot, and know the person is in breach". The enforcement of certain non-spatial conditions of release implicate Charter rights in ways that spatial conditions do not:

---

[12] Several of the Quebec actors we met told us that a distinction exists in this regard between the practice of the Municipal Court and the Quebec Provincial Court, namely, the imposition of a condition to "register one's presence at the police station", which is often seen at the Municipal Court in the case of homeless people or those whom it is feared will disappear into thin air. This condition is particularly problematic for marginalized people: "the problem with this is that if you put someone back on the street and assign a condition that they have to register at the police station once a week, well, a homeless person has no access to bus tickets. You know they won't go" (Defence lawyer, Montreal).

if somebody is prohibited from possessing something, for instance, you'd probably have to detain them, you would have to have independent reason to go into their pockets, you're engaging their Charter rights, but with a red zone you can go: "Oh, there's Mr. Smith", look [him up] in the computer: "Oh yup, that area restriction is still in place" and they've got their grounds and he is arrestable. It is a very easy one for them to enforce and it is easy for us to convict on ... *Mr. Smith is not allowed in that block. There he is in that block: pretty much case open and closed.*

(our emphasis)

The same prosecutor noted the challenges of monitoring potential criminal acts in the community through non-spatial conditions of release, such as bans on alleged drug traffickers possessing digital scales. "Who is going to monitor that?" she/he asked, and how would a police officer know unless they had reasonable and probably grounds to search that person? "There is nobody to follow them around to make sure they are behaving themselves". But a red zone, reliant only on bodily placement relative to a boundary, is a much more efficient way of monitoring compliance: "So the area restriction seems to be the best way that we have to reduce their ability to continue selling". In the case of certain crimes against the person, the conditions make it possible to take preventive action before an offence is committed.

From the moment there are conditions, as soon as there is a breach, the police officers' intervention is faster and more drastic in the sense that talking to someone is not illegal. If you have conditions, however, then it becomes illegal. That way, it is stopped immediately, and it is less likely to deteriorate. Even worse, when it comes to spousal violence, I tell the victims to tell their neighbours that there is a red zone, so that there is vigilance on the part of the people around them, that if they see him in that area, there is an immediate intervention. It's important to be able to intervene quickly. It really helps prevent other bad situations.

(Prosecutor, Montreal)

CRAFTING A REASONABLE COURT ORDER

If spatial conditions of release are a cut, they are thought of by those who craft them as surgical incisions. Like the cut of the scalpel, they are necessary, but imagined as carefully and precisely done, and responsive to the particular context of the person subject to them. The connective conditions attached to such cuts are also imagined, like the reparative nature of a surgical procedure, as clean, ameliorative, and minimal. As one Vancouver judge put it, when deciding conditions, "I'm trying to make it all personal ... I am considering the individual profile of the person". Defence attorneys described speaking directly to the accused, and determining their situation, and then liaising closely with the Crown in order to come up with tailored conditions, including area restrictions, that were not excessively constrained or unrealistic. One Vancouver legal actor noted that, as defence counsel, she would not sign off on an order until the conditions have been explored with the accused, arguing that the court is usually accommodating, and seeks to ensure compliance:

> The court doesn't ... want to see them charged with more breaches. That's not the purpose of the order, to rack up more criminal charges. So they do try and accommodate if there is anything reasonable that we can suggest as to why it won't work.

Spatial restrictions, as cuts, are thus said never to sever people from needed resources, such as their home, or access to community or health resources, it was argued, but rather are targeted and discrete. The legal cut discriminates between the necessary and the criminally risky, in other words.

> For sure, very often, a red zone will be imposed but the person will say "I live in that area", so we will try to reduce the red zone to exclude the living quarters while maybe keeping a bit of the problematic zone there, maybe reducing it to keep it from being entirely useless. It's often difficult. The problem comes from women who go to certain resources and who happen to be in that zone. Often that's the problem. It's that their life happens within that zone. So we try, as much as possible, to go with restrictions they mention to us; either we reduce the zone or place exceptions such as: you are not allowed to be in that red zone; just to go to this or that place. *We try to be accommodating.*
> (Prosecutor, Montreal; our emphasis)

Some legal actors noted that they were knowledgeable of the lived geographies of those subjected to conditions, crafting conditions accordingly:

> Some judges know Montreal better than others. There's a client, he was a drag artist, [he was] dancing at a bar in that area. The judge knew all the places that were frequented, so the prosecutor just gave up because he didn't know what they were talking about ... and I think from then on, it was obvious that the judge was just not going to impose a red zone.
> (Defence lawyer, Montreal)

Others insisted that they minimized the scope of the perimeters and ensured that they do not impose unnecessary conditions: "We use our common sense. Obviously, we won't take the whole Island of Montreal unless there are specific cases ... We're not going to put in 50 conditions just for the fun of putting in 50 of them" (Judge, Montreal). "We try to be as open as possible", noted a Prosecutor in Montreal, "precisely because the primary goal is to avoid excessive criminalization".

In this regard, prosecutors seem to develop a sensitivity to the threshold for acceptability of conditions by judges, which would, however, be likely to come into play only when there is a threat of bail hearings or when imposing a sentence:

> Because if the offence does not take place at hours like this, often the judge will tell us, "What is the reason? Why do you impose a curfew?"... Under a conditional sentence, it is a house arrest. That's why it will often be 24 hours a day and then, after a certain period of time, we'll put in a curfew, but in addition to that, we'll never put a suspended sentence with probation and a curfew because in such cases, the judges will find it much too restrictive.
>
> (Prosecutor, Montreal)

Thus, standardized templates such as the boilerplate Downtown Eastside area restriction may be modified if a person resides in the area, it was asserted. It was noted that it was hard to challenge conditions on the grounds that they were, for example, much too broad geographically (and therefore unreasonable, more likely to be broken and/or to violate the right to life, security and liberty), "if the person does not actually live in that red zone" (Defence lawyer, Montreal). For instance, Crown counsel will typically be amenable to reviewing police bail orders in order to allow a person to attend a doctor's office, a pharmacy or a bank. However, while one Vancouver Prosecutor noted that they would not red zone someone out of their home ("I can't remember one instance"), another acknowledged that such a radical cut may be called for: "If the trafficking is taking place out of a particular residence, then that is a case that I might say, 'Well, he lives there, but I want him out within 24 hours. He can attend once with a police officer to collect his belongings, but he still needs to find a new place to live'".

Others distinguish between legitimate and illegitimate activities, allowing individuals to enter certain areas for the former but not for the latter. In some cases, they may be aware (or be made aware) of the fact that individuals must visit prohibited areas for "legitimate" reasons, such as "legitimate" work, living within the perimeter, the need to visit places to access community resources and obtain health services (e.g. access to methadone), etc.

> Of course, there are situations where we will try to shorten it, let's say for reasons such as she lives there, her resources are there or she has a paid job there that is legal.
>
> (Defence lawyer, Montreal)

Similarly, when Nico was arrested during the students' strike, the police had a hard time defining his order. For one, they wished to exclude him from the university campus, but Nico was not only an activist, he was also a student, a research assistant, and a students' representative. As a result, the police officer struggled to delimit the boundaries of his exclusion given that he wanted to draw the line between legitimate activities, including studying and working and even participating in a recognized organization such as the union, and illegitimate ones, such as political organizing and demonstrating. He thus decided to ban him from the university campus altogether except to attend his classes or for work.

Thus the consensus of legal actors was that conditions of release are carefully crafted, while always operating under the shadow of legal force and constraint. Cuts and joins are both at play, in other words, according to two Montreal judges:

> I don't think we are deliberately giving conditions that we know will not be respected. We take care not to necessarily place people in breach of conditions. At the same time, if any conditions are issued, the person must comply with them.

> We're giving him a chance. If we know that he will not comply with the conditions and it is debated, there is a good chance that he will stay in custody. That's it. I remember a case where we wanted to release a guy, and he was trying to figure out whether or not he would find it difficult to adhere to the conditions. Well, I mean, it's clear that it's going to bother you, and if you don't respect the conditions, you run the risk of ending up in front of me, and maybe it's not the attitude towards conditions that you should adopt, that is very favourable to my imposing them on you. You know, at some point, it's still a repressive system, we try to prevent people from committing other offences.

That said, there were a few (particularly defence attorneys) who denounced the manner in which spatial conditions of release were crafted, noting the tendency to craft red zones that were overly large, in a manner that they deemed contemptuous and uninformed.

> It's often much too big to be really effective. I saw one where the person had been given from St. Laurent to Viau, something ridiculous; so sometimes it's just way too big. They're trying to cover a huge area of Montreal, but at the same time it does more harm than anything else.
>
> (Defence lawyer, Montreal)

So while it might make sense to red zone a drug dealer from the Metro station at which they were arrested, prosecutors (many of whom are said to be "young and have no idea that this is an exaggerated deprivation of freedom: their intellectual journey doesn't take them there" according to one defence lawyer) too often insisted on a much more expansive red zone, or a curfew, some noted. Others mentioned the lack of geographical discernment behind red zones, whereby a cut severed people from crucial timespaces. An exclusion from the subway, for example, denied people access to efficient transportation. Homeless people are immobile and tied to routines: conditions thus have to be minimal. Revealingly, however, it was observed that "it's not easy to explain such things to the Court" (Defence lawyer, Montreal)

Yet, while others admitted that red zones could be difficult to craft, given the mutual entanglements of spaces deemed risky and spaces of life, home, and resources, police logics often prevailed: "At the end of the day, who do I have to give priority to?", asked a Vancouver judge. "I have to give it to the public, I have a duty to protect the public". Similarly, a Montreal defence attorney noted the challenges in contesting conditions, remarking that "only a minority of stakeholders in the justice system is sensitive to arguments to avoid criminalization solely for breach of conditions". Thus, it is necessary to "tell the judge why you want one for the area he goes to, and these reasons must be good. I would call them humanitarian reasons: it can't just be the excessive size of the red zone". Moreover, such qualifications are limited to the concerns expressed by the defence or the accused during the bail hearing, which is sometimes difficult to anticipate at the moment. As one Montreal defence attorney noted, "often, it happens the next day; they say, 'Oh, wait, I can't go buy my food, I can't get my methadone . . .'"

EFFECTIVENESS OF CONDITIONS OF RELEASE

We asked our respondents to evaluate the effectiveness of conditions of release. While a few legal actors saw them in straightforward terms as a useful resource, most were more guarded, recognizing, as one put it, that "to determine effectiveness of those kinds of conditions is difficult" (Prosecutor, Vancouver). Several judicial actors indicated that they believed in the overall effectiveness of the conditions, presuming that they would be respected and would achieve their objectives

> I'll say yes . . . in most cases. Of course, we more often see the cases that come back for breaches, but the cases that come back for reasons other than breaches, we don't have them, they don't show up. We will get to see them when they go to trial . . . but I think in most cases, yes.
>
> (Prosecutor, Montreal)

For many, however, this confident belief was expressed as an optimistic wish:

> I personally *dare to hope* that they are useful, I dare to hope that they succeed in protecting the people they have to protect, but am I naïve? I don't know about that. I think they have their *raison d'être*, meaning that they achieve their goals . . .
>
> (Judge, Montreal; our emphasis)

As noted, others saw them at best as more or less useful stopgaps, temporary "time outs", beneficial mostly to localized publics rather than the person subject to conditions, revealing the crucial "police" temporality of these territorializations. "I don't think we were solving the person's problem", admitted one Montreal Prosecutor, "but maybe for a while the people who lived there had peace".

For some, area restrictions were effective in preventing reoffending with the main offence, while they were less useful in reducing administration of justice offences. Such may be the case because most people are not arrested for committing new substantive offences, but for being in a forbidden place, in violation of their conditions.

> It still works. I mean, unfortunately people are rarely stopped for a breach of their conditions while they are soliciting. They get arrested again for niggling things, while walking towards a resource. It's rare, very rare that someone gets arrested for solicitation. It's in that sense that I think red zones work.
>
> (Defence lawyer, Montreal)

However, many acknowledged that the effect of spatial conditions was simply to displace the problem elsewhere. For a Montreal Prosecutor, an exclusion from one convenience store chain may mean that a person simply moves to a different chain: "sometimes it just moves the problem elsewhere". Similarly, with prostitution, "we put a red zone in a place. Well, okay, maybe there will be no more prostitution in that place for a while; it will just change neigh-bourhood". Further, when asked if a one block red zone simply has the effect of dispersing criminal activity to the next block, some responded by noting police information that people tended to focus their activity on particular blocks:

> you probably could go off and deal drugs in another area, but we have found that often people have one block that they regularly deal ... But the hope is if we can't get a larger area restriction then one block, well then, at least they are not in that one block, and they will have to set up shop somewhere else.
>
> (Prosecutor, Vancouver)

Territorialized conditions are supposedly valuable, in part, because of the communicative work they facilitate, establishing clear spatial and temporal parameters for those governed by them. Yet some legal actors noted problems with their semantic effectiveness. While one Vancouver judge expressed his incomprehension of a person who repeatedly breached his red zone ("I just couldn't believe it", I said to him, "I don't get it, why are you going there?"), a Vancouver defence attorney pointed out that the temporality of territorial conditions was often unclear: "Often the guys don't know what [order] they are on, when they are in jail. Are you on bail, are you on probation, are you on a CSO? They don't know which one they are on, they just know they're supposed to be seeing somebody".

Relatedly, spatial conditions are assumed by their proponents to clearly communicate territorial messages. However, some legal actors point to their opacity and ambiguity. A "cut" might work on paper, but not on the ground, in other words. "How do you calculate a 100 metre radius from a SAQ [liquor] store?", queried a Montreal defence lawyer. "There are no guides or charts . . . For me, 100 metres is an American football field, I mean, but other than that, I'm not able to transpose a football field to a street corner. I have no idea, I mean from here to that street corner, is that 100 metres?" A Vancouver Prosecutor noted that "even for me I know I'd be thinking 'Well, 100 block of East Hastings, 2 block radius, so that is like . . .?'". Similarly, the meaning of a set of conditions may be temporally fluid. As noted earlier, the require-ment for demonstrators to avoid an illegal protest is challenging, for example, as a legal protest may become designated illegal by the police during an event.

The nature of addiction, and its relationship to the effectiveness of conditions of release, was acknowledged. One Vancouver judge insisted that many addicts actively requested red zones. For another Montreal judge, however, conditions are ineffective in cases of addiction when "the hold we have on this person is extremely weak. So they often come out of here, throw the condition in the first garbage can that see, and we pick them up again a bit later. For them, we certainly don't achieve the objectives". Addiction was acknowledged by a few as a spatiotemporal dependency, from which legal exclusion may prove ineffective. For women in the sex trade using drugs, "it was like a question of survival to go back to the same place. It was not that they wanted to break the law, but it's something like a cycle" (Judge, Montreal). Similarly, addiction is "a neces-sity for them, it's like eating for me. That's the way it is for them, so there's not much that will keep them from going back for that. . . . and a prostitute who needs her fix, she's going to do anything, anything; her priority is that, it's a matter of survival. *When you're in survival mode, you don't much care about a red zone*" (Prosecutor, Montreal; our emphasis). Yet despite such realistic recognitions, red zones continue to be routinely imposed and, as noted, regarded in at least one instant as a form of "harm reduction".

We queried the condition not to possess illicit drugs, it being pointed out that this is already an offence under the Criminal Code. The response of one

Vancouver Prosecutor was a curious one: such a condition, she noted, can serve as an index of a person's ability to adhere to conditions in general:

[It] can form part of a separate type of offence, that is that this is an individual who because of their addiction cannot abide by court orders. So for instance, if there is a condition that they not possess any drugs, then we get a measure of whether this is an individual who will comply with a court order. It's circular, right. Because the person is not going to likely be able to abstain and therefore they have drug paraphernalia and they have drugs and so . . . maybe there is a certain force . . . in enforcing that condition, telling the accused that if you are in possession of drugs, you are going to be arrested, not just for the substantive, but also breach if you are not supposed to possess it.

Yet the same Prosecutor supported the cautious use of area restrictions in the case of a street-level addicted trafficker, to protect the public interest, pointing out that the accused "always has the ability to say that 'I cannot comply with it, I won't agree to it, because I live in the area'". That said, a Vancouver defence attorney acknowledged the challenges of complying with a red zone for an addict:

keeping them from their favourite places is often . . . not a very useful condition, because a person addicted to drugs is going to go where they think they can find drugs, and they know they can find it at that corner. [But] the person will accept it almost always because they want to go out of jail and they know that the Crown is not going to give, on some of those ones.

The same defence attorney went on to muse candidly on the challenges of imposing conditions on people entangled in poverty and addiction:

I look at some of those orders and think if I were told to do as many things as these guys were told to do, and I got arrested every time I was late, I'd be in jail all the time too . . . You are dealing with a person who probably has a drug or alcohol addiction, who often has a mental illness, who doesn't have a solid living environment and being told to keep more appointments then I could handle keeping in a week. And they probably don't have an alarm clock either. *So how in the world do we expect them to comply with those kinds of things?* . . . It would be difficult for the people that are imposing those orders to live by some of those orders.

(our emphasis)

It was also noted that some imposed conditions were independent of the offence the person is charged with, particularly with bans on consumption.

In cases where alcohol is concerned, I mean, when a crime is committed, the police officers say that the accused smelled of alcohol. The Crown will impose a prohibition on using drugs and drinking alcohol. It's almost automatic, but alcohol abuse is not everyone's problem, and alcohol consumption does not automatically lead to the crime of which the person is accused, but really, there's no discernment.

(Defence lawyer, Montreal)

This echoes the comments of Justice Rosborough in the *Omeasoo* case, discussing the unreasonableness of imposing an abstinence condition on an alcoholic: imposing unreasonable and unrealistic conditions is only a disguised way of denying the accused his or her interim release:

> It is trite to say that conditions in an undertaking which the accused cannot or almost certainly will not comply with cannot be reasonable. Requiring the accused to perform the impossible is simply another means of denying judicial interim release. The same would apply to conditions which, although not impossible in a technical sense, are so unlikely to be complied with as to be practically impossible. An example of that would be to release the impecunious accused on \$1 million cash bail on the basis that he could buy a lottery ticket and potentially win enough money to post that cash bail.[13]

BREACH

One measure of the effectiveness of spatial conditions of release is the frequency with which people breached their conditions. Even for those supportive of conditions of release, the frequency of breach was hard to ignore. Yet this was sometimes met with stunning incomprehension. As noted in Chapter 5, for one Vancouver defence attorney, asking "where did all the real criminals go?", the role of the judicial system in producing crime is completely effaced.

> I have seen most stuff coming through these courts these days being failing to comply and breaches, and I don't understand. *Where did all the real criminals go?* Why isn't everybody charged with new offences? Because most of what we see on a day to day basis anymore are failures to comply and breaches.

(our emphasis)

---

[13] *R. v. Omeasoo* (2013) ABPC 328, par. 33. The Montreal Municipal Court's social programs appear to be an exception in this regard, given their special focus and the possibility of follow-ups with individuals: "In [this] program, we're going to focus a little more on the situation of the accused, contrary to what we normally would do, because we usually look essentially at the facts. If there's alcohol or if the person is still intoxicated, well, it's clear that our reflex is going to be to impose this condition, [whereas in this program] the goal is to avoid revolving doors, and to avoid over-criminalizing, so the person will be taken in hand because he or she will be willing to take the necessary steps to redress the situation. It's not always easy, we know it won't happen in a day, but at least there's a will to get out of it, so we'll perhaps be more flexible in terms of the conditions imposed, and more conciliatory on the conditions we're actually going to impose because we know that we're going to follow up with the person" (Municipal Court Prosecutor, Montreal).

Strikingly, others saw breaches less as failures than as an index of success. A Vancouver judge, noting their frequency, argued that the conditions serve valuable disciplinary purposes, communicating exclusion, while suggesting that the breaches do not constitute "real" offences. A breach shows that the conditions are:

> … working, he hasn't committed any new offences. I say well, that's the whole point. Because the only place he knows where to work is in that area. If he is on the way to work and he is stopped he spends a week in jail, and he gets out, and he thinks "Well, I guess I better get back to work" and, bang, he gets caught again.
>
> Q: And maybe the behaviour will start to change?
> A: Well exactly, that's why it's there. If he was committing crimes, actually committing additional crimes I would treat him more seriously than 7 days in jail. I'm just trying to get the message that you aren't going down there.

Similarly, a Vancouver Prosecutor characterized repeat breaches as poor choices that deserve an appropriate state response. Absent a lack of mental capacity, or a valid reason why a person accesses an area, "if the guy … has breached five times and sure he is going to breach again, that's a *choice* he keeps making, and if he can't refrain from breaching then maybe he should be detained in remand because he's imposing a threat to the community, he can't abide by these conditions" (our emphasis).[14] And yet another added that breaches of red zones are common in Vancouver, suggesting that while some may occur "because … maybe they've got drug related issues and mental related issues", it is also the case that there:

> are some people with … flagrant disregard. "Oh, nobody is going to notice me, this is where my buddy is, this is where I want to keep selling drugs". We have some people that are banned from a particular area and then they are found the following week in the same area selling drugs again, and again they keep going back to that area and selling drugs.

---

[14] During our interviews, some legal actors also challenged statistics showing increases in the remand population or AJO offences such as breach. One Vancouver Prosecutor, for example, noted that the decision to detain someone on remand is based on a case-by-case assessment, "so it can't be that there's a trend and we're going to continue that trend". It was noted that the increase in AJO offences might be a suspect statistic, given the way in which the court uses findings that do not show as a breach. As mentioned earlier, in recent years, many people have been brought to courts for a breach charge to see those charges being dropped and a warning issued. Despite the fact that the proceedings on such breach charges are stayed, it is interesting to ask what effects they may have on those subject to them.

To frame this as a "choice" or form of "flagrant disregard" is, of course, to erase the deep dependencies that compel people back to certain areas. For a Montreal judge, conditions constitute a responsibilizing contract between the state and the individual, with the latter imagined as detached subject. Breaches of conditions are thus an *individual* failure, not an *institutional* failure: "If they don't comply, it's not the fault of the Court. It's not anyone's fault. It's he or she that breached those conditions".

> The entire criminal law system is built on the idea of individual responsibility. It's *you* who are responsible for what you do. You know, the Criminal Code is a series of prohibitions for the substantive offences: you shall not steal, you shall not rape, you shall not commit wrongdoing or commit murder; it assumes that each person is responsible. You are responsible. [But] what we hear, what we constantly see, is an approach, sometimes, especially in matters of defence, that is contextual: "it's not my client's fault, it's the context, it's his mother's fault, his father's, his milieu, it's the fault of all sorts of things".
>
> (original emphasis)

At work here is a radical form of legal bracketing, that imaginatively severs the works of poverty, addiction, need, and health, situating the person as a legal individual, responsible to a set of abstract legal prohibitions. It is, in a sense, an 'anti-geography' (Pue, 1990), that abstracts people from the spaces and places they inhabit. As we shall see, however, people cannot be so easily detached from such spaces. Red zones are imposed on lived spatiotemporalities of care, citizenship, need, and affect with often devastating consequences.

7

Conditional Life inside the Red Zone

"So they're telling me basically to hide in a hole somewhere and not to come out".
(Howard, Ottawa)

TERRITORY, SPATIOTEMPORALITY, AND LEGAL VIOLENCE

The previous chapter noted the manner in which legal actors think of conditions of release as pragmatic, often rehabilitative, and carefully crafted. In this chapter, we draw from interviews with those actually subject to the cuts and joins of territorialized conditions. The contrast between the construction and experience of conditions is striking. At best, those governed by them see them as arbitrary, perplexing, and counterproductive. At worst, they are experienced as cataclysmic and injurious.

As we shall see, the experience of "release" is often one of carcerality, experienced not only as confinement – although that is powerfully present – but also as other spatiotemporal effects, that take multiple forms. In an article on police bail, Raine and Wilson (1996) suggested that we distinguish between the following spatial effects: locating (conditions assigning residences); containing (curfews, radius, no-contact orders); banning (red zones); and bounding (keep out or away from certain premises). In fact, the spatial effects here are even more diversified and overlapping. One single red zone may at once have the effects of banning as well as confining; indeed, in some cases, entrapping individuals in some neighbourhoods or areas of town and jeopardizing access to resources and community support (cf. Schuilenberg, 2015). No-contact and association orders can spatially confine people to certain places for fear of being in space visible to the authorities. Moreover, spatial restrictions rarely stand alone: most people are subject to multiple conditions at once. For instance, when combined with no-contact orders and curfews, red zones may amount to house arrest. Conditions do not only shape people's geographies, we argue. They simultaneously organize time, creating territories that come and go (Von Benda-Beckmann and Von Benda-Beckmann, 2014), territories that linger, even after being formally deactivated, and territories that remake the everyday use and experience of space and time in ways that can prove massively disruptive.

As is more immediately evident in this chapter, conditions of release act upon the body, constraining where and when a body can be, and how it should interact or associate with other bodies. Unlike the responsibilized, contractual bodies imagined by many legal actors, the bodies we encounter in this chapter are situated bodies. Many are already marked bodies, scarred by the violences of poverty, racism, patriarchy, and colonialism. Accumulated trauma generates forms of dependency and addiction. These are highly conditional lives, governed by the whims of others. Yet they are also situated within spaces of family, political engagement, memory, citizenship, and care. These are worlded bodies – in other words, shaped, like all of us by what Laurie and Shaw (2018: 7) term the geographies of being, "the existential resources that nourish and sustain, but also harm and violate". Such conditions, they suggest, are the "existential climates" that make particular lives possible. Violent conditions, conversely, are those "geographies of being that restrict the potential for life to flourish and actualize" (7).

Human flourishing may rely not only on basic capabilities, such as health and personal security, but also on forms of community participation and political engagement. Such human capacities are inherently social, dependent on and articulated through relations with others (Alexander and Peñalver, 2012: 80–101). Violence is manifested not simply as singular acts, such as detention, but also as forms of structural violence that truncate human possibility through forcefully constraining the "resources of our becoming" (16). Following Galtung (1969: 168), we can think of violence as the "cause of the difference between the potential and the actual, between what could have been and what is". Violence is evident in that which *increases* the divide between actual and potential – between the truncated and conditional life of Martine, for example, and her potential as a human being. It is also expressed, Galtung reminds us, as that which *fails* to close the divide.

It is in these terms, perhaps, that we can understand conditions of release as forms of legal violence. Legal interpretation is a practical activity that mandates others (probation officers, police, judges) to enact violence as required. As Cover (1986) reminds us, such violence may be justified. But it needs to be treated for what it is. We should not imagine that we persuade prisoners into jail or away from a red zone. Conditions of release are not the bloodless acknowledgments of "force" noted by the legal actors, in the previous chapter. These are corporeal violences. Following Cover (1986), decisions to craft, impose, and enforce conditions entail moments of legal interpretation that "signal and occasion the imposition of violence upon others. When interpreters have finished their work, they frequently leave behind victims whose lives have been torn apart by these organized, social practices of violence"(1601). Precisely because they act upon space and time, they also create "violent conditions" that make an already challenging life even harder, for many. Severing people from existential conditions, and doing so repeatedly, has predictable consequences.

In poor neighbourhoods such as Vancouver's Downtown Eastside, legal violences are territorially realized at many scales, from the organized expulsions of colonial resettlement and the spatially grounded power of state sovereignty, to the ejections of private property, or the everyday territorializing of the police. Spatial conditions of release, we argue, also express a particular territorial logic. One way in which these effects can be traced is through the boundary work (temporal and spatial) of territorialization. As is clear from our respondents, the process of cutting and joining associated with conditions of release can have wider effects. Two are particularly significant. First, conditions of release sever and rearrange spatiotemporal "geographies of being" in ways that may prove both pervasive and debilitating. Red zones are not simply discrete spacetimes, but rework extant social relations of care, need, politics, and affect, lived in and through different but entangled spatiotemporalities. Second, conditions of release, as legally enforced controls, can entangle and connect those subject to them to serial cycles of legal territorialization in ways that can prove far-reaching, calamitous, and even lethal.

This becomes clear when the experience of being governed by conditions of release begin to be more apparent. In this chapter, we document the experiences of economically marginalized people accused of petty offences involving the drug and sex trade. In the subsequent chapter, we explore their effects as applied to political protestors seeking to use public space. There are obvious differences between the two groups, in terms of both prior experience with the criminal justice system and relative social privilege. However, in both cases, the territorialized process of severance and connection is evident, producing "violent conditions" that negate or compromise their ability to access and use the urban "geographies of being" that sustain their essential human flourishing, while abrogating or effacing responsibility for such violences (Veitch, 2007).

POVERTY MANAGEMENT AND LEGAL TERRITORIALIZATION

As we shall see in chapter 8, the political activists we spoke to expressed surprise at the use of spatial conditions of release, given their relative lack of contact with the Canadian criminal justice system. This is not surprising: while conditions have indeed been used to govern political activists, they are most prevalent in the regulation of poor criminalized people. We conducted 31 interviews with individuals governed by conditions of release associated with petty street crime, particularly involving drug and sex trade offences in Montreal (6), Ottawa (7), and Vancouver (18), drawing also from 18 additional interviews conducted by Will Damon for his MA research (Damon, 2014) (a total of 49).

Like Martine or Paul, in Chapter 1, most of the informants lived in or associated with inner-city neighbourhoods such as Montreal's Centre-Sud or Hochelaga-Maisonneuve, Ottawa's Lowertown or Vancouver's Downtown Eastside, areas that were highly criminalized and closely regulated. Encounters with police, judges, lawyers, and probation officers were routine. Many informants lived in precarious forms of housing, such as shelters or residential hotels. Their use of "survival strategies", whether sanctioned or informal, ensured that they were frequently in public space, engaging in actions that placed them under potential scrutiny by legal actors. Most used drugs, some describing selling drugs for dealers as a way of accessing income and drugs, and several of them were involved in the sex trade at one point or another, primarily to sustain an addiction to drugs and to earn an income. Socially, discursively, and economically marginalized, they were members of a highly vulnerable population.

Their experiences with the criminal justice in general, and conditions of release in particular, are varied. For example, a few of our Vancouver respondents reported only a few bail or probation orders, while others noted the existence of multiple red zones throughout Canada, British Columbia (B.C.), and the Lower Mainland. For example, Sarah[1] described being red zoned from five different municipalities within Greater Vancouver. Patrick reported red zones in four Greater Vancouver cities, and one interior city, as well as being red zoned from a major Vancouver shopping centre and all Sears and Home Depot stores throughout the province. In Montreal, 5 out of 6 participants were subjected to large red zones, ranging from a specific neighbourhood to the entire Island of Montreal, in addition to abstinence clauses and, in some cases, curfews. Table 7.1, drawn from our Ottawa interviews, is illustrative of the present and past conditions of release experienced by our informants.

While most conditions were court-imposed, some respondents noted red zoning by the police, either through formal means or informal expulsion. Like

---

[1] All names have been changed.

TABLE 7.1 *Ottawa conditions of release*

Alan	Excluded from Les Suites Hotel and two Tim Hortons in Ottawa: police red zone for panhandling.
Bernice	Excluded from shelter during the day (6 a.m.–9:30 p.m.); red zoned from Salvation Army, and from Church steps; no alcohol, no association with other drinkers; red zoned for communication for the purposes of prostitution and possession of crack pipe by police (including her residence).
Chris	Red zoned for several blocks by police, no association with drug users.
Diane	Red zoned from several blocks of Lowertown area, including Salvation Army.
Howard	11 o'clock curfew from downtown Ottawa; drug abstention; not to associate with criminals; barred by police from block around Shepherds of Good Hope, a shelter and service provider, except at meal times.
John	Condition to reside at a fixed address, no-contact, no drugs, curfew 10 p.m.–6 a.m. Red zoned three years ago from area.
Ibrahim	Probation: excluded from area of offence (Augusta Street).

Martine and Paul, and not unlike some of the protesters we'll hear about in Chapter 8, many people reported that they had violated their conditions while trying to remain outside the radar. Many also noted that they had been arrested as a consequence, often experiencing police brutality, and were drawn back into the criminal justice system, with negative consequences. Informants described extensive police red zones and curfews for alleged offences such as panhandling, prostitution, and possession, as well as court-ordered conditions of release including red zones, bans on the use of alcohol or drugs, and non-association requirements. Conditions of release served as a powerful and often punitive form of territorialization, acting upon bodies in violent, oppressive, and sometimes life-threatening ways. Already vulnerable people were often made even more precarious as a consequence of conditions of release.

Some respondents seemed to understand the logic behind the imposition of a red zone from the State's perspective. Red, in Montreal, believed that the police and the courts wanted him "to change [his] lifestyle". Interestingly, in his case, he was convinced that it had worked as planned. Red reported using his red zone as an incentive to make changes in his life and moved out of the Gay Village where he used to do sex work. As a result, he turned to panhandling, which he had been doing for several years when we met him, and he stopped using crack to use opioids, which he believed was "less bad".

Red's narrative is as an exception among our respondents. While Plasma, in Montreal, also understood that the police wanted to change him, he believed that they mostly wanted him out of public spaces. This was a common observation. Sophie advised all the new women sex workers on the block in Montreal to get a cell phone and have their clients call in instead of soliciting in the streets in order to escape the police gaze and subsequent risk of red zoning. For some, the visibility of drug users and sex workers in public spaces not only made them particularly vulnerable to surveillance (Brighenti, 2006; Sylvestre et al., 2011), but it explained why red zones are issued in the first place. Plasma was convinced that red zones are used against the homeless because they do not have a fixed address and their presence is considered undesirable. If he had an apartment, he noted, he would have been curfewed. As a homeless person, "they just did not want to see me anymore. Like a cockroach, go hide in your corner". This echoes the words of Howard in Ottawa, who reported that he felt the police wanted him to dig "a hole somewhere and not come out". Titi, in Montreal, also suggested that the police aimed to discipline and subdue women and sex workers, reading a gendered dimension to their interventions: "They were trying to tame me. 'I'm going to tame you, I'm going to shut you off from all these places', they used to tell me".

Thus, rather than rational preventive or rehabilitative interventions, such conditions were frequently characterized as arbitrary, willful, or even meaningless expressions of legal power. We asked Chris in Ottawa what the purpose of his red zone was. "I'm not quite sure", he responded. "Just to . . . make life a little more difficult or horrible". How did the authorities justify it, we asked? "I don't know how, maybe with the laws, the rules or whatever", he responded, in a blunt recognition of a distant, arbitrary, but omnipresent sovereign power. Indeed, many respondents claimed not to have been given reasons for their conditions, other than outright exclusion. Judicial messaging appears to have been lost in translation. Asked how the judge explained a red zone, Juan in Vancouver responded:

> [What] I remember is if I go back, I get charged again, and they said I was looking at five months and it was going to go up.
>
> Q: Did they tell you why they kept you out of that area?
>
> A: Yeah, because I was dealing dope.

For many respondents, their conditions were simply unfair. Plasma, who did sex work in the back alleys and the motels of St Hubert Street in Montreal, believed the police and the judges did not care or understand him at all. "For judges, we're just like pieces of meat, I didn't do anything wrong, I offer a service [sex work] and I'm paid for it. We're all prostituting ourselves for something, aren't we?"

SEVERANCE: THE CUTS OF CONDITIONS

While Ibrahim saw conditions as serving a potentially useful role in serious criminal cases, he queried their relevance for minor offences, asking: "why [are] you making them suffer?" Suffering was generated, our informants explained, because of the manner in which conditions of release severed people from the everyday spatial networks and temporal rhythms of life. This, of course, was its intent. Yet it was also the unintentional effects of such cuts that proved particularly punitive. Diane was red zoned from Lowertown in Ottawa by a police officer. She characterized his move thus: "I'm gonna red zone you from the Lowertown so you stay away from drugs and you get better in life". However, she noted, he did so without:

> realizing how much *more to it there was, and how more to this area there is in concern with my life other than drugs* . . . Yes, you want to prove your point and fucking red zoned me because I was caught for doing drugs. . . [But] I can find drugs elsewhere. But *there're some things in that area* [that] are completely irrelevant to my addiction that I can't find anywhere else.
>
> (our emphasis)

In some extreme cases, this severance was profound, with people being red zoned from their homes. Lisa described being red zoned from "all of Hastings St" in the Downtown Eastside in Vancouver while on bail, noting that, for her, "it didn't make sense, my bank was there, my home was there, my probation was there, my doctor was there. Like, come on, guys! All of Hastings Street? Hello! *My whole life is there!* They're going to arrest you every time you want to go home?" (our emphasis).

Chris was red zoned from Murray street in Ottawa, but required to reside at a shelter that was only accessible from that street, which contained a soup kitchen he depended on.

> I wasn't allowed on Murray. So I have to go and come down King Edward and go in to the side building, I couldn't go into the main door on the side, which is stupid, I live here but I can't walk on the street where I live. And actually I was breaking the red zone every day because I have to go across the street to get to the Kitchen, which is on Murray. I said I couldn't be on Murray but I have to, because I live here! They tell me I have to live there but I'm not allowed being on the street. It's contradictory!

In some cases, people noted the effect of red zoning, particularly when compounded, was that they were forced to change residence. Sarah described being red zoned sequentially out of two Greater Vancouver municipalities, and then relocating to the Downtown Eastside. Others noted that the effect of conditions was to force them to live on the street, when a restriction prevented them from accessing a formal or informal place of residence. One complained of being curfewed at night from public space in Vancouver, despite being homeless, placing him in an impossible spatiotemporal predicament.

If not excluded from homes, vital resources and networks became harder if not impossible to access for many, making an already vulnerable situation even more precarious, forcing them to breach. Diane in Ottawa noted that although she was red zoned from food and shelter, she still was compelled to use these resources: "I usually have to risk to go to jail, in order to access services like that".

But beyond accessing particular spatial resources, conditions severed people from ongoing and enduring temporal connections with others, including friends and family. Chris in Ottawa put it concisely: "I can't go where other people go because of that stupid red zone". For Ron, also in Ottawa, conditions "just made me feel like I had lost a whole bunch of friends and a place to hang around", risking breach as a consequence. Respondents in Vancouver also noted the way in which their conditions of release severed vital networks, compromising everyday intimate geographies. Paul argued that the worst effects of his red zone were that he could not access valued resources: "All the resources that you need are in that red zone area. Like Carnegie [a vitally important community centre] is in there, I'm not allowed in Carnegie, which has all the resources to help get me in Social Assistance". Clyde, a gay man, noted that his red zone excluded him from a drop-in centre for men in the sex trade. The effect more generally was to prevent "access to a support group, food, resource, one of the few places I know where I feel comfortable. Kind of difficult". Such connections went both ways. For Adam, the worst consequence of red zoning was he could not provide support for others: "the worst thing is not being able to give the street youth that I'm in contact with the proper support. That's the biggest thing. I don't care about nothing else... And doing the outreach with street youth is the number one thing".

The effects of red zoning are particularly aggravated for residents of highly stigmatized neighbourhoods, such as Vancouver's Downtown Eastside. Exclusion from such places not only cuts off access to the vital resources, such as safe injection sites and low-cost housing, but also drugs, that are concentrated there. It also forces "marked" people into spaces where they are marked as "out of place", given cultural dynamics of territorial marginalization (Wacquant, 2007). For many Downtown Eastside residents:

> [I]t's as if an invisible barbed wire surrounds the area extending a few blocks from Main and Hastings in all direction. There is a world beyond, but to them it's largely inaccessible. It fears and rejects them and they, in turn, do not understand its rules and cannot survive in it.
>
> (Máté, 2008: 20)

For Sarah, being red zoned from Burnaby and New West was "shitty, because that was my life, that's where I knew everybody, that's my everyday life, that's where I live". For these and for other reasons, red zones were not experienced by many as therapeutic interventions, but as forms of exclusion and banishment: For Adam: "it doesn't feel too good. I can't go out with friends, I can't see my clients, I can't take my dogs for a walk in the area, it sucks for business for my shop. Until I can get a pardon I'm locked out of that square". Asked how it feels to be red zoned, Neil responded: "Hurtful, denied, lost . . ."

Several Vancouver respondents noted that conditions of release caused problems in maintaining and nurturing family ties because of their spatial and temporal removal from a place. Intimate networks quickly unravelled if not maintained. For Neil, the worst effect of being red zoned was "losing contact with my family, my son . . . I wanted to see my son, he is my blood, he's my boy". Conditions prevented people from participating in the vital work of commemorating and marking significant events. Patrick, who was red zoned from Vancouver, noted that one of the worst consequences was

> being separated from my nieces. When my nieces and nephews had a birthday, I could not go. Cause I had a red zone I could not go. They were like: "Uncle, Uncle, we thought you were coming?" It embarrassed my mom. I couldn't go to Vancouver cause they wouldn't allow me.

He also noted that, "I had a friend who died down here [the DTES] and I couldn't go to his funeral, which still kills me, because of the red zone". He repeatedly breached his conditions, he noted, because he was red zoned from areas where his girlfriend lived:

> by giving me a red zone all it did was initiate another charge. It is enabling me to go back to jail. It would have been better for them to lock me up for the time and then let me out. But instead I end up going right back because my girlfriend she was situated, right. She's my girl. I don't care what cops say, what judges say, if my girl's there, I'm going there. Just think, put yourself in my shoes. If you are married and your wife is in the middle of your red zone, would you go and see her?

If violent conditions are those "geographies of being that restrict the potential for life to flourish and actualize" (Laurie and Shaw, 2018: 7), forcefully constraining the "resources of our becoming" (16), then the spatiotemporal cuts of conditions of release surely qualify as forms of legal violence. While the manner in which the "cuts" of conditions sever affective ties reveal clear comparisons to the experience of political activists, their consequences proved more violent in the case of the marginalized people we interviewed. Territorial exclusions too often placed already precarious people into conditions of heightened risk, compounding pre-existing forms of vulnerability (cf. McNeil et al., 2015; Munn and Bruckert, 2013). Sex trade workers risked accessing red zoned areas, and facing detention, or used riskier areas that threatened their personal vulnerability: "Conditions don't achieve much", noted Martine. "But they create a lot of stress. They isolate us; they put the girls in harm's way". Diane in Ottawa worked in the sex trade to earn money for drugs. Already a highly risky activity, her red zone created heightened risk, she noted, when clients unwittingly drove her into her red zone after picking her up. She described how her anxiety about being driven into her red zone rubbed off onto a client, who then acted aggressively, kicking her out of his car into the middle of her red zone. Diane was also banned from having any drug paraphernalia, and red zoned from a needle exchange: "not being able to have clean paraphernalia on me: it's really frustrating when I can't have it and I need it". The result is "just again, risks for each other, like to access safe and healthy works. . .". Ironically, Diane described drug use as a coping strategy that allowed her to deal with the paranoia and stress associated with the very conditions imposed in order to prevent her drug use: "When I'm on drugs I'm just chilling out. I'm not worried about the fact that we can just got pulled over".

Other sex workers reported that red zones exposed them to further physical violence from clients or partners and rendered them less likely to rely on police protection. Sophie, for instance, was a young woman who used drugs and lived with an abusive partner. She was first red zoned from a small portion of Hochelaga-Maisonneuve in Montreal (from Papineau to Frontenac, and from Sherbrooke to Viger) for communicating for the purposes of prostitution. At the time, she lived in a rooming house right in the middle of her red zone, but the judge "couldn't care less". She moved east. After being caught in the red zone again, however ("I had no choice but to go back to Square Berri to get my dope"), her perimeter was extended to include a larger zone (from St-Laurent to Viau). "They do that to all of us, they catch you in your perimeter, and before you know it, they extend it". As Sophie lived in her perimeter, had a record of past violation of conditions, and had outstanding warrants for failure to appear before the Court to respond to those charges, she did not want to call the police for domestic violence. One evening, a neighbour called the police because her partner and her were fighting. She reported that the police "took me by the arms and feet and dragged me out of my apartment", leaving her abusive partner behind. "I'm a prostitute, a crackhead, they didn't even help me with my rights", she complained. "They treated me like shit, as if I were the criminal because I had a record . . . My partner didn't have one, so he passed as the angel".

The litany of petty and profound violences inflicted by spatial conditions of release is unrelenting. These are not abstract harms, but act upon lived, situated bodies. John in Ottawa noted that being red zoned cut him off from valuable food resources, compromising his health:

> Because of the fact that I couldn't eat, I wasn't eating as much, or my health went down, so . . . I was sick for a good while actually, after that. Not being able to eat regularly and wasn't making much money from [social assistance], so after my rent was paid, I'd have so much to buy my food. But it still doesn't last the whole month so you depend on the food kitchen and the shelters to help you and I couldn't come to them because I was red zoned.

Chris uses a wheelchair or walks with a cane, due to spinal cord and nerve damage. Walking hurts. As a result of his Ottawa red zone: "I have to take [a] lot more longer distances to go where I want, which costs me more time walking. I would rather go the quicker way . . .". One particularly brutalizing case is that of Clyde, who described being arrested for a curfew in Vancouver he was unaware of and was charged with assault on a police officer (he claimed that the police officer assaulted him). He was in remand for five months, until he was bailed out with a court-ordered curfew. He was unable to access housing, and was obliged to couch surf, where he developed a staph infection from bed bug bites. He was obliged to go to hospital every 12 hours for IV antibiotics:

> And I'm on curfew, [it's] five minutes to ten and I'm going to rip the IV. The doctor knows what's going on. Goes into the lobby . . . and talks to the officers, tells them what is going on. And [the doctor said]: "I don't care what you say about his conditions, he has to come in to the hospital every twelve hours"

Q: And what did the cops do?

A: Well they documented it, and the moment I was done with my IV antibiotics they arrested me and breached me eight counts, and I did five months.

Rather than personalized "time-outs" as imagined by legal actors, removing individuals from a finite area for a therapeutic period, red zones were seen by our respondents as inherently destructive of the spatiotemporal "conditions of existence" that sustained life for poor people. Red zones were not simply a matter of spatial access but affected the ongoing maintenance of a life. For those experiencing them, the "cuts" of conditions were not made with a scalpel, but with a meat cleaver. Bernice in Ottawa saw red zones as largely unworkable precisely for this reason. "A lot of people are in their red zones all the time", she noted, as

> we're all in a homeless situation, and mainly the people here are dealing or doing whatever … So if they red zone somebody for doing it, that person's gonna come out whether they want to or not. They might not come out in the day time so the cops can't see them, but at night time, they're all back right there doing the same thing they were because that's their money, that's how they make money or for them to take care of themselves, whether it be cigarettes, booze, drugs, doesn't matter, *that's how they take care of themselves.*
>
> (our emphasis)

Conditions of release effaced or downplayed the spatiotemporal dependencies associated with addiction, noted many. "The court will give you a red zone so you can't come into this area. But I'm an addict", noted Patrick, in Vancouver. "They sell drugs in that area. So in order for me to get drugs, I have to go to that area. So even if the court tells me not to, I still go. Even if the court tells me not to". The temporalities and rhythms of the Court clashed with that of lived experience: "you can't just tell some youth to stop using drugs and go back home, it doesn't work like that", observed Martine. "For some, it takes time to stop using and [the courts] don't respect that" (Sophie).

Drug use for many of our respondents was deeply situated, "relationally embedded" in particular places (Williams, 2016: 2). It helps to think of their drug use through a political ecology lens, that redirects us from an individualizing model to one that moves between scales: from the "internal ecologies" of the body, to the "local biologies" through which people move on a daily basis (such as neighbourhoods like the Downtown Eastside) and the "body politic" which includes the broader socio-economic context, and its dynamic shifts such as globalization. The massive dislocations of advanced capitalism and colonial racism reverberate through such scales (Alexander, 2001), producing the trauma and loss that generate the "hungry ghosts" (Máté, 2008) of inner-city addiction.

In that sense, it is unsurprising that respondents did not conform to a "rational choice" model of behaviour when it came to abiding by their conditions of release, given their drug dependency.[2] As a result, breaches were

---

[2] Máté (2008: 147) reminds us that "[t]he scientific literature is nearly unanimous in viewing drug addiction as a chronic brain condition, and this alone ought to discourage us from

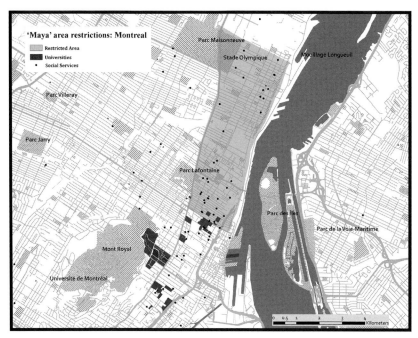

MAP 7.1 Maya's area restrictions (Montreal).
Sources: Esri, HERE, Garmin, USGS, Intermap, INCREMENT P, NRCan, Esri Japan, METI, Esri China (Hong Kong), Esri Korea, Esri (Thailand), NGCC, © OpenStreetMap contributors, and the GIS User Community

commonplace: "I was just messed up in the head really. I just didn't care. You know. And that was how I did it [breached], when I was getting high, and I needed some kind of income" (Clyde, Vancouver). "I didn't care, it didn't stop me from going. I never saw anyone complying with their red zone in Hochelaga", declared Maya, in Montreal, despite the width of her own red zone (Map 7.1).

Ultimately, Samuel argued that the only effect of a red zone, consequently, is to "ensure that a person is going to come back through jail on a new charge" because of the predictable effects of addiction:

> it's one of the areas where you go to score and you are an addict or you are severely addicted. You are not going to change to go someplace else, when all

blaming or punishing the sufferer. No one, after all, blames a person suffering from rheumatoid arthritis for having a relapse, since relapse is one of the characteristics of chronic illness. The very concept of choice appears less clear-cut if we understand that the addict's ability to choose, if not absent, is certainly impaired".

the people you know, and your dealers are in this area. You are going to go where you are comfortable. And they know that. That's the trap about the whole thing . . . it's only a matter of time until they screw up and go to jail. *It's part of a pathway that puts people back in jail.*

(our emphasis)

CONNECTIVE CONDITIONS

Samuel's characterization of conditions as a "pathway" is instructive. As noted, conditions of release, because of their status as legally consequential instructions, hook people up to a series of legal networks and actors. Of immediate significance is the manner in which conditions place people, and their movements in space and through time, into a vexed, oppressive, and sometimes violent relationship with the police, who are the everyday enforcers of these territories. Because of the spatiotemporal rhythms of inner-city neighbourhoods, people are frequently present in public space, placing them into heightened conditions of legal exposure. People are outside, often moving, and always potentially visible. As Bill in Vancouver's Downtown Eastside noted: "I spend my days downtown, running from food line, to places to go get rock and work on how to get my money for rock". For Tyrone: "my day is the same as every other day. Find something to eat. Grind [hustle] for fucking dope".

Their visibility, if governed by conditions of release, can trigger routine levels of harassment, or more overt forms of police violence. Territory can be enforced through brute, bodily force. Nathan reported breaching his curfew in Vancouver, and being picked up by the police, beaten up, and dropped off in Stanley Park, several kilometres away, to walk back to the Downtown Eastside in the rain. Juan was clear on the informal logic of police territorialization in Vancouver:

> The courts give you an order that you can't be somewhere. When the police come, he says, "look, I see you again here, and I'm going to kick your bad ass, boy". . . You go back and Oh! I'm not going to be around that damn cop, but all of a sudden, boom, it's that cop, and you are in the back alley, get beat up by these cops, and if you go complain, you get double, triple next time. That happened to me, you know.

Adam, a male sex trade worker in Vancouver, reported the following encounter in the suburbs: "six cops in an undercover car pull up at gun point, throw me in the back seat, and take me out somewhere outside of [town], and tell me, either you and your boyfriend leave, or you'll end up in jail, or worst case scenario you'll wind up in the river". Neil, red zoned from an area in

Kelowna, in the interior of B.C., described what he graphically labelled as a police "boot fucking":

> I was drunk one night, smoking crack, and it was really cold … and all of a sudden I hear: "Put your hand behind your back, you are under arrest for being in your red zone". Right away they roll in and cuff you up. RCMP [Royal Canadian Mounted Police] Kelowna detachment, that's a boot fucking.

Interviewees were thus highly attuned to the territorializing power of the police. Ron described police checks on his conditions as a routine and aggravating experience: "It bugs me, it aggravates me. It's like I'm not doing anything, and they're just, they're bugging me". Even moments of police discretion were seen as thinly veiled expressions of violence. Bernice was spotted in her red zone in Ottawa by a police officer, who recognized her: "and he … shook his finger at me like: 'you know you're in the wrong', but saying that, he walks away, so in other words [the message was] 'Go'. He gave me more like a warning then saying 'OK, you're in the red zone, let's go, you'll go to the jail'". State territorialization is enacted both viscerally and more subtly, it seems, through moments of conditional exception.

Bernice alerts us to the carceral continuum at work here. As noted, the work of carcerality extends beyond the physical space of incarceration (Moran, 2015: 100; Villaneuva, 2017). It is in this sense that we can consider the ubiquitous disciplinary power cast by the threat of "jail" attached to conditions of release, experienced as a form of spatiotemporal exclusion. The red zone at bail is sutured to the remand centre, as well as other territorialized forms of control. Jail casts a disciplinary power, even at a distance. Bernice noted that she was

> always watching for the cops, constantly watching for the cops. Somewhere else, it doesn't bother me. But because I'm here, definitely much, I'm always watching behind me 'cause *I don't wanna go back to jail … I've never spent a lot of time in jail and I really don't wanna spend time in jail…* You're always looking everywhere, behind you to see if they're around because someone know me, and the one that know me will be the one that's an asshole: "*Hey, you're in your red zone, I'm gonna take you away and go to the jail!*"

> (our emphasis)

The threat of incarceration is, however, even more powerful when combined with the realities of addiction and the intense fear of going through withdrawal. It increases the risks of violent interactions with the police as individuals are fighting for their lives: "We'd do anything not to get cuffed because we know we'll be sick, related Sophie who both experienced and witnessed such encounters.

> Once, I was with my ex and there was a police operation. The girl didn't want to get arrested and I knew her, so I knew she wouldn't let them do it. So there's nothing that she didn't do to escape. At some point, they shoved her to the back seat of the police car. But that stupid cop, he opened her window by 15–20 centimeters, so she just threw herself in the gap and escaped. Can you imagine how this police officer will interact with her in the future, can you imagine how much he'll distrust her?

People are routinely detained for breaches, noted our interviewees. In some cases, this can be short, unless – as Clyde in Vancouver noted – you're arrested on a Friday, and then "it is going to be a long fucking weekend in a cold ass fucking cell". Even shorter periods of detention, however, can be challenging:

> it is only for a couple hours, but it's mental anguish that really hurts the most, because you are in there with a whole bunch of drug addicts and people that are looking at long sentences that don't have anything to care for. Anything is possible. Your life could be threatened … Yeah, they are withdrawing, they're jonesing [craving], they're dope-sick, they're shitting and puking everywhere. I'm here for what, an area restriction violation? These guys are waiting to be put in jail. I'm waiting to be released.
>
> (Adam, Vancouver)

Adam also noted that rather than being formally arrested, he would routinely be "detained", allegedly for his own safety and that of others, and held for up to five days without access to a phone. But for people dependent on drugs, detention could have demeaning and degrading consequences. Bruce described his partner's experience of withdrawal while under detention for a breach:

> So here you have a guy who is sweating. He shat himself. And the cops said, "Clean that up". And wanted him to use his jacket to clean shit off the floor. And he said: "No, please, I'm sick, please just help me. You have a janitor". And they grabbed him and threw him on the floor.

The demeaning conditions of detention, combined with addiction, appear to be a reason for many to uncritically agree to conditions of release, confirming the findings of McNeil et al. (2015: 72) in which respondents noted that the severity of their withdrawal symptoms were such that their acceptance of the conditions of their release amounted to duress (see also Chapter 5). Patrick noted that he would agree to any restrictions to escape detention: "I know for a fact that when I go to court I will say, do whatever I can to get out". The lived experience of detention, in other words, may prompt the acceptance of an unrealistic array of conditions of release that then create the conditions for breach and subsequent detention. The carceral continuum is realized both spatially, through the production of multiple overlapping zones of confinement, and temporally, through the production of conditions that produce predictable episodes of continued discipline.

This cycle is also life-threatening for drug users upon their release. Studies have shown that people just released from prison are especially vulnerable to drug overdose: "the forced break from drug use while they are behind bars lowers their tolerance. Even if they found and used drugs in jail, the drugs they encounter afterward are often more potent. Advocates say prisoners are not getting the treatment and support they need to avoid a fatal overdose once they come out of the prison gates" (Gee, 2018). The situation is particularly worrisome in B.C., where, according to Coroners Services, about "two-thirds of those who die of drug overdose in 2016–17 have spent time in jail at some point in their lives or were under correctional supervision. Of the 1,233 fatalities in that category, 18 per cent, or 333, occurred within 30 days of release. Twenty-five per cent, or 470, died within a year" (Gee, 2018).

But it is not just prison that serves as an adjunct to conditions of release. John, in Ottawa, was obliged to relocate to another shelter because of his red zone, which he characterized in highly carceral terms:

> the staff, they're are all training to be police. So they're harder ... They got like 50,000 cameras in that place. ... We are supposed to be able to have our privacy but the only privacy we have is in our bedroom, in our room, on our bed. Other than that, you're being watched 24 hours per day. Any action you do, any bad action, they call the cops right away ... OK, yes, it's a homeless shelter but we are human ... They don't see it that way.

Also, as noted above, Patrick, who enrolled in Vancouver's community court, could only access his welfare check by conforming to the court's requirement that he present himself on a regular basis, describing the experience as like "a leash around your neck".

COMMUNICATIVE CONDITIONS

Yet, the scope, range, and duration of the "leash" is often ambiguous. The supposedly clear messaging associated with spatial conditions of release was far from evident. Several respondents noted that conditions of release were often ambiguous, or subject to communication breakdown. Some noted that they assumed that they had been exempted from certain restrictions, only to discover that the court had failed to change their record. Clyde claimed that

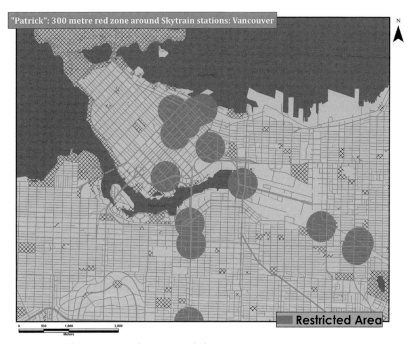

MAP 7.2 Patrick's 300-metre red zone around Skytrain stations, Vancouver.
Sources: Esri, HERE, Garmin, USGS, Intermap, INCREMENT P, NRCan, Esri Japan, METI, Esri China
(Hong Kong), Esri Korea, Esri (Thailand), NGCC, © OpenStreetMap contributors, and the GIS User
Community

he had not been given written instructions regarding a curfew after he was
released on probation. This led to a violent encounter with a police officer, he
claimed, that led to a subsequent arrest.

In part, this reflects the spatiality of the conditions. A number of Montreal
and Vancouver interviewees were vague concerning the perimeters of their
area restrictions. Plasma knew that his red zone covered the entire Centre-
Sud, including the Gay Village in Montreal, but he wasn't sure of its northern
boundaries: "Does it end at Sherbrooke or Ontario? That's a good question.
The judge told me: 'I don't want to see you again in Centre-Sud. You're a
smart guy, you'll figure it out, just check on the Internet if you're unsure'".
Patrick in Vancouver was obliged to remain 300 metres away from any Skytrain rapid transit station (Map 7.2). This proved a challenge, because he was
living rough near a station. After numerous breaches, the police paced out the
distance, and Patrick marked the perimeter with spray paint, noting:

> I don't know how far 300 meters is, I don't know how many feet a meter is.
> I can't look at a distance and say that's about 400 yards. I can't do it. So when

they say, "Stay 300 meters away", I don't even know how many feet a meter is. I have no clue. I only got through half of grade six before I got kicked out.

As we saw in chapter 6, even those who created such conditions noted the challenges of enacting their spatiality on the ground. "How do you calculate a 100 metre radius from a SAQ [liquor] store?" queried one defence attorney from Montreal.

In addition, there was uncertainty regarding the temporal duration of conditions, reinforcing an argument we made in Chapter 5 on criminal justice administration. Asked how long his red zone was in force, Chet didn't know, assuming erroneously that "once I've been dealt with, I'll still have it for a year or two". Adrian received an informal police red zone that he presumed was still operative, creating intense uncertainty. "The thing is I hesitate if I do go down there and I get stopped. Because . . . I don't know what they can carry out as charges on that. That's my concern, that's what I'm worried about". Bernice, in Ottawa, was unclear when her red zone would be lifted: "I don't know how long that's gonna be. They said 30 days, but it's been 18 now, so but I'm still, well are they gonna take the red zone thing off or not, once I go to court or not?". Even worse, Maya, in Montreal, was convinced that her red zone was effectively a lifetime condition: "I've been red zoned for 12 years; this is for life".

As with the political activists, non-association requirements created a mobile, changing geography. The requirement that people not have contact with drug users, in particular, proved perplexing. An abstract requirement was complicated by the lived realities of inner-city life, in which many people were likely drug users, moving through the shared dense spaces at the same time. For Bernice, in Ottawa, this created an almost impossible situation:

> One of my friends, he's not allowed to hang around with anybody that does alcohol. Now, he can't talk to these people either, so that means you can't talk to fifty percent of the people around here. How do they know or how can they justify that, if they don't know? Like if I walk up to you, I don't know. I can start to talking to you and [them] the cops come around: "Oh, she's an alcoholic, you're not supposed to be around her" and you get arrested, that doesn't make any sense.

Ibrahim faced a similar dilemma: "How do you know if the person had something [e.g. a criminal record]? I hate breaking the law, but you don't know". The consequences of such ambiguous, discretionary, and extensive forms of spatial regulation are profound. Carcerality becomes a form of subjectivity, a mobile territorial condition that is carried with the subject, in much the way that undocumented migrants or those subject to electronic tags (Keenan,

2018) experience legal geographies. Forced to enter red zones to secure vital resources, yet unsure where such red zones extend, or how long they operate, or how to interpret related conditions, such as non-association, while confronting the ever-present possibility of discretionary police enforcement, red zones are experienced not as fixed sites of containment or banishment, but as hybrid and fluid legal forms that simultaneously expel, move, confuse, come and go, and detain (Miéville, 2010). The red zone is not simply a single bounded space. In many ways it becomes a generalized legal condition of spatial access and prohibitions realized throughout urban space, echoing the "roving exclusion zone" described by political activists, discussed below.

All of these entanglements, not surprisingly, make the breach of conditions not only possible but also highly likely. This creates the "revolving door", in which the breach of conditions leads to new, and often more constraining conditions, which are perhaps even more likely to be breached. Rather than a stepping-stone, allowing for advancement and improvement, many respondents indicated that conditions of release ensure that people constantly cycle through the criminal justice system or, at worse, become further entangled. Territorialized conditions at one moment thus easily cascade into an ongoing cycle of territorialization. For Nathan, in Vancouver, red zones and other conditions ensure that "you are prone to fail". For many, breaches were a routine experience:

> Oh, I used to get arrested and put in jail for 3 to 4 days at a time, every couple of week, because of [red zones] and charges, charges. So my criminal record is 3 months. Nothing is for anything criminal, it is always for breaching, possession, breaching, breaching, breaching. They would kick in your door and get you for breach so you would have a possession and a breach.
>
> (Anne, Vancouver)

This ensured criminality even absent any formal breaches, according to some. Adam noted that his red zone "used to be like a revolving door for me", noting that he would be routinely arrested for breaching his red zone, even though he was not engaged in criminal behaviour:

> I could be standing on the corner in my red zone and then, boom, "Mr. X you are in your red zone. And you are standing on the corner. Are you soliciting sex?", "No officer, I'm not soliciting sex, thank you very much, I'm just waiting for a friend". "Bullshit!" Then they throw me in the city jail 3 to 5 days.

Some noted the manner in which subsequent breaches lead to an escalation of negative consequences, such that the revolving door becomes a penal escalator:

For your first breach they will be lenient, give you a slap on the wrist, then kick you out the door. The second time they might do that, or they will just hold you over, so the more breaches that you accumulate on your record, the punishment gets more severe. Next time you get two weeks, maybe the next time you get 30 days, next time 3 months. It just goes *higher and higher and higher.*

(Rob, Vancouver; our emphasis)

Patrick described being on the "step up" program, whereby subsequent sentences are automatically doubled. So a breach that led to a ten-month sentence becomes a twenty-month sentence when repeated. This applied to probation. Ibrahim in Ottawa described those he met in jail, reflecting on their ambitions after release. "But by the time they come out, reality will set in, all their plans will crumble, because [of] conditions, and probation, and 'you can't go there, you can't go there'". Using a highly embodied metaphor, he described probation as:

like you're *standing on one leg,* man. You come out of jail early, you're standing on one leg still. You're not standing on two legs. You're standing on one leg and how you gonna move on? You can't, you're a loser basically ... *because everything is closed.* So what's the options that you have then? The only option is that you do to commit more crime, I guess, to survive. O.K., why do you need a condition? He did his time. If he do something crazy then do it. But if you put him how you gonna move on.

(our emphasis)

Those governed by conditions of release thus become entangled in legal infrastructures. As such, they become increasingly visible to legal actors, such as the police. But the neighbourhoods they occupy are already highly monitored. Here, criminal law may become hooked up to regulatory criminal law, as police use minor infractions, such as jaywalking, street vending, public drinking, or intoxication as grounds for stopping inner-city residents and running their names, revealing the presence of red zones that then allow for more aggressive forms of enforcement (King, 2013a; b; Sylvestre, Bernier, and Bellot, 2015).

Such a proactive policing strategy should not be underestimated in cities like Montreal where at least 65,000 statements of offences (tickets) for violations of the City by-laws or regulations have been issued to homeless individuals between 1994 and 2010, and more than half (30,500) within the last five of those 15 years (Sylvestre et al., 2011; Bellot and Sylvestre, 2017).[3] According to

---

[3] Although these are striking numbers, we should note that the methodology used by the researchers only provides a conservative account of the number of tickets issued to homeless

Bellot and Sylvestre (2017), the most frequent violations for which statements of offence were issued are public consumption of alcohol and public drunkenness (over 60% of all statements of offences), loitering, or obstruction on the public domain (12%), and sleeping in a park after closing hours (5%). This is also true of Vancouver, where 95% of all tickets issued for sidewalk vending and sidewalk obstruction between 2008 and 2012 were concentrated within three blocks of the Downtown Eastside (King, 2013a; b: see also Chesnay and Sylvestre, 2013 and O'Grady, Gaetz, and Buccieri, 2013 for similar results from Ontario).

One rationale for this intensified by-law blitz, targeted at marginalized communities, is that it provides an opportunity for the police to discover bail or probation breaches which would otherwise have been left unchecked for lack of legal justification. Indeed, it is often easier for the police to observe that someone is committing a minor offence than to find out that this person is breaching his or her court order. The violation of by-laws thus offers police officers the reasonable and probable grounds to believe that an offence has been committed, grounds that they would perhaps not have had *but for* the initial by-law violation. One consequence for the person subject to a red zone in those blocks, therefore, is that a minor by-law infraction, a matter of regulatory criminal law, can lead to a more serious criminal law charge. Moreover, the by-law infraction itself may be elevated to a criminal offence as it may constitute a breach of the general requirement to keep the peace and be of good behaviour imposed in most bail orders and all probation orders.

A few respondents responded to the possibility of police surveillance with bravado. For Howard, in Ottawa: "You might be able to lock me up, but that's OK, one day I'm gonna get out, and when I get out, I'm going right back to the same way, because *nobody, nobody* tells me what, or when, or where, to do what I want to do. I'm my own person". Some participants even deliberately breached their conditions, as an act of resistance. This is the case of Plasma in Montreal, who, as a matter of fact and without us first noticing, we ended up interviewing in the middle of his red zone. "Not everyone would do it", he said as we started to feel uncomfortable, "you've got to be brave, but nothing will happen. I've dressed up today and you're with me!" But, much more common, however, were intensified forms of self-territorialization, as people governed by conditions of release regulated their comportment, interactions, and spatial and temporal presence. So Diane noted that she made "constant

individuals in Montreal. Indeed, they only considered tickets for which individuals had given the address of a shelter or community group that support homeless people in the city. The extent of the phenomenon is thus probably underestimated.

efforts. I don't have paraphernalia in my bag when I'm not using it, for keeping the peace and things like that". Yet, as noted, for many other requirements (notably access to her red zone) "I don't really have any other options".

With no options but to enter red zones, many informants were forced to adopt a variety of strategies, predicated on avoiding exposure, including concealment, camouflage, and subterfuge. The case of Diane, in Ottawa, is illustrative. She described how she and her partner would surreptitiously access a highly patrolled drug market, from which she was red zoned:

> There's a building . . . and we have friends up there, so if we walk up and see a bunch of cops, we just go up into the building or we cut around the Metro parking lot and come back around the other way. But usually we go into the apartment building and we can see through the window if the cops are coming. Take turns trying to run out, and the other person keeping watch for cops.

But, unsurprisingly, this generated anxiety, even paranoia. The word "territory" derives in part from the Latin verb "terrere", to frighten or terrify. For Diane, incessant fear and anxiety, generating panic attacks, was the worst effect of her red zone. Forced to access her red zone, which includes resources such as a needle exchange, as well as allowing her to access drugs, generated "constant fear and worries. . . *There's always a fear, there's already a fear, whatever I'm doing*" (our emphasis)

This fear was omnipresent, for Diane, shaping her everyday social encounters:

> If a friend calls my name, I'm just: [whispers] "Shut the fuck up!" They don't fucking know [I'm red zoned], they're just saying hi, but I'm like [whispers] "I'm not supposed to fucking be here, *shut up!* I'll be in trouble!"

The situation for Diane was compounded by the fact that her husband, on probation, has also been red zoned. A breach would be more serious for him: "he could be looking at 6 months if he got pulled over, you know breach after breach, and then a charge, and he'd be fucked". Their collective predicament is a powerful indictment of the dynamics of legal territorialization. Conditions, notably the red zone, seek to sever them not only from the spaces they need to sustain themselves, but also threaten to detach them from each other, by virtue of the way in which conditions of release are connected to grids of territorial power, operative in the past (previous encounters with conditions), the present (omnipresent police patrols), or the future (the threat of future detention). Red zones are spaces of fear.

Legal territorialization is highly embodied. Excluded by shelter rules and red zones, Diane and her husband were forced to sleep rough, so they could sleep together. But the internalized anxiety induced by their conditions meant that sleep was hard to come by at night, forcing them to take turns to nap: "The whole point of it is so we can be together, but then the whole purpose is completely defeated, when one of us is sleeping at a time", she noted. Anxiety induced conflict. They fought a lot, more so than before the red zone, often quarrelling about the red zone, while worrying that the conflict attracted unwanted police attention. She became furious when he took risks, like jaywalking, or not wearing a hat: "We're both constantly worried, and we're both trying to watch each other's asses", she noted. Yet the individualizing nature of the conditions negate affective connections:

> At the same time I've got to look out for mine too, 'cos I can't blame him if he wasn't able to. But we both damn well know that if anything happens, we're both blaming each other. And that's just the frustrating part of being on the streets, using drugs, in a committed relationship … It's tiring, and it's stressful.

RIGHTS AND RED ZONES

Informants were clear in characterizing red zones as not only ineffective and punitive, but as immoral and unjust, violating their rights. Conditions of release severed not only spatiotemporal networks, but also foundational norms of citizenship and legality. Howard, in Ottawa, was old enough to reflect on the emergence of conditions in the 1990s ("Oh, we'll red zone you, we're gonna do this, we're gonna do that") as "not legal, you can't tell somebody that he can't walk down the street". "It's a free country", he noted, "we're in Canada, we're not in Syria!"

For some, conditions of release were seen as violating basic due process rights. Chris in Ottawa itemized his conditions, but then noted ironically, but correctly: "But you're still innocent, innocent until proven guilty". The seemingly arbitrary application of conditions – particularly by police – was seen as an illegitimate and discriminatory expression of state power.[4] "They pick and choose who they wanna charge and who they don't wanna charge. It's not a good thing", complained Bernice in Ottawa:

> It's not fair to a lot of people. I understand why people are saying that they are being prejudiced against other people. You know, some of them they don't

---

[4] Unlike judges, the police were seen as overly aggressive: "the cops are too ready to give away a red zone to everybody; here, you're red zoned, you're red zoned, you're red zoned, you're red zoned! So like 50% of the people that live here are red zoned" (Bernice, Ottawa).

like them, they just pick on that person, pick, pick, pick, and eventually the
person's gonna break, right, that's what going to happen.

But the territorializing effects of red zones, and the way in which they severed
lived timespaces, was more strongly challenged.

> I don't think anybody should have the right to deny you a safe place to be, a
> safe place to sleep, safe equipment . . . You know for an officer to decide that
> ok, I'm going to take away all of this from her . . . the Sheps, and the Sally,[5]
> just for doing drugs . . .
>
> (Bernice, Ottawa)

The arbitrary power of the police, "who put a little red zone on you", were
challenged. They shouldn't have the power to tell you where you can walk, on
which street" (Chris, Ottawa).

As powerful as they may be, however, as alluded to in Chapter 5, these
arguments rarely reach the courtroom. The legal professionals we interviewed
seemed frankly surprised or confused by questions of rights. "In what sense?",
queried a prosecutor in Vancouver. "What do you mean by fundamental rights?",
asked a Montreal judge, noting that he/she was "kind of stumped to answer you in
one way or another. The viewpoint of curtailing fundamental rights in this sense or
according to the Charter is not a viewpoint that is often raised, and that is quite
present; no".

Although some confirmed their importance in general terms, most legal actors
confirmed that the invocation of rights was infrequent in relation to conditions of
release: "It is rare that we are arguing really big rights issues at bail. Because
generally the Crown isn't pounding the table about things unless there is a good
reason for it as well", noted a defence attorney in Vancouver. Another acknowledged the *Reid* case: "There was, I think out of Victoria a challenge to area
restrictions based on an argument that it restricted a person's right to mobility under
section 6 of the Charter of Rights and Freedoms".[6] That said, "that is rarely raised,

---

[5] The references are to the Shepherds of Good Hope and the Salvation Army, faith-based service
providers to the homeless in Ottawa's Lowertown.

[6] In *R. v. Reid* (1999) B.C.P.C. 12, the defence argued that the Public Prosecution Service of
Canada's practice of seeking a standardized "one square mile red zone" in order to keep drug
offenders away from the downtown area of Victoria for bail and probation in every case of drug
trafficking and possession for the purpose of trafficking regardless of the specifics of the case or
of the offender was unconstitutional and violated the offender's rights protected by s. 2b), 6, 7,
12, 15 of the Canadian Charter. Judge Gove, who is now a judge at the Downtown Community
Court in Vancouver, vehemently criticized this practice of the federal Crown. Although he did
not go through each Charter claim made by the defence, he found that excluding an
individual from the downtown of his city clearly interfered with his participation in the
community and to do so without demonstrating that it is necessary and justified in the case of

at least here" (Prosecutor, Montreal). Rights? "No. I don't know, I haven't seen any" (Judge, Montreal). A rights-based argument is "rare, it's very rare" . . . I never personally ever heard such an argument" (Prosecutor, Montreal).

If rights are present, for legal actors, they tend to be juxtaposed to the rights of "the public":

> The person has their liberty rights, their section 7 right to life, liberty and security of the person, they've got those rights, but the community also has a vested interest in being protected from these individuals who are accused of crime . . . individual rights are at play but they have to be balanced by the needs and rights of individuals in our communities.
>
> (Prosecutor, Vancouver)

There are multiple barriers to making rights claims. First, legal remedies are limited.[7] Further, as exposed in Chapter 5, the context in which such orders are issued does not provide any space or time for rights arguments, especially when the accused is held in the remand centre. This does not mean that certain conditions are not contested or that there is no request for amendments once they have been imposed. In the case of release orders, these requests for amendments are made at *pro forma* releases sometime after the appearance or bail hearing, and are obtained with the consent of counsel.[8] According to all the actors interviewed, it is, however, very rare that lawyers go to the Superior Court for a judicial review unless the person remains in custody. Several actors informed us of the pitfalls inherent in any subsequent challenge to the conditions, given the difficulty of ensuring the presence of people in Court.

---

this individual would interfere with his liberty and violate the principles of fundamental justice (in particular here, arbitrariness, overbreadth and disproportionality) (par. 57, 61, and 63). More specifically, red zone conditions cannot solely be based on the type of offence or a class of offenders. Judge Gove insisted, however, that his ruling should not be interpreted to hold all red zone conditions unconstitutional *per se*, but he suggested that such conditions be based on the unique circumstances of each case.

7   A release order imposed by the Court can only be reviewed before the trial with the written consent of the prosecutor or by a Superior Court judge: ss. 520–521 Cr. C. (judicial review), referring to s. 493 Cr.C "judge". According to the Supreme Court of Canada in *R.* v. *St Cloud* (2015) SCC 27, the judicial review process is not a *de novo* hearing providing open-ended discretion to the reviewing judge, but a hybrid remedy. The reviewing judge can only intervene "where relevant new evidence is tendered, where an error of law has been made or, finally, where the decision was clearly inappropriate" (par. 139). Furthermore, in accordance with the rule against collateral attacks on court orders, bail or probation conditions cannot be challenged during the trial or raised in defense to a breach charge: s. 687 Cr. C. With respect to sentencing decisions, appellate courts should only consider the "fitness of the sentence" and refrain from interfering with the trial judge's unless there was an error of law or the sentence was clearly unreasonable: *R.* v. *Shropshire*, [1995] 4 SCR 227, par. 46; *R.* v. *Lacasse*, 2015 SCC 64, [2015] 3 SCR 1089, par. 42–48.

8   S. 515.1 Cr. C.

You can go to the Superior Court; if you can't do it here, you must go to the top, but it takes time, it may be seven days before you have a date, you have to have the person show up and testify about how his or her situation has changed . . . but you know, for a homeless person it's already tough to make them come to Court. You happen to meet them at the corner of Berri the day before and give them their date. They swear they will be there but sometimes they aren't. It's not bad faith. He'll see you two weeks later and tell you: "I forgot, you know, you won't believe what happened to me, do you think we can . . . and then you release them from their default. So, going to Superior Court, it's delusional, it's not realistic . . .".

(Defence lawyer, Montreal)

CONCLUSION

In sum, court-imposed conditions of release appear to be often catastrophic for many. For Chad, the effects of being red zoned while on bail in Vancouver were felt as punitive:

A: Yeah, big punishment and for nothing.

Q: how has the restriction affected your everyday life?

A: it is uncomfortable, everyday I wake up I have to hide to go where I need to go, or else they send me to jail, for nothing.

Q: has it made it harder to get to resources, to VANDU [drug users resource centre]?

A: Of course it does.

Q: can you list some of the things?

A: I can't go . . . like meet my friend at Columbia and Hastings, I can't visit nobody, I got to hide around, I can't do that. So I don't know what to do.

Neat cartographic distinctions, reliant on naive conceptions of rational, individualized actors moving through tidy criminogenic landscapes confront the dense relational topologies of dependency, poverty, and radically constrained choices. In cutting people from localized resources and joining them to networks of legal force and surveillance, spatial conditions of release constitute a form of territorialized legal violence, rendering vulnerable people all the more precarious. Such forms of legal violence are part of the everyday experience for many marginalized Canadians, it seems, compounding systemic forms of racism, oppression, and state power. But it is not only the poor who find themselves subject to law's territory. Certain political activists, deemed a threat to security, also become entangled in the red zone. It is to their experience that we turn next.

8

Red Zoning Politics

"I don't think I can map it out for you.
It felt like I just couldn't be anywhere".
(Zora, Toronto)

The largest mass-arrest in Canadian peace-time history occurred between June 26 and 27, 2010, when over a thousand people were arrested in Toronto during demonstrations protesting the G20 Summit. As many commentators noted, the policing response to this political gathering was unjustified and unwarranted:

> Media, human rights monitors, protestors and passers-by were scooped up off the streets. Detained people were not allowed to speak to a lawyer or to their families. Arbitrary searches occurred in countless locations across the city, in many instances several kilometres from the G20 Summit site. Peaceful protests were violently dispersed and force was used. In an effort to locate and frustrate a small cohort of vandals, police disregarded the constitutional rights of thousands.
> (National Union of Public and General Employees, and Canadian Civil Liberties Association, 2011: 11)

Two years later, mass protests in Quebec were met with similar aggressive policing. The "Quebec Maple Spring", which began on February 13, 2012, started with a series of student demonstrations against the provincial Liberal government's plan to nearly double tuition fees over a three-year period, thus threatening accessibility to public education, but soon turned into the most important social movement in Quebec modern history (Speigel, 2014). At its peak, 300,000 students were on strike in the province (Ancelovici and Dupuis-Déri, 2014). On May 18, 2012, in an attempt to quash the movement, the Quebec National Assembly enacted Bill 78, a special law that suspended the school semester and declared it illegal for students to block access to classes and to participate in a public gathering of more than 50 people without providing an itinerary to the police. Defying the law, some 400,000 people gathered in the streets of Montreal on May 22 to mark the 100th day of the strike (Cox, 2012; Speigel, 2016), with solidarity protests held simultaneously in Toronto, Calgary, Vancouver, as well as New York and Paris.

According to the Quebec La ligue des droits et libertés (2013), there was a total of 3,509 arrests between February 16 and September 3, 2012 in the province, leading to the issuance of 2,433 statements of offence pursuant to by-laws and provincial statutes, and at least 471 criminal charges. As in Toronto, the police used a variety of tactics, many of them territorial, in order to monitor, regulate, and suppress political action, as evidenced by the use of security fences, the kettling of protestors, a massive police presence, and arrests. The timely control of space, clearly, was a significant priority.

In the course of this project, we met with ten individuals who were arrested during these two high-profile events. We also interviewed two environmental activists in Vancouver. For the activists we spoke to, caught up in state territorialization, the occupation and use of space – mostly public, but also semi-private and private space, as well as networks of communication and mobilization – was crucial to their politics. Indeed, in order to make clear how the regulation of dissent relies on specific spatial and temporal forms of territorialization, one has to understand how dissent itself relies on public spaces and takes a particular spatial form (Starr, Fernandez, and Scholl, 2011).

For some activists, public space was a space of representation (cf. Mitchell 1995): occupying public space "made our politics visible" (Rick), forcing "others to listen to our claims" (Nico).[1] Visibility, however, was only one of their actions' many goals that also included empowerment, resistance, and democratic participation. Demonstration changed the power dynamic and empowered demonstrators who felt they "were able to overcome any obstacle" (Mary). For Steve and Anita, public space was a "convergence space" (Routledge, 2003), a space of political deliberation where people could network and create connections. In particular, the duration of the student strike created a "'liberating space-time' during which people paused and creative political discussions emerged" (Nico: cf. Speigel, 2014). The experience of the demonstration was thus transformative, serving to imagine emancipatory possibilities.

But simple presence or connection were not sufficient for some protestors such as Carrie. Rather than conventional protest, which she characterized, acidly, as "look at the space we are taking up and please, because we are here,

---

[1] All names have been changed.

consider our point of view", she endorsed a more active strategy: "I find it more strategically useful to ... challenge how that space is constituted... [I]t's about trying to challenge the meaning of space rather than occupying it and taking it for what it is. It's about *reconstituting* space" (our emphasis). As Pile suggested in relation to resistance, protest is a means by which people "occupy, deploy and create alternative spatialities from those defined through oppression and exploitation" (1997: 3).

Thus, space was understood, for Sam, as "really strategic", to the extent that protestors are capable of occupying and "holding space", or through reclaiming space that should belong to the public and had been appropriated by private interests (Anita). Thus, this may entail a territorial reconstitution, potentially through disruption or blockage. For Zora, a successful demonstration usually means "interrupting, disrupting, or stopping something that you feel is an oppressive force", by physically slowing or halting spatial access to a meeting, for example. For others, such as Marius, occupying space is a political alternative in itself: for them, it is important to challenge capitalism without playing its game or resorting to its own reformist means, such as our broken electoral process.

Police tactics reconstituted these spaces of political possibility. Interviewees spoke of policing through a territorial lens, including the use of kettling, police surveillance, and the creation of "boundaries" through the implementation of the Toronto security fence, with checkpoints throughout the city. The experience of arrest, for the activists, was also territorial. Carrie, for example, became aware that she was on a list of arrest warrants, and, knowing that the criteria for arrests at a private house were more rigorous compared to the street, elected to remain at home. Sam also suggested that the police chose to arrest people when they were on their own, in public space, and in "vulnerable positions". Arrests were experienced as traumatic, and highly embodied, infiltrating personal living spaces. Emma, in Toronto,

> heard a bang on the door, and they used the battering ram to bust through. It felt like it was all in super slow motion ... There were little red dots [from the police weapons] on us. Then they just did the whole "down on the ground, hands on your head". It was all very slow motion and weird.

Marius, in Montreal, compared the tactics used by the police when they arrested him and some other 30 people on the morning of the Formula 1 Grand Prix on June 7, 2012 that overlapped with the students' strike, to those used against organized crime:

> it was a large-scale planned operation like we had never seen used with students. They entered my apartment with search warrants at 6 a.m. in the

morning while I was still sleeping, rushing through the front and the back door all at once, about 10 of them, pointing their weapons at me, telling me to get dressed and lie down face on the floor so I could be handcuffed. My vision was blurred. I felt I was gonna lose consciousness.

Rick described the experience of being thrown inside a police vehicle and systematically assaulted by an officer. Detention was also experienced temporally. Rick contrasted his intensely rapid and violent arrest with the subsequent mundane two-hour wait before transportation to detention.

The activists were held in detention for several days or weeks (e.g. Zora was held in custody for three weeks, Emma, for a month), and then released on bail, under wide-ranging conditions. In general, these entailed a diverse, overlapping mix of financial sureties, red zones, non-association conditions with other activists on bail, bans on participation in unlawful demonstrations, or any demonstration, curfews, as well as the unusual adoption of house arrest. Unlike many of our other respondents, this was often their first experience with bail (see Table 8.1).

Perhaps unsurprisingly, the activists saw the conditions as politically motivated, designed to control dissent and disrupt political activity. Zora noted that as a result of her conditions, she "shut down completely. I became uninvolved politically for over a year of my life", while for others the nature of their political participation changed. Nico, for instance, an experienced activist, used to be a leader and organizer in the Montreal students' movement. After his first arrest, he "only went to pots and pans" demonstrations[2] and stopped going to the heavily policed night protests. In Anita's case, as well as Nico, conditions not only broke the movement but also negated their identity as activists, striking at their existential core. "As an activist", noted Anita, "I was completely broken". Their "geographies of being" relied on access to political space. "Political action is at the heart of my life; everything revolves around it, my friendships, my studies, my relationship to the State, to authority and others", noted Nico. Bail conditions violently truncated the spatiotemporal conditions that sustained them as political beings.

Conditions not only curtailed individual expressions of activism, but also created a "chilling effect on political organizing" more generally, Sam noted. These sentiments were echoed by Anita, subject to multiple bail conditions during the students' strike in Montreal: "Conditions are only a means to break people, to break the movement, to make sure people get scared and become

---

[2] Referring to the banging of pots and pans that occurred on the front porch and balconies of Montreal dwellings starting in May 2012. See Speigel, 2014: 778 for an interesting discussion of this creative tactic.

TABLE 8.1 *Conditions imposed on demonstrators*
First published in Sylvestre, Villeneuve Ménard, Fortin, Bellot, and Blomley, 2018.

First name Type of condition	Montreal					Toronto					Vancouver		Total of individuals
	Anita	Marius	Mary	Nico	Steve	Carrie	Emma	Rick	Sam	Zora	Barbara	Greg	
Amount of surety (the highest amount where applicable) c = surety d = deposit		Over $1000 (d) + Over $5000 (c)	Over $500 (d)		Over $2000 (d)	Over $50 000 (c)	Over $50 000 (c)	$1000	Over $25 000 (c)	Over $50 000 (c)			8
Keep the peace and be of good behaviour	X		X	X	X	X	X	X		X	X	X	8
Do not contact or associate with certain individuals or groups	X	X	X	X	X	X	X		X	X			9
No-go, radiuses, or red zones	X	X	X	X	X			X	X		X	X	9
Reside at X address and notify the court of any change of address	X	X	X	X	X	X	X						7
Remain within the jurisdiction of the court			X		X								2
Curfew or house arrest	X		X		X	X	X		X	X			8
Outside of their residence, be in the presence of a surety					X	X	X		X	X			4
Do not participate in certain or any kinds of demonstrations	X	X	X	X	X	X	X	X	X	X		X	10
No masks or disguises in a	X		X		X								3

Condition				Cases							Total
No bags/backpacks or any containers in a demonstration	X		X		X						3
No weapons, explosives, weapon licensing requirement	X		X	X	X	X	X	X	X	X	8
Carry a copy of the court order	X		X		X	X	X	X	X	X	7
No cell phones or other communication devices			X			X	X			X	4
Do not copy or divulge evidence to third party			X					X	X	X	2
Other conditions*	X	X	X	X	X	X	X	X	X	X	10
Approx. duration of conditions (months) b = bail p = probation	20 m. (b)	27 m. (b) + 36 m. (p)	22 m. (b) + 12 m. (p)	20 m. (b) + 12 m. (p)	15 m. (b) + 12 m. (p)	16 m. (b)	18 m. (b)	10 m. (b)	17 m. (b)	16 m. (b)	
Max. number of conditions applying simultaneously	7	25	15	5	18	11	10	8	15	13	17

* Other conditions included conditions to appear before the Court at a certain date (10), abstain from using unprescribed drugs or alcohol (4), community service (3), and make reasonable efforts to find a job and keep it (1).

'good activists'". By (re)controlling space, it was felt, the authorities could (re) control time. The activist energy around the G20, she noted, had been palpable. But the subsequent repression, including the bail conditions, "really killed the momentum" (Rick). The fact that all charges were subsequently dropped was noted.

> If they had never convicted us, if we had never done jail time, they still would have got two years of a bunch of people not being able to really do anything political . . . I think the bail conditions makes people nervous even more than the possibility of going to jail. I think they use bail conditions as a deterrent and as a restriction on protest.
>
> (Emma)

Some protesters even went further, suggesting that criminalization and the imposition of restrictive conditions were not only targeted at protesters themselves, but aimed at delegitimizing the social movement by depicting those associated with it as dangerous criminals. This was not only reflected in the surveillance and arrest tactics deployed by the police, but also at a judicial level. Marius, for instance, was convinced that the conditions imposed, much like the serious charges that were first laid in some cases (including terrorism in Montreal and conspiracy to commit an indictable offence, such as rioting, and obstruction and mischief in Toronto), were part of a deliberate operation to deter demonstrators and scare people off: "This was massive State propaganda with deliberate disinformation to marginalize some organizations and scare people in order to justify the repression used against others".

EXPERIENCES OF CARCERALITY

Of particular significance to the activists involved in the G20 protests in Toronto was the widespread adoption of house arrest, experienced by many as a form of carcerality. For Sam, house arrest was "like being in jail". Operative for lengthy periods (a year and a half, for most people), house arrest constituted a clear severing, cutting the activists off from their vital spatial and temporal networks and rhythms. Indeed, for Zora, the severing effect was even more pronounced than pre-release detention. While in jail, Zora noted that she could engage with others, talk to her co-accused, and think about her situation theoretically and politically. Her body and brain, as she put it, were not detached. But when she was under house arrest:

> I felt that my mind part of me was more controlled . . . [N]ot only was I not allowed to go places, I was also not allowed to speak publicly. I couldn't

interact with people . . . I would just sit, and was angry. . . But I was incredibly fearful too.

Strikingly, Zora described her experience as one of a present absence. Required to reside at her sister's house in Toronto, her conditions, excluding visitors to her residence, meant she was effectively "outside of Toronto for nine months". In terms of "community and support structure, it didn't feel like I was in Toronto while staying at my sister's place". The experience, as she put it, was one that, "I don't think I can map it out for you. *It felt like I just couldn't be anywhere*" (our emphasis). In at least one case, that of Barbara, an environmental activist from Vancouver, the threat of having to endure such restrictive conditions made her refuse to sign an undertaking. In her case, she appeared to be willing to endure one territorial constraint in order to avoid another.

Feelings of confinement and isolation were felt by all of our respondents, although they originated from different sources. Mary, for example, who was subject to a complete ban from the Island of Montreal and a prohibition to demonstrate, remembered fighting the hardest against her non-association clause. She said she could deal with material restrictions to her livelihood, but couldn't accept sociospatial constraints. If this were to apply, she believed, the court would extend its territorial reach to her friends. While she was ready to take the personal risk of violating her conditions, she could not force her friends to do the same: "Even if I think it's worth the risk to keep talking with someone, it doesn't mean that they are going to feel the same. And I can't expect them or ask them to be willing to do so".

The non-association clauses similarly had important consequences on the maintenance of personal and political connections. Rick, who lived in Ottawa but had family in Guelph, was red zoned from downtown Toronto. Carrie noted that she was unable to associate with her partner, who was also on bail, except in the company of both their sureties: "We had been living together for a few years at that point, and then, all of sudden – bam! – We were separated for a year". But it also severely constrained her mobility. As an activist, her personal and political spaces tended to fuse: "there was so much shared space that even to go to a meeting would be a risk".

Such clauses thus severed people from the vital spatiotemporal political infrastructures of activist politics. The lead up to the protests, Sam noted, had generated wonderful camaraderie and a sense of collective struggle. "Then – bam! – It was all gone". Emma also worried that her conditions "would leave me behind", as activism moved on without her, particularly in light of the emergence of the Occupy movement, and the Arab Spring: "this is such a stupid time to have these conditions and to be in jail!" The conditions led Zora to worry that she would be "forgotten" by her activist community. When she was finally able to resurface, "there was a temporal displacement of being stuck nine months earlier … People had moved on".

This temporal disconnection was perhaps heightened during the students' strike in Montreal given that the strike was ongoing while demonstrators were on bail. Anita, for example, explains how she was confined in her apartment, bound to comply with a prohibition to demonstrate, with a red zone covering a large portion of downtown, and a curfew, while "all of her friends" were busy with the strike, leaving her feeling powerless and fearful that she'd "never be able to catch up later".

Confinement and disconnection sometimes combined with complete banishment. Most demonstrators in Montreal were red zoned or banned from multiple sites of protests. As 75% of the student population was on strike and demonstrations were organized all across the city, these could translate into many widely dispersed, large perimeters. Marius, for instance, was prohibited from being within 300 metres of any postsecondary institution as well as from the downtown core (Map 8.1).

Thus, taken in isolation, these conditions had a direct impact on individuals' mobility and their access to public spaces and activism, but they were even more restrictive when they combined and overlapped, producing a multiplier effect with important and sometimes unexpected spatial consequences. Steve's example is instructive. He was arrested multiple times during the students' strike, including once for mischief and assault on a police officer after participating in a demonstration in April 2012 at the Montreal Convention Centre where the Quebec Premier was unveiling his "Northern Plan" to develop the mining industry in Quebec's North before the business community. The protest had turned into a violent confrontation, with police firing chemicals, rubber bullets, and tear gas at protesters.[3] As summarized in Table 8.1, Steve was released under more than a dozen extremely restrictive conditions, including a cash deposit of several thousand dollars, a prohibition not to be found on the Island of Montreal, a curfew, a no-contact condition with anyone who had a criminal record or pending cases, and a prohibition "not to be found inside any building or on any land owned by any learning institution or within a

---

[3] The social unrest was only exacerbated when the Premier joked that, as part of his Plan, "employers could offer the protesters jobs 'as far North as possible'" (Peritz, 2012).

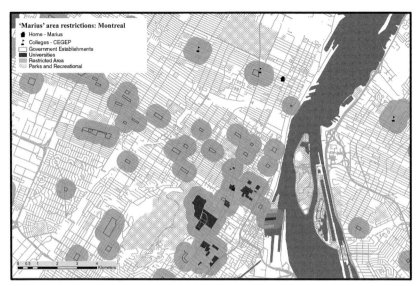

MAP 8.1 Marius's area restrictions (Montreal). First published in Sylvestre, Villeneuve Ménard, Fortin, Bellot, and Blomley, 2018
Source: Esri

100 metre radius of those, except to circulate on the public thoroughfare".[4] The last condition was particularly challenging. First, it was not place-specific, and could include the Island of Montreal as well as other surrounding cities, or even the entire province of Quebec. Secondly, but for the last part of the sentence, "except to circulate on the public thoroughfare", this condition would have basically prevented Steve from going anywhere. As Map 8.2 shows, if someone were to drive across the city, he or she would soon bump into important obstacles, let alone, as was the case for Steve, if he were to travel by bus or by foot. But, taken as a whole, this condition seems to support a particular form of urban governance: it supports the view that the public spaces surrounding any learning institution could be used in order to facilitate pedestrian flow and circulation, but not occupation, or the promotion of public citizenship and democracy (Blomley, 2010).

Perhaps even more importantly, for 15 months while he was on bail, Steve was evicted from his apartment, living right across the bridge on the south

[4] In the original, the condition requires that Steve "ne pas se trouver à l'intérieur de tout bâtiment ou sur tout terrain appartenant à une institution d'enseignement ou à moins de 100 m de ceux-ci sauf sur la voie publique pour y circuler".

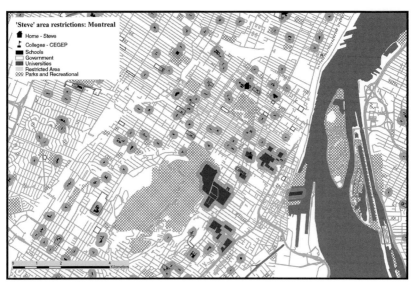

MAP 8.2 Steve's area restrictions (Montreal).
Sources: Esri, HERE, Garmin, USGS, Intermap, INCREMENT P, NRCan, Esri Japan, METI, Esri China
(Hong Kong), Esri Korea, Esri (Thailand), NGCC, © OpenStreetMap contributors, and the GIS User
Community

shore of Montreal, on the margins of his former existence. He used to spend
time at the Longueuil subway station, where he would wait for friends to visit
him at scheduled times, often in violation of his bail order, loitering, as he put
it, in a space of non-existence (Coutin, 2000):

> I had never lived in Longueuil. I had nothing to do but life went on for my
> friends. I sat on the same bench at the station for days and I waited for them
> to come and visit. I had put together a pseudo-schedule and my friends came
> in turn and stayed for 20 to 25 minutes before someone else came, and so
> on ... In a way, I was forced to loiter.

A Montreal student and experienced activist with an interest in women's
rights and prisoners' justice, Mary was arrested five times during the student
strike. Like Steve, she experienced the cumulative and intersecting force of
legal territorialization. She was first released on bail with a prohibition to
participate in any non-peaceful demonstration and to use any disguise in a
demonstration. She was caught a few weeks later wearing a mask and charged
with failure to comply. She was released under the same conditions but
caught the same evening while participating in a non-peaceful demonstration.
After her fourth breach, the justice of the peace was unforgiving. He gave her
three days to move out of her apartment and leave the "judicial district of

Montreal" (including the entire Island) completely, setting a curfew in the interim. During those three days, time was compressed as Mary scrambled to pack up her things and move out of her apartment to meet her deadline. Mary was banished from Montreal for most of the students' strike (from April to October), but then her conditions were modified, and a somewhat smaller red zone applied.

Interviewees struggled to cope with these forms of territorialized control. Like Steve, Emma relied on spatiotemporal schedules to endure house arrest: "I would have a different time of the day that I would be in different rooms of the house". She also developed projects, like reading, as coping mechanisms to mitigate against her sense of uselessness and inability to contribute to social movements. Zora largely confined herself to her bedroom in her parents' house while under arrest, carving out a form of autonomy, as "almost like a reclamation of my own life".

Many protesters resisted territorialization, creating spaces of resistance. Steve, for example, was allowed to be on the Island of Montreal to attend court, for medical appointments, or to meet with his lawyer. On those days, he also took the liberty to stop by his apartment and meet with a few friends, in violation of his conditions. Mary chose to ignore most of her conditions except those related to political participation, following what she described as "a risk management strategy": "the chances that cops at a demonstration recognize me … is a lot higher that a cop in the street, where there is a hundred of people and they are not really looking for me". In order to access downtown Montreal where she was prohibited, she let her hair grow long and changed the way she dressed. Finally, for Mary, the rhythm of the protest became crucial. The longer the conditions prevailed, the more comfortable she was in violating them, convinced that the police cared less about conditions once the students' strike started losing its momentum. As time passed, Nico also felt more comfortable violating his conditions. While he first started cooking for his friends instead of participating in demonstrations, he slowly became willing to take greater risks, expressing "the right to be in public space", wearing a mask, or using back alleys and demonstrating in other police precincts where he was less likely to be recognized. However, others were less daring: "many of my friends were careless about their conditions, but I couldn't make it work. If everyone is in jail for the cause, it doesn't help" (Anita).

Territorialization was deeply internalized, shaping prior understandings of personal autonomy and agency. For Sam, "what I realized the most was that I had a lack of control over my life. That was terrifying. My parents had control over my life. The court had control over my life. These undercovers had fucked up my life". Sam notes that she developed a stress-related illness while under house arrest, recognizing that she was in denial regarding its lingering traumatic effects. Other protestors suffered from poor mental health as a result of social precarity and political marginalization. Marius, who had been arrested in his apartment, experienced extreme anxiety problems. Convinced that he was under strict police surveillance, he didn't leave his apartment for at least two months except to buy groceries, and when he did, he hid in small laneways. Rick, assaulted and beaten by police after his arrest, and then threatened not to talk about it, noted that he was really scared after the G20 and so didn't talk about his experience. But he decided that "not talking about it was stressing [him] out and so [he] felt [he] needed to talk about it". He therefore risked breaching his no-protest condition and accepted an invitation from an activist group to speak at a library about his G20 experience, finding the experience to be "very therapeutic".

Sam's recognition that "the court had control over my life", and Marius's experience with confinement, speaks to the way in which legal territorialization not only severs but also connects. The conditionality of conditions of release presumes a system of surveillance and discipline, predicated on physical presence in space and time. The activists noted the manner in which they internalized the conditions, driven by fear. Zora admitted that she was "scared shitless ... I didn't want to do anything to rock the boat". Sam characterized this as "that panopticon effect, where you don't need to be there to be watching someone, because the threat of being watched is making them comply". Territorial control was thus achieved through self-surveillance and interiorization of disciplinary rules. For instance, Nico distinguished between the objective effects of conditions, and their internalized experience:

> It doesn't prevent you from being in the city and doing a little bit of what you want, *but it's like there's a prison in the city* ... where you always have a police officer in your head telling you that you can go this way, and that you cannot go that way ... and if you happen to go in the wrong direction, then watch yourself.
> (our emphasis)[5]

Activists thus internalized a territorialized grid that was at once seen as nakedly visible yet entirely opaque. While in a bakery with her mother, a surety, Sam reflected on this paradox:

---

[5] Foucault, 1977: 202): "He [*sic*] who is subjected to a field of visibility and who knows it, assumes responsibility for the constraints of power; he makes them play spontaneously upon himself; he inscribes in himself the power relation in which he simultaneously plays both roles; he becomes the subject of his own subjection".

I remember thinking like the person working here has no idea that I am potentially facing eight years in jail right now and on house arrest. I looked like a regular person, but I felt like there was this flashing sign above my head that only I can see – "house arrest, house arrest"!

Their potential visibility to the State shaped their encounters in space. "Every cop I saw", noted Carrie,

I sort of worked on the presumption that I could be having a very personal relationship with that person in that they know me and that they are looking for me rather than ... walking around the city and seeing the police and thinking it's not a big deal. In this case it was ... cops were no longer inconspicuous, like they were very conspicuous and *I presumed that I was conspicuous to them all the time'*.

(our emphasis)

Perhaps because of this sense of radical exposure in public space, some retreated into private space. Constantly afraid of being picked up, Mary confided that she avoided public space and "would always go to someone's house". Being in public space had become a very stressful experience, even after her conditions had been lifted: "I was walking home from my friend's house last night and there were several cops at each block, and there were no reasons for them to look at me, but there is always that fear that somebody will say 'wait a second!' and identify you from a crowd. So I felt better indoors". Steve concurred, yet resisted: "Public space is not that public. Most cops tell you to move on, to circulate, but you have no obligation to circulate. It just speaks to the fact that public space is *their* space" (original emphasis).

If territory communicates (Chapter 2), its meaning is not always clear to those governed by it, as we noted in the previous chapter. For example, conditions of release often required that activists avoid public demonstrations. Emma adopted the broadest interpretation, further constraining her political activity, and her spatial movements. This affected her use of space. She made a large detour to avoid the Occupy Ottawa encampment, for example, "just to be absolutely clear that I was going nowhere near it". Carrie was banned from associating with any "political groups", yet was unsure "if they consider so and so part of a banned group or not".

While the restrictions designated specific spaces to which people were confined or excluded, the nature and open-ended character of the conditions also created forms of temporal territorialization, activated at often unpredictable times. Zora noted that she was forbidden to associate with a list of 19 people, reading association as including simple co-presence ("anything from being in a room with them to being on a streetcar with them"). She described the resultant ban not as a fixed location, but as a "moving geography". Carrie similarly described this as a "roving exclusion zone":

> There would be times when I would walk into the room and one of my co-accused was there and one of us would have to go and it would be hard to figure that out despite not being able to talk . . . [I]t's like this *roving exclusion zone* that necessarily meant that when one person was in a space another couldn't be. So aside from hard geographic restrictions it was super fluid.
>
> (our emphasis)

Even after the removal of formal conditions, legal territorialization had an after-life, it seems, shaping the activist's engagement with space and time:

> While we were under conditions, we didn't go to a demo because we were too scared, and then when our conditions fell, they continued to affect our choices. Up until now, whenever I see a police officer, I freak out. I'm like, "don't look at me, don't talk to me", I keep my distances.
>
> (Anita)

Carrie noted that she still avoids certain spaces in Toronto, fearing that they will trigger anxiety: "these spaces have a history, for sure". Zora continues to participate in demonstrations but has learnt that the State uses people's position within a demonstration as an index of their political power within a movement. Her thought is, "Oh, I am at the front of the demo and I am talking to this person who is carrying a flag. I wonder if the cops are videotaping me right now . . . So, it's this extra layer of knowing what they are looking for and being aware of it". She describes how her formerly extroverted self has become socially anxious and paranoid: "I still sort of find myself hiding from being in a centre of a large room".

Given their political fluency, it is not surprising that many respondents were outspoken as to how they "had been completely deprived of all my rights as an individual", as Anita noted. Yet, there was little evidence of rights-based challenges by their lawyers: "there was not much taste for challenging it on, like, constitutional grounds", noted Carrie. The activists' lawyers were described by Zora as wanting "to be nice and not too pushy" [with the courts] or of trying to "get into the good graces of the Crown" (Carrie), with lawyers seeking small, incremental relaxation of the conditions. As a result, changing Zora's conditions from house arrest to living with her partner had "twelve or fifteen steps in it, according to my lawyer's friendly amendment mindset".

Given their political disposition, the activists sought to act collectively, and bring a group challenge to their conditions. However, this seemed to collide with the lawyer's client-based approach, whose "job is to look after one client [while] we wanted them to look after all twenty of us and they were like, 'what do you mean, that doesn't work, I am supposed to look after you?'" (Sam). But it could also have been in anticipation of the limits of rights-based challenges in similar cases, as hinted by Carrie: "I get it ... I'm in law school now and I looked into these things and the courts suck at protecting constitutional rights like freedom of assembly and freedom of association and expression ... The courts don't actually hold those things in very high esteem".[6]

As noted above, the legal actors we interviewed acknowledged that there were multiple obstacles facing those who wanted to challenge their conditions, including legal and contextual barriers related to spatiality and temporality of criminal justice administration (see Chapters 5 and 7 and Sylvestre et al., 2018), also expressing, when asked whether certain bail or probation conditions might impact fundamental rights, incomprehension and surprise. Of course, expressive rights in relation to demonstrations were recognized, but also seen as justifiably constrained by conditions of release if the rights of the "public" were unduly compromised:

---

[6] As a matter of fact, prohibitions to demonstrate have been found unconstitutional in the 1980s and 1990s, but more readily accepted by the courts after 2007. In 1982, a condition "not to attend at, demonstrate, obstruct or in any way cause a disturbance within a radius of one-half mile of the Litton systems" was found in violation of s. 2b) and c) of the Canadian Charter (freedom of expression and freedom of association and peaceful assembly), and not justified under s. 1 (*R. v. Collins* (1982) 31 C.R. (3d) 283 (Ont. Co. Ct.). The Ontario County Court held that rights could not be restricted based on speculative concerns and that the Crown must show compelling reasons to curtail them. In the *Fields* case, a condition imposing a complete ban to participate in "any strike or lockout of a firm, industry shop or any other employee/employer establishment" was found too broad and narrowed down to a specific labour conflict in Cambridge, Ontario. And a few years later the Quebec Superior Court made an important ruling in *R. v. Manseau* (1997) JQ no. 4553 (S.C.) (QL), holding that in order to respect individual rights, complete bans on demonstrations should not be imposed. Instead, they should be replaced by more circumscribed and tailored restrictions, such as prohibitions to demonstrate on any private property without the owner's consent or prohibitions to participate in any unlawful or illegal demonstrations as well as requirements to leave any demonstration as soon as it becomes non-peaceful or illegal. These conditions were subsequently followed, including outside of Quebec *R. v. Clarke* (2000) OJ No. 5738 (Ont. Sup. Ct.) (QL). In this case, the Ontario Superior Court found that both a condition not to demonstrate and a condition restricting the applicants from communicating with any member of the Ontario Coalition Against Poverty were in violation of s. 2b) and c) of the Charter. According to the Court, conditions not to communicate should also be individualized in order to withstand Charter scrutiny. See also *R. v. Gamblen*, 2013 ONCJ 661 with respect to non-association clauses (rejecting a constitutional argument based on s. 9 of the Charter). The situation started to change in 2007, however. For instance, in *R. c. Hébert* (2007 QCCS 7175 (Qc Sup. Ct.)); appeal dismissed on other grounds in (2010) QCCA 2210, the Quebec Superior Court upheld a probation condition imposing a complete ban on demonstrating and the Ontario courts soon followed in a series of cases growing out of the G20 protests and associated arrests, confirming restrictive bail conditions that included complete prohibitions from "organizing, participating in or attending any public demonstrations" (*R. v. Hundert* 2010 ONCJ 343; *R. v. Singh* (2011) ONSC 717). See Sylvestre et al., 2018.

Freedom of expression, of course, you can't keep people from expressing themselves, they just have to do it ... He has an individual right, but we also have collective rights, so his freedom stops where the freedom of others begins. From the moment he starts making trouble when he demonstrates, well ..., that's why I tell you that the condition happens when he sees that it's no longer peaceful, then he has to leave. But freedom of expression is a fundamental right, you can't really touch that.

(Prosecutor, Montreal)

As we have already noted, spatialized conditions of release were also seen by some legal actors as pragmatic means by which Charter rights could be circumvented by the police. As shown in Chapter 6, physical presence in a territorialized red zone is easier to monitor than, for example, possession of controlled substances. Similarly, spatial conditions of release (or temporal constraints) were seen by some legal actors as less likely to trigger a rights concern than more apparently personalized restrictions.

Similarly, when asked to comment on the decision to use a red zone rather than a ban on demonstrations, one legal actor indicated that a red zone did not immediately raise the same constitutional concerns:

We know that any restriction on participating in a demonstration is offensive because people may think that it entails a limit to freedom of expression, whereas *we do not have the same reservation for a red zone*. The ban on demonstrations directly attacks freedom of expression which is jealously guarded by everyone.

(Prosecutor, Montreal; our emphasis)

Similarly, when questioned in connection with an arrest during the student strike in Montreal, the spokesperson for the Director of Criminal and Penal Prosecutions indicated that prosecutors would generally not ask that the Court impose a condition not to demonstrate. According to him, "[t]he problem is not the demonstration. But demonstrating doesn't mean breaking windows ... We care about fundamental freedoms", he told a journalist from *La Presse* before mentioning that "*there are other ways of monitoring an individual* who tends to end up in the wrong place at the wrong time: *defining a red zone where he won't have the right to be, imposing a curfew*" (Desjardins, 2012; our emphases).

CONDITIONS OF RELEASE AND THE REMAKING OF URBAN SPACE

As our participants suggested, public spaces are strategically important because it is where dissent becomes visible. Being in public spaces with others in particular is crucial for political messaging and communication. For protesters, the choice of a site of protest is key to the message being proposed (Zick,

2009). Thus, by denying access to certain places, such as Toronto's financial district, university premises, or a specific meeting place such as Emilie Gamelin Park, courts directly participate in the definition and regulation of a particular "landscape of dissent" (Mitchell and Staeheli, 2005), where not only protests are confined to certain places and certain times, but certain messages associated to such places are silenced. When someone is red zoned from a certain place with symbolic or strategic relevance, he or she is prevented from expressing a particular message on certain issues. Indeed, "*where* voices are silenced makes a huge difference as to *which* voices are heard" (Mitchell and Staeheli, 2005, 798). Conditions of release regulate who can access designated spaces at specific times, thus playing a crucial role in the regulation of political dissent.

Similarly, as we saw in Chapter 7, the territorializing effect of conditions of release in controlling who can access space, and when, shapes the city and the possibilities it affords. This can have violent consequences, we demonstrated, placing already vulnerable bodies into enhanced forms of precarity. Conditions of release, far from a technical or dispassionate form of judicial regulation, are a powerful vector of discipline and control, deserving of our attention. In the concluding chapter, we reflect on our findings, and consider alternatives.

Conclusion

9

Red Zones in and out of the Courtroom

Spatial restrictions are concealed in plain sight. Sam, one of the Toronto protestors we interviewed, noted the paradox that her restrictions were invisible to outsiders, yet highly evident for her and legal actors: "I looked like a regular person but I felt like there was this flashing sign above my head that only I could see – "house arrest, house arrest!", she noted. Similarly, during a break from courtroom observations in Vancouver, we dropped into a community meeting of current and former drug users in Vancouver's Downtown Eastside. Our hardworking research assistant, Will Damon, knew many of the people in the room, and so we were welcomed warmly. Reminded of our interest in spatial restrictions, the people in the room became animated. One by one, they recounted, in detail, the often multiple red zones they had been subject to, or continued to be subject to, noting the petty tyrannies they experienced with their enforcement by police, their minimal but frustrating encounters with court actors, their daily negotiations and attempts at clandestine concealment when breaching their conditions, the legal violence they had undergone, and the impacts upon their most fundamental rights.

These people could attest to the significance and scope of spatial restrictions. Our primary goal in this project has been to make the work of red zones and other territorial conditions of release legible to others – notably scholars, policy-makers, and legal actors- documenting their widespread use and their often-violent effects on marginalized populations.

In order to do so, we conceptualize these conditions through the lens of territory, a bounded spacetime through which access is regulated or, in other words, a legal technology that organizes space and time in order to regulate relations of power within its boundaries through classification, communication, enforcement, displacement, and the cutting and joining of socio-legal relations. Such legal territory is also most immediately corporeal, acting on bodies: containing, directing, or excluding them. Where and when certain bodies are, and what those bodies are doing at any time, is a central concern of the criminal justice system, we show. In general, it seems, conditional orders are designed to position, remove, locate, or contain bodies that are deemed to be at risk to engage in objectionable legal acts (bodies having sex, consuming drugs, engaging in protests) (Chapter 2).

Red zones and other territorial conditions of release are a contemporary expression of a longstanding set of common law tools, many of them targeted at marginalized people, entailing the use of spatial strategies of containment, exclusion, and expulsion. Highly flexible and discretionary, such tools have served historically to advance state interests, rather than protecting individual liberties. They are now situated within wider shifts happening in the criminal justice system. In particular, the spatiotemporality of criminal justice administration has the effect of reducing resistance and rights-based challenges (Chapters 3 and 5).

Quantitative data presented in the first part of this book reveal that spatiotemporal restrictions have become pervasive, often imposed in contravention to the law and generating an important number of offences against the administration of justice through breaches of court orders. Initially conceived as an alternative to incarceration, such orders have effectively become a supplement to it. Failures to comply with a bail or probation order have consistently been the top two most common offences in adult criminal courts for at least a decade in Canada, amounting to approximately 25% of all criminal cases. Put bluntly, conditions of release generate crime, and in so doing the judicial system has enlarged itself while pushing vulnerable people into cycles of incarceration and surveillance (Chapter 4).

In the last part of the book, we suggested that territories were not inert spacetimes, but were actively made and experienced. As such, we exposed the context in which the work of territorialization is achieved, emphasizing how legal actors – and in particular state legal actors such as prosecutors, justices of the peace, and judges – actually performed the work of territorialization as well as illustrating their effects on those subject to such court orders.

The imposition of spatial conditions of release by legal actors, we revealed, is often highly routinized, and draws from a flexible interpretation of the legally sanctioned conditions for release in cases of bail and probation. Motivated by therapeutic, criminogenic, or "police" rationales, the effect is to enforce a territorial "cut" that simultaneously "joins" those subject to them to networks of legal surveillance and carceral control, placing already vulnerable bodies in situation of enhanced risk. The experience of spatial conditions of release is thus often far removed from these rationales. They are experienced as confusing, ambiguous, irrational, counterproductive, but also, more importantly, lived as forms of carceral violence. For protesters, the conditions had a direct impact on political organizing, neutralizing their voices during highly strategic times while also deeply affecting their personal lives. In short, we argued, legal actors perform the work of territorialization following rationalities that often directly clash with the lived experience and rationalities suffered by marginalized individuals (Chapters 6, 7, and 8).

In what follows, we begin by drawing together some scholarly threads. In addition to its most immediate goals, we hope this book also makes a wider contribution to related scholarship in law, space, and social ordering. We then go on to note the significant and curious absence of rights challenges to conditions of release, before concluding with our own rights-based argument for necessary reforms to the oppressions of the red zone.

SCHOLARLY CONTRIBUTIONS

A *Focus on Courts in the Production of Urban Space*

The first contribution of this book is the focus on the legal geographies of court-imposed spatial and temporal tactics. As noted, a great deal of scholarship concentrates on the specific role of the police and of legislatures in regulating urban public spaces through forms of spatial tactics. This entails forms of banishment, exclusion, and other forms of spatiotemporal regulation. While there are many useful insights to be garnered from this research, it is striking that very little has been written on the ways in which courts, and legal actors working within the criminal justice system (e.g. judges, justices of the peace, prosecutors, and defence lawyers) contribute, directly or indirectly, to the production of spatial governance. We have sought to fill this gap.

A *Focus on General Provisions of the* Criminal Law

Moreover, the overwhelming tendency is to confine the analysis to relatively visible (and occasionally controversial) legislative acts, as opposed to the often more quotidian forms of law's technical practice, such as the venerable instrument of bail or the use of probation. In contrast, the spatial restrictions we trace are not exceptional tools or the result of particular legislative interventions or policing strategies. Instead, they are rooted in technical criminal procedure or sentencing practices, relying on the general provisions of the Criminal Code of Canada and on common law principles. They are part of the mundane fabric of petty offences, deriving from the everyday processes and routines of criminal courts and of legal actors (Stuntz, 1997). This creates a sense of naturalness which makes challenges less likely to occur. This peculiarity has also allowed us to think directly about the nature and characteristics of contemporary criminal law and punishment, in particular as criminal law builds and incorporates administrative law logics and *dispositifs*, such as informality and minimal procedural safeguards (Vieira Velloso, 2013; Sylvestre et al., 2015).

A Deeper, Richer, and More Complex Understanding of Law and a Focus on Legal Practices

We engage with critical socio-legal and geographical scholarship by emphasizing the importance of understanding better the specifics of legal knowledge and processes in the analysis of the spatial regulation of urban spaces. While the tendency for social scientists interested in law might be to treat legal knowledge and technicalities as uninteresting, Riles insists on their importance, arguing that critical scholars "should care about technical legal devices because the kind of politics that they purport to analyze is encapsulated here" (2005: 975). Law's technicalities are political because they are linked to epistemological questions related to the production of knowledge, science, and truth (Riles, 2005; Valverde, 2009). More specifically, they are political because they serve as crucial "passage points" through which social contests pass. As such, the institutional frameworks they foreground may or may not close the door to certain types of arguments, such as rights. We also build on Silbey (1985) and other socio-legal scholars' conception of law as a social practice emphasizing the importance of court dynamics and context and the relationships between the different actors (judges, prosecutors, defence lawyers, court personnel, bail supervisors, etc.).

The Emphasis on Time, as Intimately Connected to Space

Legal geographers have paid insufficient attention to the different temporalities of law (Valverde, 2015), and the manner in which time and space are inseparable. We have focused on both. Conditional orders have important temporal dimensions that are intrinsically related to their spatiality. Technically speaking, they often include time, combined with curfews of specific duration (pending trial, probation orders can be up to three years). Designed to instantiate forms of behaviour, such as abstaining from involvement in the sex trade, drug use, or social protest, they rely on the assumption that behaviour may change over time, requiring repeated regulation. However, as demonstrated, the longer someone is required to comply with conditions, the more likely he or she is to be found in breach of these conditions. On a systemic level, we emphasize the peculiar spatiality and temporality of criminal justice administration, which are characteristic of a system in which people are managed over time through their engagement with particular spaces, such as the streets, the remand centre, or the courtroom.

Territory as a Violent Legal Technology

We have also tried to contribute to emergent scholarship on territory as a particular legal technology, structuring social relations through forms of classification, communication, enforcement, and displacement, organizing both space and time. We make sense of the work of territory as attempts at simultaneously *cutting* and *joining* socio-legal relations that acts upon bodies: directing them, containing them, and excluding them. Enrolling and legitimating force, law's territory also easily becomes a form of legal violence, curtailing the spatiotemporal potential for life to flourish.

THE RED ZONE: A RIGHTS-FREE TERRITORY?

Throughout the book, we have suggested that conditions of release trigger different rights violations, including the right to be presumed innocent and the right to bail, or, more specifically, demonstrators' expressive rights and a marginalized population's rights to life, liberty, and security of the person. Yet these issues rarely come to the forefront. When asked whether certain bail or probation conditions might impact fundamental rights during our interviews, legal actors almost systematically expressed incomprehension and surprise. They confirmed that it was unusual for them to make or hear such arguments.

The curious absence of rights is related to many factors that we tried to highlight, and which are worth restating here as this book comes to a close. These might include, as noted above, the routinized and technical nature of bail proceedings or sentencing practices. The fact that in some jurisdictions a specific bail form is in use, with boxes to check, or lists of conditions from which to choose, exemplifies the bureaucratic character of court-imposed condition-making.

More importantly, as explained in Chapter 5, the context in which conditional orders are imposed and policed on the street, particularly in the case of bail, does not provide the necessary space to discuss rights issues or challenges conditions. More specifically, our interviews and observations suggest a compounding set of circumstances that militates against a rights-based challenge to the prevailing system. First, alleged offenders are often in no position to raise these issues: they are held in overcrowded remand facilities while awaiting bail determination. Many use drugs, and thus undergo withdrawal or become dope sick: they wish to be released at any cost and will often readily accept the suggested bail conditions, having understood that "if you plead guilty, you get out today, but if you're innocent, you have to stay in" (Mills, 1971), and wait for a bail hearing; or after going through multiple adjournments, will be ready to plead guilty and be sentenced to a probation order. Furthermore, under pressure and struggling to survive, alleged offenders often forget crucial details (such as their doctor's office or harm reduction services being within a red zone).

Legal actors also have different limitations. Prosecutors are not always in a position to assess the significance of the spatial restrictions imposed by the police, to whom they tend to defer for their knowledge of where the "shifting hot spots" are located. While they will sometimes consider housing and access to services, including social, health, and legal services, they are also sensitive to the public interest, as filtered through community complaints and police concerns about certain neighbourhoods. Further, they are often tempted to follow established, if sometimes arbitrary, spatial templates. In turn, duty counsels, representing the alleged or convicted offenders, only have a few minutes to discuss what the conditions entail, and they sometimes advise their clients to accept all the conditions the prosecutor consents, given a concern that bail may be denied altogether at a hearing. Unless an objection is raised, judges will typically defer to prosecutors or are tempted to accept stricter conditions to avoid sending the accused to a remand centre. Overall, the prevalence of policing considerations can take precedence over and interfere with legislative and judicial objectives.

Other factors that militate against the possibility of raising legal or rights-based challenges also include, as alluded to in Chapter 7, limited legal remedies. Once they have been imposed, bail conditions can only be reviewed before the trial with the written consent of the prosecutor or in a separate proceeding before a Superior Court judge, and appellate courts will only intervene in sentencing conditions if there is an error of law or if the sentence is clearly unreasonable. As such, it never seems to be the right place and the right time to raise these questions.

Moreover, legal actors frequently trade off individual rights against other legal considerations and priorities, including the prevention of crime or of so-called recidivism (which too often only refers to breaches of court orders), the necessity of providing temporary relief to certain residents in the city, or even good-faith efforts to help or rehabilitate alleged offenders that often go unquestioned.

Further, the curious absence of rights may also be a function of their spatialization. Not only do State-scale constitutional rights rarely apply to "low-level" regulations (Valverde, 2015) or everyday court processes, but also, by developing conditions of release via quasi-technical and cartographic tools, the effect is to divert attention from the person – the bearer of rights – to the space itself. To the extent that red zones appear to act on spaces rather than people, they appear less contentious (Blomley, 2010). The governance of space, of course, entails the governance of the person. However, the effect of focusing on the former is to make rights-based arguments that much harder. As Cresswell puts it, spaces "appear to have their own rules, not the rules constructed for them" (1996: 159). As we noted in Chapter 2, territorialization operates not only through forms of practical classification, communication, and enforcement, but can also entail forms of "displacement", such that territorialization may serve to obfuscate the power relations that work in and through it, presumably because of the reified manner in which space is so often viewed. This can be highly consequential. In the specific context of demonstrators, Zick (2006), for example, notes the widespread use of spatial tactics in the regulation of speech, arguing that it is able to withstand judicial scrutiny because of a view of space as a passive container, rather than as itself constitutive of speech. As mentioned in Chapters 6 and 8, spatialized conditions of release were actually perceived by some legal actors as pragmatic means by which Charter rights could be circumvented (see also Sylvestre et al., 2018).

MAKING CHANGE

While those inside the red zone factory may have given up on rights, we refuse to do so. It is the recognition of the routine legal violences inflicted by spatial conditions of release that is at the heart of this book, and it is to those that we finally turn. It is deeply ironic that a set of legal techniques designed to inculcate forms of legal responsibility ultimately deny their own responsibility in the commission of human suffering and harm (Veitch, 2007). Spatial conditions of release sustain the divide between the actual and the potential, between the truncated lives of those we encountered and their full potential as human beings.

When we first started our project, one important and surprising finding was the relative lack of institutional reflection on conditions of release. Highly routinized, legal actors tend not to recognize their effects, intentional or otherwise. Fieldwork itself has provided some opportunities to raise awareness among legal actors on the extent of the phenomenon of spatial restrictions and their impact on the lives and rights of marginalized people. In British

Columbia, Quebec, and Ontario, community groups and civil liberties associations have long been active in documenting these violations (e.g. John Howard Society of Ontario, 2013; Canadian Civil Liberties Association and Education Trust, 2014; Pivot Legal Society, 2018). Our own research results were shared in two public reports in Vancouver (Sylvestre, Bellot, and Blomley, 2017) and Montreal (Sylvestre et al., 2018) and have attracted important media coverage (e.g. Dhillon, 2017; Lupick, 2017b; Corriveau, 2018; Winter, 2018). As a result, we have also been asked to speak and provide training to legal actors on conditions of release. We met with policy-makers and addressed parliamentarians (Sylvestre, 2018). And, thankfully, there is some momentum towards change. A series of institutional reformers in the last decade, including Geoffrey Cowper (2012; 2016) and Murray Segal (2016) in British Columbia, Raymond Wyant (2016) in Ontario, the members of the Justice Table in Quebec (Table Justice-Québec, 2016), and the most recent federal report by the Standing Senate Committee on Legal and Constitutional Affairs (2017), have belatedly recognized the need for sustained analysis and reform (although it should be noted that much of this has been driven by a desire to reduce court delays and institutional costs). Cowper, for instance, called for further study of offences against the administration of justice, and for appropriate reform, stating that administrative offences, directly generated by numerous and unreasonable conditions of releases, "is an area which remains in need of a system-wide response that will necessarily include careful research, sound data and evidence, and exploring collaborative alternatives through pilot programs" (2016: 8).

Most significantly, on April 1, 2019, the Public Prosecution Service of Canada (PPSC), which has participated to this study, released a new guideline "addressing bail conditions for accused with substance abuse disorders", in order to "address the epidemic of opioid overdoses". PPSC is responsible for the prosecution of offences against the Controlled Drugs and Substances Act in British Columbia. Relevant sections of the new guideline reads as follows:

> Public Prosecution Services of Canada (PPSC) prosecutors are directed, unless required by the circumstances of the case to address public safety or as part of a drug treatment court initiative, to adopt the following practices:
>
> 1. Seek to minimize or eliminate the imposition of certain bail conditions for individuals with a substance use disorder with the goal of minimizing short-term detentions for breaches of bail conditions. The determination of whether an individual has a substance use disorder should be based upon reliable information that may, for example, include representations provided by the Crown by the accused, defence counsel, caregivers, counsellors or the police.

2. The conditions that should generally not be imposed include:
   a. "not to be in possession of controlled substances";
   b. "not to be in possession of drug use paraphernalia"; and
   c. broad area restrictions. Area restrictions conditions, if imposed, must be carefully tailored to the specific offence and location.
3. Where, despite this such conditions having been imposed, and breach charges or new simple possession charges are being proposed as a result of an arrest, federal prosecutors should take steps to have the new charges dealt with on an out-of-custody basis unless public safety concerns require them to be dealt with on an in custody basis.

PPSC [···] should undertake discussions with the police and provincial prosecutors services and health care providers (as well as the judiciary and defence cousel as determined to be appropriate) in order to assist with the establishment of the specific regional practices that will help to ensure that such pre-trial custody not required to address public safety concerns are minimized and that conditions such as and conditions are avoided on police-release documents.

As will be discussed below, these changes should be commended and served as an example to provincial prosecution services.

Further, as mentioned in Chapter 4, in June 2019, the Canadian Parliament adopted Bill C-75 in order to

modernize and clarify interim release [bail] provisions to simplify the forms of release that may be imposed on an accused, incorporate a principle of restraint and require that particular attention be given to the circumstances of Aboriginal accused and accused from vulnerable populations when making interim release decisions.[1]

As will shall see below, many of C-75's amendments to the Criminal Code are steps in the right direction. For the most part, however, the changes are simply restatements of the status quo and do not go far enough to protect the rights of marginalized people and address the over-representation of those groups in the criminal justice system. As such, these amendments are not likely to trigger significant systemic changes to deeply ingrained legal practices.

The solutions to the situation we document here are not straightforward. We know that law plays a much wider and more powerful role in producing the marginalization that conditions of release respond to and often intensify. Many of those subject to conditions of release are already highly policed

---

[1] Bill C-75 has received royal assent on June 21, 2019 and can now be referenced to as S.C. 2019, c. 25.

and criminalized. The colonial conditions that propel large numbers of Indigenous people into the criminal justice system are, in many ways, a product of law. Despite important advances in fields such as harm reduction, the war against drugs continues to punish marginalized people even in the midst of the opioid crisis plaguing North America, one of the most important public health emergencies of recent times. Sex work also continues to be stigmatized and criminalized, putting everyday women, and men, in harm's way. Police power can often be expressed in highly discriminatory and capricious ways, with particular intensity in public spaces. In one sense, reforming conditions of release is in danger of overlooking the more systemic changes that are needed, requiring us to remember the perils of "non-reformist reform" (Gorz, 1968). Yet, on the principle that the legal technicalities and processes do, indeed, matter, it is appropriate to take on these technicalities, and seek to reduce the violent work they often do. In that light, some immediate changes to conditions of release need to be embraced. We suggest that the law and practices surrounding the imposition and negotiation of conditions of release, including red zones, should be completely revised. We start with bail.

As pointed out in Chapter 4, there is a pressing need for the recognition of prevailing law governing bail. *Unconditional release must be the norm for granting release*, as required by the Criminal Code, and must serve as a real alternative to remand, not a conduit to detention. We can only hope that the 2017 decision from the Supreme Court of Canada in *R. v. Antic*, and the adoption of a principle of restraint in Bill C-75, will send an important message to lower courts. As our data confirmed, at the moment, however, conditions of release have completely supplanted unconditional release. When the alternative to custody is unconditional release, it suddenly becomes easier to challenge unreasonable conditions of release. It also radically changes the power dynamic among legal actors, in particular for defence attorneys. Specifically, in order to reduce the prevalence of conditional release across the board, *we suggest that peace officers should not have the power to temporarily detain a person who does not pose a real and imminent threat to the safety of another person (a victim or a witness) or where there is little or no likelihood that the accused would be sentenced to incarceration if found guilty of the alleged offence.*[2] If incarceration following arrest is drastically limited

---

[2]   A similar provision was introduced in England in 2012 with respect to the powers of justices of the peace. The Bail Act 1976 was amended as follows: "A Justice of the Peace may not remand a person in, or commit a person to, custody under subsection (5) if . . . d) it appears to the justice of the peace that there is no real prospect that the person will be sentenced to a custodial sentence in the proceedings": Legal Aid, Sentencing and Punishment of Offenders Act 2012, Schedule 11, par. 8, as referred to in Ashworth and Zedner, 2014: 71.

and alleged offenders first appear before the court on interim release (as opposed to from custody), conditions of release may not be interpreted by legal actors, as they are now, as the lesser evil compared to remand.

The Criminal Code should also be amended so as to clarify the legitimate objectives of bail. In this regard, Bill C-75 left those completely untouched. In our view, conditions should only be imposed to ensure the accused's attendance in court (first ground) or in order to avoid serious and imminent harm (second ground), as per s. 515 (10) Cr. C. *Conditions imposed to ensure that the accused will appear in court should also be proportionate to the gravity of the alleged offence.* For instance, it is hardly justifiable to keep a drug user in remand or under restrictive, and sometimes life-threatening, conditions of release in order for them to appear in court for minor offences, such as drug possession for the purposes of trafficking (often to sustain an addiction), small theft or fraud, or breaches.

Conditions imposed following the second ground (i.e. avoiding serious and imminent harm) should only be imposed if there is a substantial likelihood that, if released, the accused will commit a criminal offence involving serious harm.[3] At the moment, legal actors tend to focus on the likelihood that the accused, if released, might be committing *any* criminal offence or interfere with the administration of justice, regardless of the gravity or seriousness of the future offence, or of any kind of proportionality between the nature of the restrictions imposed and that of the interference. The importance legal actors attach to crime prevention regardless of its gravity is particularly problematic, as courts often do not have adequate evidence to sustain any risk analysis or base their decisions on evidence that would not be sufficient to justify a conviction (Ashworth and Zedner, 2014: 70). The fact that the accused are subject to reverse onus in many cases, including in the context of breach and drug charges, only adds to the problem.[4] Bill C-75 did not repeal such reverse onuses.

Bail conditions should also *not be used to facilitate the surveillance and arrest of marginalized people.* Most conditions of release are first imposed by the police and, more often than not, ratified by prosecutors or courts (or slightly revised to ensure enforceability). Policing objectives are often at odds with judicial objectives, including the protection of fundamental rights.

---

[3] Note that this is exactly what the Bail Reform Act of 1970 implied. After the Act came into force, it was, however, amended to drop the words "involving serious harm" so that an accused could be denied bail if there was a likelihood that he or she could commit any offence, not just an offence involving serious harm. See Friedland, 2012: 320.

[4] See e.g. subsections 515(6) c) and d) Cr. C.

Courts should not be used to relay or respond to surveillance or bureaucratic imperatives.

Finally, bail conditions should not seek rehabilitation. Although legal actors are aware that rehabilitation should not be pursued at bail, in practice, the boundary between crime prevention and rehabilitation is often blurred. Many marginalized individuals who end up in the criminal justice system do so as a result of prior massive rights violations, including violations to their rights to life and security, equality without discrimination, health, housing, and to a minimum income. It is only fair to suggest that their most fundamental needs should be met. Yet, the criminal system justice, and bail in particular as individuals are still presumed innocent, cannot be the main point of entry to have access to such services. Diversion and the use of "appropriate measures"[5] in partnership with community groups and health and social services should become the norm with respect to dealing with minor offences, such as breaches, drug offences, and crimes against property, insofar as they are often directly connected to survival in the streets, or physical and mental health issues.

In fact, imposing unreasonable conditions amounts to denying judicial interim release and denying the right to reasonable bail, as Judge Rosborough reminded us in *R. v. Omeasoo*. These comments are worth repeating:

> It is trite to say that conditions in an undertaking which the accused cannot or almost certainly will not comply with cannot be reasonable. Requiring the accused to perform the impossible is simply another means of denying judicial interim release. The same would apply to conditions which, although not impossible in a technical sense, are so unlikely to be complied with as to be practically impossible. An example of that would be to release the impecunious accused on $1 million cash bail on the basis that he could buy a lottery ticket and potentially win enough money to post that cash bail.[6]

As such, certain conditions, including those targeted by PPSC's new Guideline, should be avoided at all costs. Red zones and other territorial

---

[5] "An important point raised by Kevin Fenwick, then Deputy Minister and Deputy Attorney General with the Government of Saskatchewan's Ministry of Justice, was of the need to be wary of using the term 'alternative' when talking about programs that divert accused persons and offenders away from the traditional courthouse route, saying that he preferred the term 'appropriate measures'. The committee concurs, since 'alternative' suggests that such measures present a separate kind of justice or a different legal culture. What became clear from our study is that these measures have support across a diverse range of stakeholders in the justice system": Standing Senate Committee on Legal and Constitutional Affairs, 2017: 143.

[6] *R. v. Omeasoo* (2013) ABPC 328, par. 33.

conditions of release, our study showed, are particularly problematic for marginalized populations. They are among the most commonly imposed and the most commonly breached. *It is essential that territorialized conditions be used only in cases where the accused poses a real and imminent threat to the safety of another person* (see also Pivot Legal Society, 2018: 102). Prior to the adoption of Bill C-75, section 503(2.1) of the Criminal Code did not contain specific provisions allowing peace officers to impose geographical conditions and we are concerned that the newly enacted section 501(3) will create an incentive to impose such conditions and remain unchecked. Indeed, when a police officer releases an accused, conditions are not systematically reviewed by prosecutors except at the request of the accused. It may take several weeks, or even months, before the accused appears and those conditions are revised for the first time. In some cases, the charges will be never be filed by the prosecution leading to abuses of authority.

Finally, let us emphasize that *legal aid programs should be adequately funded* to make sure that the right to a reasonable bail is respected.

At the sentencing stage, *legal actors should be much more parsimonious in the manner in which they craft individualized legal orders*, while paying attention to the type of conditions they impose to facilitate offenders' rehabilitation. They should create and reinforce their *partnerships with health and social services as well as community groups* who should be consulted about rehabilitation programs. Such groups should not, however, be enrolled in the enforcement of conditions of release. The *number of conditions should be strictly limited.* Our regression analysis clearly showed that multiplying restrictive conditions in probation orders increases the likelihood of breach significantly. Moreover, our interviews with individual subject to court orders demonstrated how counterproductive and life threatening some of these conditions are. Legal actors are not social workers, and despite the fact that they are constantly asked to deal with social problems, they should defer to those who have the relevant expertise, including marginalized populations themselves. In doing so, legal actors have to accept that there are no single or customized answer to the profound traumas experienced by marginalized people. While they need to get involved, they also need to stop reinforcing criminalization patterns and realize that a series of court-imposed conditions is not likely to resolve years of suffering and violence without proper peer and community support.

In particular, in crafting sentencing orders, legal actors should avoid imposing red zones and other territorial restrictions that *fail to sustain rehabilitation and that, in some cases, significantly increase the likelihood of breaching.* Keeping a person away from a specific area does not necessarily produce the intended results. Moreover, although this type of conditions was not at the heart of this study, we know from research that imposing prohibitions to use drugs or alcohol only set up drug users to fail and increase their vulnerability (e.g. Pivot Legal Society, 2018). This is particularly true of Indigenous individuals struggling with addiction (e.g. *R. v. Omeasoo* (2013)). As such, harm reduction programs, as opposed to complete abstinence, need to become part of court orders. Although harm reduction strategies are only one step towards recovery, they are life-saving and an important signal to users that they matter and are equal in security and dignity. As mentioned in our regression analysis, requiring people to stay in a treatment centre for short periods of time seems to have a positive impact on their ability to abide by their court order, but law abidance cannot be an end in itself, nor the only response to addiction problems. In many cases, this will also require investing in supported housing and social programs. As a result, legal actors should aim at better identifying the problems in a person's life and the appropriate resources they need in order to protect them from reoffending, instead of creating the conditions that maintain them under judicial supervision while interfering with important care. The same principles should apply to conditional sentences with the necessary adjustments in light of the fact that they are incarceration sentences.

Important changes should also be put in place with respect to offences against the administration of justice. Our research has shown the importance of such offences and their impact on the likelihood that an accused will remain in custody, be found guilty, and sentenced to imprisonment (see Chapter 4). Marginalized people quickly sink into a downward spiral of broken conditions and subsequent incarceration. In Montreal, there is a strong correlation between breaching and the accumulation of court cases. In this sense, recidivism is *institutional rather than criminal*: that is, people accumulate cases because they do not respect their conditions, often for predictable and understandable reasons, rather than because they commit new substantive criminal offences.

We thus suggest that police and prosecution services across the country develop *guidelines and set institutional targets in order to reduce significantly the number of offences against the administration of justice*. Such guidelines could in part be modeled on PPSC's. They could also include the obligation for police officers and prosecutors to justify the conditions imposed in release orders and to make sure that defendants can comply with those conditions before imposing them. Targets should be monitored and reviewed annually, and the data should be publicly available.

Bill C-75 also created a new process, the "judicial referral hearing", to deal with administration of justice offences. During this hearing, if the justice of the peace or judge, who hears the matter is satisfied that the failure to comply with a court order did not cause a victim physical or emotional harm, property damage or economic loss, he or she shall review any conditions of release imposed on the accused and may decide to take no action, make a new release order, or remand the accused to custody. Such a decision involves dismissing any charge for breach that had been laid against the accused. It is possible (and desirable) that this new process will have a dissuasive effect on prosecutors and ultimately reduce the number of offences against the administration of justice. But it is also possible that these changes will only institutionalize an unofficial practice that is already before the courts (especially in Vancouver) and where prosecutors repeatedly bring the accused who breach their conditions back before the judge so that they receive a simple "warning" and then withdraw the breach charges. This round of court appearances, which are often accompanied by short periods of pre-trial detention, might therefore continue to clog the justice system while having significant consequences for the most vulnerable of the accused, including, for example, by exposing them to a state of withdrawal, increasing the risk of overdosing, and depriving them of the health services they need. In addition, it is possible that this new process will have a net-widening effect (see Chapter 4), increasing the control on persons who would not have been subject to such a review for breach of conditions because of the low severity of the alleged breach. It would be more effective to *completely decriminalize the breaching of conditions that do not cause harm or threaten to cause harm to victims*. In doing so, peace officers, prosecutors, and justices would be required strictly to define conditions of release and to limit themselves to a series of conditions that concern the safety of victims or witnesses and attendance in court. Let us not forget that at the bail stage the person subject to conditions is always presumed innocent under law.

Such legislative changes, if adopted, are likely to provide the right kind of incentives, but may not change deeply ingrained cultural risk-aversion practices, unless courts and legal actors acknowledge how counterproductive and harmful these practices are and accept that they are a small, but essential, part of the solution. This can start with the development of a spatiotemporal imaginary, that is an understanding of how law, space, and time, when combined, represent powerful techniques of power and regulation and how they could be curtailed. We hope this book has helped in advancing the significance and value of such a critical legal geographical sensibility.

Ultimately, we hope that this book has contributed to rendering visible previously invisible practices of discrimination that have a disparate impact on marginalized people at a systemic level, and that it will provide the basis for significant changes in how we deal with the social problems that criminalization tends to hide and reproduce. Spatiotemporal conditions of release constitute a vast matrix of territorial control, invisible to most. In making the "red zone", and the work it does, legible, we hope to reveal these hidden legal geographies, and name and contest the violences they produce.

Bibliography

Adam, B. (1990) *Time and Social Theory.* Philadelphia, PA: Temple University Press.

Agamben, G. (2005) *State of Exception.* Chicago, IL: University of Chicago Press.

Alexander, B. K. (2001) "The Roots of Addiction in Free Market Society". Canadian Centre for Policy Alternatives. www.policyalternatives.ca/publications/reports/roots-addiction-free-market-society.

Alexander, G. S., and E. M. Peñalver (2012) *An Introduction to Property Theory.* Cambridge: Cambridge University Press.

Allen, J. (1999) "Spatial Assemblages of Power: From Domination to Empowerment", in D. Massey, J. Allen, and P. Sarre (eds) *Human Geography Today.* Cambridge: Polity Press.

(2011) "Topological Twists: Power's Shifting Geographies". *Dialogues in Human Geography* 1(3): 283–298.

Allspach, A. (2010) "Landscapes of (Neo)Liberal Control: The Transcarceral Spaces of Federally Sentenced Women in Canada". *Gender, Place, and Culture* 17(6): 705–723.

Ancelovici, M., and F. Dupuis-Déri (2014) *Un printemps rouge et noir: regards croisés sur la grève étudiante de 2012.* Montreal: Écosociété.

Ares, C. E., A. Rankin, and H. Sturz (1963) "The Manhattan Bail Project: An Interim Report on the Use of Pre-Trial Parole". *New York University Law Review* 38: 67–95.

Ashworth, A., and L. Zedner (2008) "Defending the Criminal Law: Reflections on the Changing Character of Crime, Procedure, and Sanctions". *Criminal Law and Philosophy* 2(1): 21–51.

(2010) "Preventive Orders: A Problem of Undercriminalization", in R. A. Duff, L. Farmer, S. E. Marshall, M. Renzo, and V. Tadros, *The Boundaries of the Criminal Law.* Oxford: Oxford University Press.

(2014) *Preventive Justice.* Oxford: Oxford University Press.

Attorney General of the United States (1963) *Report of the Attorney General's Committee on Poverty and the Administration of Federal Criminal Justice,* Submitted to the Honorable Robert F. Kennedy, Attorney General of the United States, February 25, 1963. Washington, DC: Government Printing Office.

Auditor General of British Columbia (2011) Effectiveness of BC Community Corrections, 7 December. www.bcauditor.com/pubs/2011/report10/bc-community-corrections-cccp.

Baer, L. D. (2005) "Visual Imprints on the Prison Landscape: A Study on the Decorations in Prison Cells". *Tijdschrift voor economische en sociale geografie* 96(2): 209–217.

Balbus, I. D. (1973) *The Dialectics of Legal Repression: Black Rebels before the American Criminal Courts*. New York: Russell Sage Foundation.

Beattie, K., A. Solecki, and K. E. Morton Bourgon (2013) *Police and Judicial Detention and Release Characteristics: Data from the Justice Effectiveness Study*. Research and Statistics Division, Department of Justice Canada. http://publications.gc.ca/collections/collection_2018/jus/J4-65-2013-eng.pdf.

Beckett, K., and S. Herbert (2008) "Dealing with Disorder: Social Control in the Post-industrial City". *Theoretical Criminology* 12(1): 5–30.

(2010a) *Banished: The New Social Control in Urban America*. Oxford: Oxford University Press.

(2010b) "Penal Boundaries: Banishment and the Expansion of Punishment". *Law & Social Inquiry* 35(1): 1–38.

Beckett, K., and H. Evans (2015) "Crimmigration at the Local Level: Criminal Justice Processes in the Shadow of Deportation". *Law & Society Review* 49(1): 241–277.

Beckett, K., and N. Murakawa (2012) "Mapping the Shadow Carceral State: Toward an Institutionally Capacious Approach to Punishment". *Theoretical Criminology* 16(2): 221–244.

Bellot, C. (2003) "Les jeunes de la rue: disparition ou retour des enjeux de classe?" *Lien social et politiques* 49 : 173–182.

Bellot C., and M.-E. Sylvestre (2017) "La judiciarisation de l'itinérance à Montréal: les dérives sécuritaires de la gestion pénale de la pauvreté", *Revue générale de droit* 47: 11–44.

Betina, B. (2010) "From Disciplining to Dislocation: Area Bans in Recent Urban Policing in Germany". *European Urban and Regional Studies* 14(4): 321–334.

Bisharat, G. (2014) "The Plea Bargain Machine". *Dilemas: Revista de Estudos de Conflito e Controle Social* 7(3): 767–795.

Blomley, N. (2003) "From 'What?' to 'So What?' Law and Geography in Retrospect", in J. Holder and C. Harrison (eds) *Law and Geography*, Current Legal Issues, vol. 5. Oxford: Oxford University Press: 17–33.

(2004) *Unsettling the City: Urban Land and the Politics of Property*. London: Routledge.

(2007) "How to Turn a Beggar into a Bus Stop: Law, Traffic and the Function of Place". *Urban Studies* 44(9): 1697–1712.

(2008) "Civil Rights Meet Civil Engineering: Urban Public Space and Traffic Logic". *Canadian Journal of Law and Society* 22(2): 55–72.

(2009) "Homelessness and the Delusions of Property". *Urban Geography* 30(6): 577–590.

(2010) *Rights of Passage: Sidewalks and the Regulation of Public Flow*. London: Routledge.

(2012) "Coloured Rabbits, Dangerous Trees and Public Sitting: Sidewalks, Police and the City". *Urban Geography* 33(7): 917–935.

(2014a) "Disentangling Law: The Practice of Bracketing". *Annual Review of Law and Social Science* 10: 133–148.

(2014b) "The Ties That Blind: Making Fee Simple in the British Columbia Treaty Process". *Transactions of the Institute of British Geographers* 40(2): 168–179.

Blomley, N., and J. Bakan (1992) "Spacing Out: Towards a Critical Geography of Law". *Osgoode Hall Law Journal* 30(3): 661–690.

Bogomolny, R., and M. Sonnenreich (1969) "The Bail Reform Act of 1966: Administrative Tail Wagging and Other Legal Problems". *Arizona Law Review* 11: 201–228.

Bourdieu, P. (1977) *Outline of a Theory of Practice*, Cambridge Studies in Sociology, vol. 16. Cambridge: Cambridge University Press.

(1985) "The Social Space and the Genesis of Groups". *Theory and Society* 14(6): 723–744.

Braverman, I., N. Blomley, D. Delaney, and A. Kedar (2014) *The Expanding Spaces of Law: A Timely Legal Geography*. Stanford, CA: Stanford University Press.

Brighenti, A. (2006) "On Territory as Relationship and Law as Territory". *Canadian Journal of Law and Society* 21(2): 65–86.

Bright, D. (1995) "Loafers Are Not Going to Subsist upon Public Credulence: Vagrancy and the Law in Calgary, 1900–1914". *Labour/Le Travail* 36 (1995): 37–58.

Brown, E. (2014) "Expanding Carceral Geographies: Challenging Mass Incarceration and Creating a 'Community Orientation' towards Juvenile Delinquency". *Geographica Helvetica* 69: 377–388.

Bryan, J. (2012) "Rethinking Territory: Social Justice and Neoliberalism in Latin America's Territorial Turn". *Geography Compass* 6(4): 215–226.

Burczycka, M., and C. Munch (2015) "Trends in Offences against the Administration of Justice". 15 October. Statistics Canada. *Juristat* 35(1). www150.statcan.gc.ca/n1/en/pub/85-002-x/2015001/article/14233-eng.pdf?st=INq2Xv4K.

Caldeira, T. P. R. (2000) *City of Walls: Crime, Segregation, and Citizenship in São Paulo: Crime, Segregation and Citizenship in Sao Paulo*. Berkeley: University of California Press.

Callon, M. (1998a) "Introduction: The Embeddedness of Economic Markets in Economics", in M. Callon (ed.) *The Laws of the Markets*. Oxford: Blackwell: 1–57.

(1998b) "An Essay on Framing and Overflowing: Economic Externalities Revisited by Sociology". *Sociological Review* 46(1 suppl.): 244–269.

Canadian Civil Liberties Association and Education Trust [A. Deshman and N. Myers] (2014) *Set up to Fail: Bail and the Revolving Door of Pre-Trial Detention*. Toronto: Canadian Civil Liberties Association.

Cape, E., and R. A. Edwards (2010) "Police Bail without Charge: The Human Rights Implications". *Cambridge Law Journal* 69(3): 529–560.

Carnegie Community Action Project (2016) *Out of Control: The Rate of Change and Rents in the Downtown Eastside*. Vancouver: Carnegie Community Centre. www.carnegieaction.org/wp-content/uploads/2017/03/CCAP-SRO-HOTEL-REPORT-2016.pdf.

Carr, J., E. Brown, and S. Herbert (2009) "Inclusion under the Law as Exclusion from the City: Negotiating the Spatial Limitation of Citizenship in Seattle". *Environment and Planning A: Economy and Space* 41(8): 1962–1978.

Carson, E. A. (2014) *Prisoners in 2014*. Washington, DC: Bureau of Justice Statistics of the U.S. Department of Justice. www.bjs.gov/content/pub/pdf/p14.pdf.

Chesnay, C., C. Bellot, and M.-E. Sylvestre (2013) "Taming the Disorderly One Ticket at the Time: The Penalization of Homeless People in Ontario and British Columbia". *Canadian Journal of Criminology and Criminal Justice* 55(1): 161–186.

Cheung, C. (2018) "By the Numbers: Metro Vancouver's Increasing Inequality and Division". *The Tyee*. 15 November 2018. https://thetyee.ca/News/2018/11/15/Metro-Vancouver-Inequality-Division/.

Chiste, K. B. (2005) "The Justice of the Peace in History: Community and Restorative Justice". *Saskatchewan Law Review* 68: 153–172.

Chowdhury, G. (2003) "Natural Language Processing". *Annual Review of Information Science and Technology* 37: 51–89.

Chute, G. R. (1928) "The Totuava Fishery of the California Gulf". *California Fish and Game* 14(4): 275–281.

Clare, N., V. Habermehl, and L. Mason-Deese (2018) "Territories in Contestation: Relational Power in Latin America". *Territory, Politics, Governance* 6(3): 302–321.

Cloatre, E., and N. Wright (2012) "A Socio-Legal Analysis of an Actor-World: The Case of Carbon Trading and the Clean Development Mechanism". *Journal of Law and Society* 39(1): 76–92.

Cohen, S. (1979) "The Punitive City: Notes on the Dispersal of Social Control". *Contemporary Crises* (3): 339–363.

   (1985) *Visions of Social Control: Crime, Punishment, and Classification*. Cambridge: Polity Press.

Collins, D., and N. Blomley (2003) "Private Needs and Public Space: Politics, Poverty and Anti-Panhandling By-Laws in Canadian Cities", in Law Commission of Canada, *New Perspectives on the Public–Private Divide*. Vancouver: UBC Press: 40–67.

Commission for Public Complaints against the RCMP (2001) *Commission Interim Report: Following a Public Hearing into the Complaints Regarding the Events That Took Place in Connection with Demonstrations during the Asia Pacific Economic Cooperation Conference in Vancouver, B.C. in November 1997 at the UBC Campus and at the UBC and Richmond Detachments of the RCMP*. Ottawa: Commission for Public Complaints against the RCMP.

Correctional Services Program (2017) "Trends in the Use of Remand in Canada 2004/2005 to 2014/2015". Statistics Canada. *Juristat* 37(1). www150.statcan.gc.ca/n1/pub/85-002-x/2017001/article/14691-eng.htm.

Corriveau, J. (2018) "Plaidoyer contre les dérives des conditions de libération". *Le Devoir*. 9 April 2018. www.ledevoir.com/societe/524759/plaidoyer-pour-mettre-fin-au-cycle-infernal-du-non-respect-des-conditions.

Costello, K. (2014) "'More Equitable than Justice of the Peace': The King's Bench and the Poor Law, 1630–1800". *Journal of Legal History* 35(1): 3–26.

Coutin, S. B. (2000) *Legalizing Moves: Salvadoran Immigrants' Struggle for U.S. Residency*. Ann Arbor: University of Michigan Press.

Cover, R. M (1986) "Violence and the Word". *Yale Law Journal* 95(8): 1601–1629.

Cowper, D. G. (2012) "A Criminal Justice System for the 21st Century". Final Report to the Minister of Justice and Attorney General Honourable Shirley

Bond. 27 August. www2.gov.bc.ca/assets/gov/law-crime-and-justice/about-bc-just
ice-system/justice-reform-initiatives/cowperfinalreport.pdf.

(2016) "A Criminal Justice System for the 21st Century". Fourth Anniversary Update
to the Minister of Justice and Attorney General, Suzanne Anton, QC. 19 October.
www2.gov.bc.ca/assets/gov/law-crime-and-justice/about-bc-justice-system/justice-
reform-initiatives/cowper-report-4-anniversary-update.pdf.

Cox, E. (2012) "400,000+ in the Streets? Quebec's Students Are Winning. . ." [blog].
http://rabble.ca/blogs/bloggers/ethan-cox/2012/05/500000-streets-quebecs-students-
are-winning.

Craig, E. (2011) "Sex Work by Law: Bedford's Impact on Municipal Approaches to
Regulating the Sex Trade". *Review of Constitutional Studies* 16(1): 97–120.

Crawford, A. (2008) "Dispersal Powers and the Symbolic Role of Anti-Social Behaviour
Legislation". *Modern Law Review* 7: 753–784.

(2015) "Temporality in Restorative Justice: On Time, Timing and Time- Consciousness". *Theoretical Criminology* 19(4): 470–490.

Crawford, C. E. (ed.) (2010) *Spatial Policing: The Influence of Time, Space, and
Geography on Law Enforcement Practices.* Durham, NC: Carolina Academic Press.

Cresswell, T. (1996) *In Place/Out of Place: Geography, Ideology and Transgression.*
Minneapolis: University of Minnesota Press.

Damon, W. G. (2014) "Spatial Tactics in Vancouver's Judicial System". MA thesis,
Simon Fraser University.

Davis, M. (2011) *City of Quartz: Excavating the Future in Los Angeles.* London: Verso.

De Haas, E. (1940) *Antiquities of Bail: Origin and Historical Development in Criminal
Cases to the Year 1275.* New York: Columbia University Press.

DeCicco, J. (1973) "Pretrial Bail". *Criminal Justice Quarterly* 1: 66.

DeL., H. F. (1940) "'Preventive Justice': Bonds to Keep the Peace and for Good
Behavior". *University of Pennsylvania Law Review and American Law Register*
88(3): 331–347.

DeVerteuil, G., J. May, and J. von Mahs (2009) "Complexity Not Collapse: Recasting
the Geographies of Homelessness in a 'Punitive' Age". *Progress in Human Geography* 33(5): 646–666.

Delaney, D. (2005) *Territory: A Short Introduction.* Oxford: Blackwell.

(2010) *The Spatial, the Legal and the Pragmatics of World-Making: Nomospheric
Investigations.* New York: Routledge.

dell'Agnese, E. (2013) "The Political Challenge of Relational Territory", in D. Feath-
erstone and J. Painter (eds) *Spatial Politics: Essays for Doreen Massey.* Chichester:
John Wiley & Sons: 115–124.

Department of Justice Canada (2009) "The Justice System Costs of Administration of
Justice Offences in Canada". Research and Statistics Division, January 2013. http://
publications.gc.ca/collections/collection_2018/jus/J4-64-2013-eng.pdf.

Dépelteau, F. (ed.) (2018) *The Palgrave Handbook of Relational Sociology.* Basingstoke:
Palgrave Macmillan.

Derrida, J. (1990) "Force of Law: The 'Mystical Foundation of Authority'". *Cardozo
Law Review* 11(5): 919–1045.

Desjardins, C. (2012) "Une manifestante derrière les barreaux". *La Presse.* 26 April.
www.lapresse.ca/actualites/dossiers/conflit-etudiant/201204/26/01-4519274-une-man
ifestante-reste-derriere-les-barreaux.php.

Desmond, C. E. (1952) "Bail: Ancient and Modern". *Buffalo Law Review* 1: 245–248.

Dhillon, S. (2017) "Report Slams Use of Court-Imposed 'Red Zones' in Vancouver". *Globe and Mail.* 31 October. https://beta.theglobeandmail.com/news/british-col umbia/report-slams-use-of-court-imposed-red-zones-in-vancouver/art icle36792921/?ref=http://www.theglobeandmail.com&.

Dirsuweit, T. (1999) "Carceral Spaces in South Africa: A Case Study of Institutional Power, Sexuality and Transgression in a Women's Prison". *Geoforum* 30(1): 71–83.

Douzinas, C. (2006) "Thesis on Law, History and Time". *Journal of International Law* 7: 13–27.

Dubber, M. (2005) *The Police Power: Patriarchy and the Foundations of American Government.* New York: Columbia University Press.

Duker, W. (1977) "The Right to Bail: A Historical Inquiry". *Albany Law Review* 42: 33–120.

Dumontier, A. (1972) *La loi sur la réforme du cautionnement.* Les Cahiers de droit. Quebec: Faculté de droit de l'Université Laval.

Duneier, M. (2000) *Sidewalk.* New York: Farrar, Straus & Giroux.

Dupuis-Déri, F. (2013) *À qui la rue?: répression policière et mouvements sociaux,* Montreal: Les Éditions Écosociété.

Ehrlich, J. W. (1959) *Blackstone's Commentaries on the Laws of England.* New York: Capricorn Books.

Elden, S. (2005) "Missing the Point: Globalization, Deterritorialization and the Space of the World". *Transactions of the Institute of British Geographers,* 30(1): 8–19.

——— (2010) "Land, Terrain, Territory". *Progress in Human Geography* 34(6): 799–827.

Emirbayer, M. (1997) "Manifesto for a Relational Sociology". *American Journal of Sociology* 103(2): 281–317.

England, M. (2008) "Stay Out of Drug Areas: Drugs, Othering and Regulation of Public Space in Seattle, Washington". *Space and Polity* 12(2): 197–213.

Ericson, R., and A. Doyle (2003). *Risk and Morality.* Toronto: University of Toronto Press.

Esmonde, J. (2002) "Criminalizing Poverty: The Criminal Law Power and the Safe Streets Act". *Journal of Law and Social Policy* 17: 63–86.

——— (2003) "Bail, Global Justice and the Limits of Dissent". *Osgoode Hall Law Journal* 41 (2): 323–359.

Farmer, L. (2010) "Time and Space in Criminal Law". *New Criminal Law Review: An International and Interdisciplinary Journal* 13(2): 333–356.

——— (2014) "Response 2: Criminal Law as a Security Project". *Criminology & Criminal Justice* 14(4): 399–404.

Feeley, M. (1992) [1979] *The Process Is the Punishment: Handling Cases in a Lower Criminal Court.* New York: Russell Sage Foundation.

——— (1997) "Legal Complexity and the Transformation of the Criminal Process: The Origins of Plea Bargaining". *Israel Law Review* 31: 183.

Feeley, M., and J. Simon (1992) "The New Penology: Notes on the Emerging Strategy of Corrections and Its Implications". *Criminology* 30(4): 449.

——— (1994) "Actuarial Justice: The Emerging New Criminal Law", in D. Nelken (ed.) *The Futures of Criminology.* London: Sage: 173–201.

Feldman, A. (1991) *Formations of Violence: The Narrative of the Body and Political Terror in Northern Ireland.* Chicago: University of Chicago Press.

Fernandez, L. (2008) *Policing Dissent: Social Control and the Anti-Globalization Movement*. New Brunswick, NJ: Rutgers University Press.

Fishwick, E., and M. Wearing (2017) "'Unruly Mobilities' in the Tracking of Young Offenders and Criminality: Understanding Diversionary Programs as Carceral Space", in Jennifer Turner and Kimberley Peters (eds) *Carceral Mobilities*. London: Routledge.

Foote, C. (1956) "Vagrancy-Type Law and Its Administration". *University of Pennsylvania Law Review* 104(5): 603–650.

Ford, R. (1999) "Law's Territory (A History of Jurisdiction)". *Michigan Law Review* 97: 843–930.

Forest, P. (ed.) (2009) *Géographie du droit: épistémologie, développement et perspectives*. Quebec: Les presses de l'université Laval.

Fortin, V. (2018) "The Control of Public Spaces in Montreal in Times of Managerial Justice". *Penal Field* 15: (unpag.). http://journals.openedition.org/champpenal/10115.

Foucault, M. (1977) *Discipline and Punish: The Birth of the Prison*. London: Allen Lane.

(1980) "Questions on Geography", in C. Gordon (ed.) *Power/Knowledge: Selected Interviews and Other Writings, 1972–77*. New York: Pantheon Books: 63–77.

French, R. (2001) "Time in the Law". *University of Colorado Law Review* 72: 663–748.

Friedland, M. L. (1965) *Detention before Trial: A Study of Criminal Cases Tried in the Toronto Magistrates' Courts*. Toronto: University of Toronto Press.

(2012) "The Bail Reform Act Revisited". *Canadian Criminal Law Review* 16: 315–322.

Fukuda, K. (2016) "Incarceration and Incorporation: The Infrastructures of Japanese-Canadian Internment and Redress". *Society + Space*. http://societyandspace.org/2017/10/03/incarceration-and-incorporation-the-infrastructures-of-japanese-canadian-internment-and-redress/.

Fuller, L. L. (1963) "Collective Bargaining and the Arbitrator". *Wisconsin Law Review* 1: 3–46.

(1978) "The Forms and Limits of Adjudication". *Harvard Law Review* 92(2): 353–409.

Fyson, D. (2006) *Magistrates, Police, and People: Everyday Criminal Justice in Quebec and Lower Canada (1764–1837)*. Toronto: University of Toronto Press.

Galanter, M. (1991) "Punishment: Civil Style". *Israel Law Review* 25(3–4): 759–778.

Galtung, J. (1969) "Violence, Peace, and Peace Research", *Journal of Peace Research* 6(3): 167–191.

Gard, R. (2014) *Rehabilitation and Probation in England and Wales, 1876–1962*. London: Bloomsbury.

Garland, D. (2014) "What Is a 'History of the Present'? On Foucault's Genealogies and Their Critical Preconditions". *Punishment & Society* 16(4): 365–384.

Gee, M. (2018) "Danger beyond the Prison Gates: One in 10 Overdose Deaths Happen to Ex-Inmates within Year of Release". *Globe and Mail*. 30 November. https://www.theglobeandmail.com/canada/article-within-a-year-of-release-one-in-10-ex-prisoners-die-of-overdose/.

Gilham, P. (2011) "Securitizing America: Strategic Incapacitation and the Policing of Protest since the 11 September 2011 Terrorist Attacks". *Sociology Compass* 5(7): 636–652.

Gilham, P., B. Edwards, and J. Noakes (2013) "Strategic Incapacitation and the Policing of Occupy Wall Street Protests in New York City, 2011". *Policing & Society* 23(1): 81–102.

Gill, N., D. Conlon, D. Moran, and A. Burridge (2016) "Carceral Circuitry: New Directions in Carceral Geography". *Progress in Human Geography*. https://jour nals.sagepub.com/doi/abs/10.1177/0309132516671823?journalCode=phgb.

Girard, P., J. Philips, and R. B. Brown (2018) *A History of Law in Canada*, vol. 1, *Beginnings to 1866*. Toronto: University of Toronto Press.

Gittens, M., and D. Cole (1995) *Report of the Commission on Systemic Racism in the Ontario Criminal Justice System*. Toronto: Queen's Printer for Ontario.

Goebel J., and T. R. Naughton (1944) *Law Enforcement in Colonial New York: A Study in Criminal Procedure (1664–1776)*. New York: The Commonwealth Fund.

Goffman, E. (1974) *Frame Analysis: An Essay on the Organization of Experience*. Cambridge, MA: Harvard University Press.

Goldfarb, R. (1965) *Ransom: A Critique of the American Bail System*. New York: Harper & Row.

Goodrich, P. (1990) *Languages of Law: From Logics of Memory to Nomadic Masks*. London: Weidenfeld & Nicolson.

Gordon, T. (2004) "The Return of Vagrancy Law and the Politics of Poverty in Canada". *Canadian Review of Social Policy* 54: 34–57.

Gorz, A. (1968) *Strategy for Labor: A Radical Proposal*. Boston: Beacon Press.

Grabham, E. (2016) *Brewing Legal Times: Things, Form, and the Enactment of Law*. Toronto: University of Toronto Press.

Greenhouse, C. J. (1989) *Praying for Justice: Faith, Order, and Community in an American Town*. Ithaca, NY: Cornell University Press.

Grinnell, F. W. (1917) "Probation as an Orthodox Common Law Practice in Massachusetts Prior to the Statutory System". *Massachusetts Law Quarterly* 2(6): 591–639.

Grunhut, M. (1958) "New Projects for Probation in France and Belgium". *British Journal of Delinquency* 8: 219–222.

Hannah-Moffat, K., and P. Maurutto (2012) "Shifting and Targeted Forms of Penal Governance: Bail, Punishment and Specialized Courts". *Theoretical Criminology* 16(2): 201.

Harcourt, B. E. (2001) *Illusion of Order: The False Promise of Broken Windows Policing*. Cambridge, MA: Harvard University Press.

(2007) *Against Prediction: Profiling, Policing and Punishing in the Actuarial Age*. Chicago: University of Chicago Press.

(2013) "Punitive Preventive Justice: A Critique", in A. Ashworth, L. Zedner, and P. Tomlin (eds) *Prevention and the Limits of Criminal Law*. Oxford: Oxford University Press.

Harvey, D. (1996) *Justice, Nature and the Geography of Difference*. Oxford: Blackwell.

Hay, D. (1975) "Property, Authority, and the Criminal Law", in D. Hay, P. Linebaugh, J. G. Rule, et al. (eds) *Albion's Fatal Tree: Crime and Society in Eighteenth Century England*. New York: Pantheon.

Hayward, K. J. (2012) "Five Spaces of Cultural Criminology". *British Journal of Criminology* 52(3): 441–462.

Herbert, S. (1996) "The Geopolitics of the Police: Foucault, Disciplinary Power and the Tactics of the Los Angeles Police Department". *Political Geography* 15(1): 47–59.

(1997) *Policing Space: Territoriality and the Los Angeles Police Department.* Chicago: University of Chicago Press.

Hermer, J., and J. E. Mosher (eds) (2002) *Disorderly People: Law and the Politics of Exclusion in Ontario*. Halifax, NS: Fernwood Publishing.

Hill, G. (2005) "The Use of Pre-Existing Exclusionary Zones as Probationary Conditions for Prostitution Offenses: A Call for the Sincere Application of Heightened Scrutiny". *Seattle University Law Review* 28: 173–208.

Hopper, T. (2014) "Vancouver's 'Gulag': Canada's Poorest Neighbourhood Refuses to Get Better despite $1M a Day in Social Spending". *National Post*. 14 November. https://nationalpost.com/news/vancouvers-gulag-canadas-poorest-neighbourhood-refuses-to-get-better-despite-1m-a-day-in-social-spending.

Hubbard, P., and T. Sanders (2003) "Making Space for Sex Work: Female Street Prostitution and the Production of Urban Space". *International Journal of Urban and Regional Research* 27(1): 75–89.

Hubbard, P., R. Matthews, and J. Scoular (2008) "Regulating Sex Work in the EU: Prostitute Women and the New Spaces of Exclusion". *Gender, Place and Culture: A Journal of Feminist Geography* 15(2): 137–152.

Hucklesby, A. (1994) "The Use and Abuse of Conditional Bail". *Howard Journal of Criminal Justice* 33(3): 258–270.

(2001) "Police Bail and the Use of Conditions". *Criminology & Criminal Justice* 1(4): 441–463.

(2002) "Bail in Criminal Cases", in M. McConville and G. Wilson (eds) *The Handbook of the Criminal Justice Process*. Oxford: Oxford University Press: 115–136.

(2009) "Keeping the Lid on the Prison Remand Population: The Experience in England and Wales". *Current Issues in Criminal Justice* 21(1): 3–23.

(2013) *Bail: Law, Policy and Practice*. London: Routledge.

Hulchanski, D. (2016) "Vancouver Region Neighbourhood Change Research Partnership". http://neighbourhoodchange.ca/.

Hyde, A. (1997) *Bodies of Law*. Princeton, NJ: Princeton University Press.

John Howard Society of Ontario (2013) *Reasonable Bail?* Toronto: John Howard Society of Ontario. https://johnhoward.on.ca/wp-content/uploads/2014/07/JHSO-Reasonable-Bail-report-final.pdf.

Johnsen, S., and S. Fitzpatrick (2007) *The Impact of Enforcement on Street Users in England*. York: Joseph Rowntree Foundation.

(2010) "Revanchist Sanitisation or Coercive Care? The Use of Enforcement to Combat Begging, Street Drinking and Rough Sleeping in England". *Urban Studies* 47(8): 1703–1723.

Kärrholm, M. (2007) "The Materiality of Territorial Production: A Conceptual Discussion of Territoriality, Materiality, and the Everyday Life of Public Space". *Space and Culture* 10(4): 437–453.

(2017) "The Temporality of Territorial Production: The Case of Stortorget, Malmö". *Social & Cultural Geography* 18(5): 683–705.

Keenan, S. (2018) "A Prison around Your Ankle and a Border in Every Street: Theorising Law, Space and the Subject", in A. Philippopoulos-Mihalopoulos (ed.) *Routledge Handbook of Law and Theory*. London: Routledge: 71–88.

Kellough, G., and S. Wortley (2002) "Remand for Plea: Bail Decisions and Plea Bargaining as Commensurate Decisions". *British Journal of Criminology* 42: 186–210.

Kelman, M. (1981) "Interpretative Construction in the Substantive Criminal Law". *Stanford Law Review* 33(4): 591–673.

Khan, L. A. (2009) "Temporality of Law". *McGeorge Law Review* 40(1): 55–106.

King, D. (2013a) "When Proactive Policing Crosses the Line". *Pivot*. www.pivotlegal .org/when_proactive_policing_crosses_the_line.

(2013b) "Pivot and VANDU Slam VPD over City Bylaw Enforcement". *Pivot* Press Release. 6 June. www.pivotlegal.org/pivot_and_vandu_slam_vpd_over_city_ bylaw_enforcement.

Klingele, C. (2013) "Rethinking the Use of Community Supervision". *Journal of Criminal Law and Criminology* 103(4): 1015–1070.

Klinke, I. (2012) "Postmodern Geopolitics? The European Union Eyes Russia". *Europe-Asia Studies* 64(5): 929–947.

(2013) "Chronopolitics: A Conceptual Matrix". *Progress in Human Geography* 37(5): 673–690.

Kohler-Hausmann, Issa (2013) "Misdemeanor Justice: Control without Conviction". *American Journal of Sociology* 119(2): 351–393.

(2014) "Managerial Justice and Mass Misdemeanors". *Stanford Law Review* 66(3): 611–694.

(2018) *Misdemeanorland: Criminal Courts and Social Control in an Age of Broken-Windows Policing*. Princeton, NJ: Princeton University Press.

Kohler-Hausmann, Julilly (2015) "Welfare Crises, Penal Solutions, and the Origins of the 'Welfare Queen'". *Journal of Urban History* 41(5): 756–771.

Lacey, N. (2001) "Social Policy, Civil Society and the Institutions of Criminal Justice". *Australian Journal of Legal Philosophy* 26: 7–25.

Lambarde, W. (1581) *Eirenarcha, or, Of the Office of the Iustices of Peace, in Two Bookes*. London: R. Newbery and H. Bynneman.

Langbein, I. L. (1933) "The Jury of Presentment and the Coroner". *Columbia Law Review* 33(8): 1329–1365.

Langbein, J. H. (1974) *Prosecuting Crime in the Renaissance*. Cambridge, MA: Harvard University Press.

(1979) "Understanding the Short History of Plea Bargaining". *Law & Society Review* 13: 261–272.

(1983) "Shaping the Eighteenth-Century Criminal Trial: A View from the Ryder Sources". *University of Chicago Law Review* 50(1): 1–136.

Langdell, C. C. (1871) *A Selection of Cases on the Law of Contracts: With References and Citations*. Boston: Little, Brown, and Co.

Laurie, E. W., and I. G. R. Shaw (2018) "Violent Conditions: The Injustices of Being". *Political Geography* 65: 8–16.

Law, J. (1999) "After ANT: Complexity, Naming and Topology". *Sociological Review*, 47(1_suppl): 1–14.

Lefebvre, H., and D. Nicholson-Smith (1991) *The Production of Space*. Oxford: Blackwell.

Lermack, P. (1976) "Peace Bonds and Criminal Justice in Colonial Philadelphia". *Pennsylvania Magazine of History and Biography* 100(2): 173–190.

Lewis, P., and R. Evans (2009) "High Court Injunction: The Weapon of Choice to Slap down Protests". *Guardian*. October 27.

La ligue des droits et libertés (2013) *Répression, discrimination et grève étudiante: analyse et témoignages*. http://liguedesdroits.ca/wp-content/fichiers/rapport-2013-repression-discrimination-et-greve-etudiante.pdf.

Lippert, R. (2007) "Urban Revitalization, Security and Knowledge Transfer: The Case of Broken Windows and Kiddie Bars". *Canadian Journal of Law and Society* 22(2): 29–53.

Lippert, R., and M. Sleiman (2012) "Ambassadors, Business Improvement District Governance and Knowledge of the Urban". *Urban Studies* 49(1): 61–76.

Liu, S., and N. Blomley (2013) "Making News and Making Space: Performing the Geographies of Poverty in Vancouver's Downtown Eastside". *Canadian Geographer* 57(2): 119–132.

Low, S. (2000) *On the Plaza: The Politics of Public Space and Culture*. Austin: University of Texas Press.

Low, S. M., and D. Lawrence-Zúñiga (2003) "Locating Culture", in S. M. Low and D. Lawrence-Zúñiga (eds) *The Anthropology of Space and Place: Locating Culture*. Oxford: Blackwell Publishing: 1–48.

Lupick, T. (2017a) *Fighting for Space: How a Group of Drug Users Transformed One City Struggle's with Addiction*. Vancouver: Arsenal Pulp Press.

(2017b) "No-Go Zones for People on Bail Creating Tough Choices for Drug Users in Vancouver". *Georgia Straight*. 31 October. www.straight.com/news/988846/no-go-zones-people-bail-creating-tough-choices-vancouver-drug-offenders-study-finds.

Lynch, G. E. (1998) "Our Administrative System of Criminal Justice". *Fordham Law Review* 83(4): 2117–2151.

MacDonald, A. (2012) "The Conditions of Area Restrictions in Canadian Cities: Street Sex Work and Access to Public Space". MA thesis, University of Ottawa.

McNeil, R., H. Cooper, W. Small, and T. Kerr (2015) "Area Restrictions, Risk, Harm, and Health Care Access Among People Who Use Drugs in Vancouver, Canada: A Spatially Oriented Qualitative Study". *Health and Place* 35: 70–78.

McPhail, C., J. D. McCarthy, and A. W. Martin (2004) "Protest and Place: The Shrinking Effective Size of the U.S. Public Forum", American Sociological Association, San Francisco, 16 August. www.asanet.org/sites/default/files/2004_annual_meeting_program.pdf.

Malakieh, J. (2018) "Adult and Youth Correctional Statistics in Canada, 2016/2017". 19 June. Statistics Canada. *Juristat* 38(1). https://www150.statcan.gc.ca/n1/en/pub/85-002-x/2018001/article/54972-eng.pdf?st=Mt_BmjtK.

Marinos, V. (2006) "The Meaning of 'Short' Sentences of Imprisonment and Offences against the Administration of Justice: A Perspective from the Court". *Canadian Journal of Law and Society* 21(2): 143–167.

Massé, R., F. Desbiens, and M.-F. Raynault (2017) "La pauvreté et les inégalités sociales, de graves menaces à la santé des populations: mémoire des

Directeurs de santé publique de Montréal et de la Capitale-Nationale". Government of Quebec. https://santemontreal.qc.ca/professionnels/drsp/publications/pub lication-description/publication/la-pauvrete-et-les-inegalites-sociales-de-graves-menaces-a-la-sante-des-populations-memoire-des-d/.

Massey, D. (1991) "A Global Sense of Place". *Marxism Today* 38: 24–29.

(2004) "Geographies of Responsibility". *Geografiska Annaler: Series B, Human Geography* 86(1): 5–18.

Máté, G. (2008) *In the Realm of Hungry Ghosts: Close Encounters with Addiction*. Toronto: Alfred A. Knopf.

Matthews, R. (2005) "Policing Prostitution: Ten Years On". *British Journal of Criminology* 45(6): 877–895.

Maurutto, P., and K. Hannah-Moffat (2006) "Assembling Risk and the Restructuring of Penal Control". *British Journal of Criminology* 46(3): 438–454.

Mawani, R. (2015) "The Times of Law". *Law & Social Inquiry* 40(1): 253–263.

Maxwell, A. (2017) "Adult Criminal Courts Statistics in Canada, 2014/2015". 21 February. Statistics Canada. *Juristat* 37(1). www150.statcan.gc.ca/n1/en/pub/85-002-x/2017001/article/14699-eng.pdf?st=X9hxXmHW.

Mayor's Task Force on Housing Affordability (2012) "Bold Ideas towards an Affordable City", Interim Report. June. https://vancouver.ca/files/cov/mayors-task-force-hous ing-affordability-interim-report-june-2012.pdf.

Meloche, S. (2014) Notes Sent by Sylvain Meloche from the Information Technologies Services of the City of Montreal, May 23.

Merry, S. (2001) "Spatial Governmentality and the New Urban Social Order: Controlling Gender Violence through Law". *American Anthropologist* 103(1): 16–29.

Mertens, D. M., and S. Hesse-Biber (2012) "Triangulation and Mixed Methods Research: Provocative Positions". *Journal of Mixed Methods Research* 6(2): 75–79.

Meyer, H. H. (1972) "Constitutionality of Pretrial Detention". *Georgetown Law Journal* 60(6): 1381–1474.

Miéville, C. (2010) *The City and the City*. New York: Del Rey Ballantine Books.

Mills, J. (1971) "I Have Nothing to Do with Justice". *Life*. 12 March: 56–69.

Ministère de la sécurité publique du Québec (2013) *Profil des personnes condamnées à une courte peine d'incarcération en 2010–2011*. www.securitepublique.gouv.qc.ca/fileadmin/Documents/services_correctionnels/publications/profil_courte_peine/profil_courte_peine_2010-2011.pdf.

Ministry of Justice, British Columbia (2013) Downtown Community Court in Vancouver: Efficiency Evaluation. September 6. www.provincialcourt.bc.ca/downloads/dcc/DCCEfficiency_Evaluation.pdf .

Ministry of the Attorney General of Ontario (2014) "Update on G20 Prosecutions". 20 June. Queen's Printer for Ontario. www.attorneygeneral.jus.gov.on.ca/english/g20_case_update.php.

Mitchell, D. (1995) "The End of Public Space? People's Park, Definitions of the Public, and Democracy". *Annals of the Association of American Geographers* 85(1): 108–133.

(1997) "The Annihilation of Space by Law: The Roots and Implications of Anti-Homelessness Laws in the United States". *Antipode: A Journal of Radical Geography* 29(3): 303–337.

Mitchell D., and L. A. Staeheli (2005) "Permitting Protest: Parsing the Fine Geography of Dissent in America". *International Journal of Urban and Regional Research* 29 (4): 796–813.

Moore, D. (2011) "The Benevolent Watch: Therapeutic Surveillance in Drug Treatment Court". *Theoretical Criminology* 15(3): 255–268.

Moore, D., L. Freeman, and M. Krawczyk (2011) "Spatio-Therapeutics: Drug Treatment Courts and Urban Space". *Social & Legal Studies* 20(2): 157–172.

Moran, D. (2012) "'Doing Time' in Carceral Space: Timespace and Carceral Geography". *Geografiska Annaler: Series B, Human Geography* 94(4): 305–316.

(2013) "Between Outside and Inside? Prison Visiting Rooms as Liminal Carceral Spaces". *GeoJournal* 78(2): 339–351.

(2015) *Carceral Geography: Spaces and Practices of Incarceration*. Farnham: Ashgate.

Mulcahy, L. (2010) *Legal Architecture: Justice, Due Process and the Place of Law*. London: Routledge.

Munn, M. (2011) "Living in the Aftermath: The Impact of Lengthy Incarceration on Post-Carceral Success". *Howard Journal of Criminal Justice* 50(3): 233–246.

Munn, M., and C. Bruckert (2013) *On the Outside: From Lengthy Imprisonment to Lasting Freedom*. Vancouver: UBC Press.

Murphy, E. (2009) "Manufacturing Crime: Process, Pretext, and Criminal Justice". *Georgetown Law Journal* 97: 1435–1507.

Myers, N. M. (2017) "Eroding the Presumption of Innocence: Pre-Trial Detention and the Use of Conditional Release on Bail". *British Journal of Criminology* 57(3): 664–683.

Myers, N. M., and S. Dhillon (2013) "The Criminal Offence of Entering Any Shoppers Drug Mart in Ontario: Criminalizing Ordinary Behaviour with Youth Bail Conditions". *Canadian Journal of Criminology and Criminal Justice* 55(2): 187–214.

Myhre, K. C. (2013) "Cutting and Connecting: 'Afrinesian' Perspectives on Networks, Relationality, and Exchange". *Social Analysis* 57(3): 1–24.

Natapoff, A. (2013) "Aggregation and Urban Misdemeanors". *Fordham Urban Law Journal* 40(3): 1043.

National Union of Public and General Employees, and Canadian Civil Liberties Association (2011) "Breach of the Peace: G20 Summit 'Accountability in Policing and Governance'". Public Hearings, 10–12 November, Toronto and Montreal. https://ccla.org/cclanewsite/wp-content/uploads/2015/02/Breach-of-the-Peace-Final-Report.pdf.

Neely, A. H. (2015) "Internal Ecologies and the Limits of Local Biologies: A Political Ecology of Tuberculosis in the Time of AIDS". *Annals of the Association of American Geographers* 105(4): 791–805.

Neocleous, M. (2000) *The Fabrication of Social Order: A Critical Theory of Police Power*. London: Pluto Press.

NETPOL (The Network for Police Monitoring)(2011) *Report into the Policing of Protest 2010/2011*. London. https://netpol.files.wordpress.com/2012/07/wainwright-report-final1.pdf.

"Note" (1961) "Bail: An Ancient Practice Reexamined" *Yale Law Journal* 70: 966–977.

"Note" (1966) "Preventive Detention before Trial". *Harvard Law Review* 79(7): 1489–1510.

O'Grady, B., S. Gaetz, and K. Buccieri (2013) "Tickets . . . and More Tickets: A Case Study of the Enforcement of the Ontario Safe Streets Act". *Canadian Public Policy* 39(4): 541–558.

O'Malley, P. (2006) "Criminology and Risk", in G. Mythen and S. Walklate (eds) *Beyond the Risk Society: Critical Reflections on Risk and Human Security* New York: McGraw-Hill: 43–59.

Office of the Auditor General of British Columbia (2013) "Securing the JUSTIN System: Access and Security Audit at the Ministry of Justice", 24 January. www.bcauditor.com/pubs/2013/report9/securing-justin-system-access-and-security-audit-ministry.

Osborn B., and W. Small (2006) "'Speaking Truth to Power': The Role of Drug Users in Influencing Municipal Drug Policy". *International Journal of Drug Policy* 17(2): 70–72.

Ouimet Committee (1969) *Report of the Canadian Committee on Corrections*. 31 March. Halifax: Queen's Printer.

Paasi, A. (2003) "Region and Place: Regional Identity in Question". *Progress in Human Geography* 27(4): 475–485.

Packer, H. L. (1964) "Two Models of the Criminal Process". *University of Pennsylvania Law Review* 113(1): 1–68.

Painter, J. (2010) "Rethinking Territory". *Antipode: A Journal of Radical Geography* 42(5): 1090–1118.

Pasternak, S. (2017) *Grounded Authority: The Algonquins of Barriere Lake against the State*. Minneapolis: University of Minnesota Press.

Pauly, B., G. Cross, and D. Weiss (2016) "No Vacancy: Affordability and Homelessness in Vancouver". University of Victoria, Centre for Addictions Research of BC and Union Gospel Mission. www.ugm.ca/wp-content/uploads/2016/10/HAW_Report_Final-Oct11.pdf.

Pelvin, H. (2017) "Doing Uncertain Time: Understanding the Experiences of Punishment in Pre-trial Custody". Ph.D. thesis, University of Toronto.

Peritz, I. (2012) "Quebec Premier Jokes with Business Leaders as Police Beat Back Protesters". 20 April. www.theglobeandmail.com/news/politics/quebec-premier-jokes-with-business-leaders-as-police-beat-back-protesters/art icle41019965/.

Phillips, J. (2012) "Poverty, Unemployment, and the Administration of Criminal Law: Vagrancy Laws in Halifax, 1864–1890", in P. Girard and J. Phillips (eds) *Essays in the History of Canadian Law: Nova Scotia*, vol. 3. Toronto: University of Toronto Press/Osgoode Society: 128–162.

Pile, S. (1997) "Introduction: Opposition, Political Identities and Spaces of Resistance", in S. Pile and M. Keith (eds) *Geographies of Resistance*. London: Routledge: 1–32.

Pitsula, J. M. (1980) "The Treatment of Tramps in Late Nineteenth-Century Toronto". *Canadian Historical Association: Historical Papers* 15(1): 116–132.

Pivot Legal Society (2018) "Project Inclusion: Confronting Anti-Homeless & Anti-Substance User Stigma in British Columbia". Full Report. Vancouver, B.C.: Pivot Foundation. www.pivotlegal.org/full_report_project_inclusion_b.

Poutanen, M. A. (2015) *Beyond Brutal Passions: Prostitution in Early Nineteenth-Century Montreal*. Montreal: McGill-Queen's University Press.

Prince, R. J. (2006) "A Line in the Sand: Implementing Scene of the Crime Stay-Away Orders as a Condition of Pretrial Release in Community Prosecution". *Virginia Law Review* 92: 1899–1956.

Prior, J., and P. Hubbard (2017) "Time, Space, and the Authorisation of Sex Premises in London and Sydney". *Urban Studies* 54(3): 633–648.

Provincial Court of British Columbia (2017) "Bail Orders Picklist". 1 May. https://docs .google.com/viewer?url=http%3A%2F%2Fwww.provincialcourt.bc.ca%2Fdown loads%2Fcriminal%2FBAIL%2520PICKLIST%2520-%2520MAY%25201% 25202017%2520-%2520LETTER%2520SIZE_%2520ENDNOTE.docx.

Pue, W. Wesley (1990) "Wrestling with Law: (Geographical) Specificity vs. (Legal) Abstraction". *Urban Geography* 11 (6): 566–585.

——— (2000) *Pepper in Your Eyes: The APEC Affair*. Vancouver: University of British Columbia Press.

Puttkammer, E. W. (1953) *Administration of Criminal Law*. Chicago: Chicago University Press.

Raine J. W., and M. J. Wilson (1996) "The Imposition of Conditions in Bail Decisions: From Summary Punishment to Better Behaviour on Remand". *Howard Journal of Criminal Justice* 35(3): 256–270.

——— (1997) "Police Bail with Conditions: Perspectives on the Use, Misuse and Consequences of a New Police Power". *British Journal of Criminology* 37(4): 593–607.

Reid, A. (2017) "Extending a Relative Methodological Perspective to Sentencing Outcome Analysis". Ph.D. thesis, Simon Fraser University.

Reitano, J. (2017) "Adult Correctional Statistics in Canada, 2015/2016". 1 March. Statistics Canada. *Juristat* 37(1): Table 5. www150.statcan.gc.ca/n1/en/pub/85-002-x/2017001/article/14700-eng.pdf?st=scCCjZPj.

Riles, A. (2005) "A New Agenda for the Cultural Study of Law: Taking on the Technicalities". *Buffalo Law Review* 53: 973–1033.

Ross, B. L. (2010) "Sex and (Evacuation from) the City: The Moral and Legal Regulation of Sex Workers in Vancouver's West End, 1975–1985". *Sexualities* 13(2): 197–218.

Routledge, P. (2003) "Convergence Space: Process Geographies of Grassroots Globalization Networks". *Transactions of the Institute of British Geographers* 28(3): 333–349.

Sack, R. D. (1983) "Human Territoriality: A Theory". *Annals of the Association of American Geographers* 73(1): 55–74.

Samaha, J. (1981) "The Recognizance in Elizabethan Law Enforcement". *American Journal of Legal History* 25(3): 189–204.

Sanchez, L. (2004) "The Global E-rotic Subject, the Ban, and the Prostitute-Free Zone: Sex Work and the Theory of Differential Exclusion". *Environment and Planning D; Society and Space* 22(6): 861–883.

Sarat, A., and T. R. Kearns (1992) "Making Peace with Violence: Robert Cover on Law and Legal Theory", in A. Sarat and T. R. Kearns (eds) *Law's Violence*. Ann Arbor: University of Michigan Press: 49–84.

Schuilenburg, M. (2015) "Behave or Be Banned? Banning Orders and Selective Exclusion from Public Space". *Crime, Law and Social Change* 64(4–5): 277–289.

Schwan, K. J. (2016) "Why Don't We Do Something? The Societal Problematization of 'Homelessness' and the Relationship between Discursive Framing and Social Change". Ph.D. thesis, University of Toronto. https://tspace.library.utoronto.ca/bitstream/1807/76837/1/Schwan_Kaitlin_J_201611_PhD_thesis.pdf.

Segal, Murray D. (2015) "Independent Review of the Police and Prosecution Response to the Rehtaeh Parsons Case". https://novascotia.ca/segalreport/Parsons-Independent-Review.pdf.

(2016) "Championing Positive Change: Findings of the Review of the BC Prosecution Service". www2.gov.bc.ca/assets/gov/law-crime-and-justice/criminal-justice/prosecution-service/reports-publications/cjb-segalreport-2016.pdf.

Sentencing Guidelines Council (2004) "New Sentences: Criminal Justice Act 2003. Guideline". https://consult.justice.gov.uk/digital-communications/imposition-consultation/supporting_documents/SGC%20New%20Sentences%20CJA%202003%20PDF%201.pdf.

Shandley, C. (2013) Vancouver Provincial Court: Vancouver Drug Court and Downtown Community Court Breach Analysis, Record Level Data and Methodology Notes, 9 December.

Sibley, D. (1995) *Geographies of Exclusion*. London: Routledge.

Silbey, S. S. (1985) "Ideals and Practices in the Study of Law". *Legal Studies Forum* 9 (7): 7–22.

Soja, E. (1989) *Postmodern Geographies: The Reassertion of Space in Critical Social Theory*. New York: Verso.

Speigel, J. B. (2014) "Rêve général illimité? The Role of Creative Protest in Transforming Space and Time during the 2012 Quebec Student Strike". *Antipode: A Journal of Radical Geography* 47(3): 770–791.

(2016) "Performing 'In the Red': Transformations and Tensions in Repertoires of Contention during the 2012 Quebec Student Strike". *Social Movement Studies* 15(5): 531–538.

Sprott, J. B. (2015) "How Court Officials 'Create' Youth Crime: The Use and Consequences of Bail Conditions". *Canadian Criminal Law Review* 19(1): 27–39.

Sprott, J. B., and N. Myers (2011) "Set Up to Fail: The Unintended Consequences of Multiple Bail Conditions". *Canadian Journal of Criminology and Criminal Justice* 53(4): 404–423.

Standing Senate Committee on Legal and Constitutional Affairs (2017) "Delaying Justice is Denying Justice: An Urgent Need to Address Lengthy Court Delays in Canada" (Final Report). https://sencanada.ca/content/sen/committee/421/LCJC/reports/Court_Delays_Final_Report_e.pdf.

Starr, A., and L. A. Fernandez (2009) "Legal Control and Resistance Post-Seattle". *Social Justice* 36(1): 41–60.

Starr, A., L. A. Fernandez, and C. Scholl (2011) *Shutting Down the Streets: Political Violence and Social Control in the Global Era*. New York: New York University Press.

Statistics Canada (2016) Data Products, 2016 Census. www12.statcan.gc.ca/census-recensement/2016/dp-pd/index-eng.cfm.

(2017) Uniform Crime Reporting Survey. www23.statcan.gc.ca/imdb/p2SV.pl?Func
tion=getSurvey&SDDS=3302.

(2019) "Adult Criminal Courts, Guilty Cases by Type of Sentence". Table 35-10-
0030-01. www150.statcan.gc.ca/t1/tbl1/en/tv.action?pid=3510003001.

Steiker, C. S. (1998) "The Limits of the Preventive State". *Journal of Criminal Law and Criminology* 88(3): 771–808.

Stewart, W. (2016) "Situating Drugs and Drug Use Geographically: From Place to Space and Back Again". *International Journal of Drug Policy* 33: 1–5.

Strathern, M. (1996) "Cutting the Network". *Journal of the Royal Anthropological Institute* 2(3): 517–535.

Stumpf, J. (2006) "The Crimmigration Crisis: Immigrants, Crime, and Sovereign Power". *American University Law Review* 56(2): 367–419.

Stuntz, W. J. (1997) "The Uneasy Relationship between Criminal Procedure and Criminal Justice". *Yale Law Journal* 107(1): 1–76.

(2004) "Plea Bargaining and Criminal Law Disappearing's Shadow". *Harvard Law Review* 117(8): 2548–2569.

Sylvestre, M.-E. (2010a) "Disorder and Public Spaces in Montreal: Repression (and Resistance) through Law, Politics, and Police Discretion". *Urban Geography* 31(6): 803–824.

(2010b) "Rethinking Criminal Responsibility for Poor Offenders: Choice, Monstrosity, and the Logic of Practice". *McGill Law Journal*, 55(4): 771–817.

(2018) "Towards Real Implementation of the Right to Reasonable Bail and Respect for the Rights of Marginalized People". Brief Submitted to the Standing Committee on Justice and Human Rights Relating to Bill C-75: An Act to Amend the Criminal Code, the Youth Criminal Justice Act and other Acts and to make consequential amendments to other Acts. www.ourcommons.ca/Content/Committee/421/JUST/Brief/BR10008630/br-external/SylvestreMarieEve-9897935-e.pdf.

Sylvestre M.-E. and D. Bernier (2012) "Les arrestations préventives sont illégales et illégitimes". *Le Devoir*. June 12. www.ledevoir.com/opinion/idees/352178/les-arrestations-preventives-sont-illegales-et-illegitimes.

Sylvestre, M.-E., C. Bellot, and N. Blomley (2017) "Une peine avant jugement? La mise en liberté provisoire et la réforme du droit pénal canadien", in J. Desrosiers, M. Garcia, and M.-E. Sylvestre, *Réformer le droit criminel au Canada : défis et possibilités/Criminal Law Reform in Canada: Challenges and Possibilities* Montreal: Éditions Yvon Blais: 189–228.

Sylvestre, M.-E., C. Bellot, A. Duchesne-Blondin, V. Fortin, and N. Blomley (2018) "Les conditions géographiques de mise en liberté et de probation et leur impact sur les personnes marginalisées à Montréal". Research Report. https://www.researchgate.net/publication/329218501_Les_conditions_geographiques_de_mise_en_liberte_et_de_probation_et_leur_impact_sur_les_personnes_marginali sees_a_Montreal.

Sylvestre, M.-E., C. Bellot, P. A. C. Ménard, and A. C. Tremblay (2011) "Le droit est aussi une question de visibilité: l'occupation des espaces publics et les parcours judiciaires des personnes itinérantes à Montréal et à Ottawa". *Canadian Journal of Law and Society* 26(3): 531–561.

Sylvestre, M.-E., D. Bernier, and C. Bellot (2015) "Zone Restrictions Orders in Canadian Courts and the Reproduction of Socio-Economic Inequality". *Oñati Socio-Legal Series* 5(1): 280–297.

Sylvestre, M.-E., N. Blomley, W. Damon, and C. Bellot (2017) "Red Zones and Other Spatial Conditions of Release Imposed on Marginalized People in Vancouver". Research Report. www.researchgate.net/publication/320740634_Red_zones_and_Other_Spatial_Conditions_of_Release_Imposed_on_Marginalized_People_in_Vancouver.

Sylvestre, M-E., W. Damon, N. Blomley, and C. Bellot (2015) "Spatial Tactics in Criminal Courts and the Politics of Legal Technicalities". *Antipode: A Journal of Radical Geography* 47(5): 1346–1366.

Sylvestre, M.-E., F. Villeneuve Ménard, V. Fortin, C. Bellot, and N. Blomley (2018) "Conditions géographiques de mise en liberté et de probation imposées aux manifestants: une atteinte injustifiée aux droits à la liberté d'expression, de réunion pacifique et d'association". *McGill Law Journal* 62(4): 923–973.

Table Justice-Québec (2016) "Action Plan to Reduce Delays in Criminal and Penal Cases 'Pour une justice en temps utile en matière criminelle et pénale'". https://www.justice.gouv.qc.ca/en/department/issues/action-plan-to-reduce-delays-in-criminal-and-penal-cases-pour-une-justice-en-temps-utile-en-matieres-criminelle-et-penale/.

Thompson, E. P. (1967) "Time, Work-Discipline, and Industrial Capitalism". *Past & Present* 38: 56–97.

Thorner, T., and N. Watson (1981) "Patterns of Prairie Crime: Calgary, 1875–1939", in L. A. Knafla (ed.) *Crime and Criminal Justice in Europe and Canada*. Waterloo, Ontario: Wilfrid Laurier University Press: 219–256.

Timasheff, N. S. (1941) *One Hundred Years of Probation 1841–1941, Part One: Probation in the United States, England and the Commonwealth of Nations*. New York: Fordham University Press.

Toronto Police Service (2011) "Planning for the Future … Scanning the Toronto Environment". www.torontopolice.on.ca/publications/files/reports/2011envscan.pdf.

Trotter, G. (2010) *The Law of Bail in Canada*. 3rd edn Toronto: Carswell.

Trought, T. W. (1927) *Probation in Europe*. Oxford: Blackwell.

Turnbull, S., and K. Hannah-Moffat (2009) "Under These Conditions: Gender, Parole and the Governance of Reintegration". *British Journal of Criminology*, 49(4): 532–551.

Turner, A. J. (2016) *Anthony and Berryman's Magistrates' Court Guide 2016*. London: Butterworths.

Turner, J. (2016) *The Prison Boundary: Between Society and Carceral Space*. London: Palgrave Macmillan.

Turner, J., and K. Peters (eds) (2017) *Carceral Mobilities*. London: Routledge.

Valverde, M. (2009) "Jurisdiction and Scale: Legal 'Technicalities' as Resources for Theory". *Social & Legal Studies* 18(2): 139–157.

——— (2014) "'Time Thickens, Takes on Flesh': Spatiotemporal Dynamics in Law", in I. Braverman, N. K. Blomley, D. Delaney, and A. Kedar (eds) *The Expanding Spaces of Law: A Timely Legal Geography*. Stanford, CA: Stanford University Press: 53–76.

(2015) *Chronotopes of Law: Juridiction, Scale and Governance.* London: Routledge.

Vanhamme, F. (2014) "Les conditions judiciaires du maintien en liberté", in M. Vacheret and F. Prates (eds) *La détention avant jugement, une pratique controversée.* Montreal: Presses de l'université de Montréal : 83–104.

(2016) "Organisation sociale de la mise en liberté provisoire: des effets de profilage?" *Reflets* 22(1): 28–55.

Vanstone, M. (2008) "The International Origins of Probation". *British Journal of Criminology* 48(6): 735–755.

Veitch, S. (2007) *Law and Irresponsibility: On the Legitimation of Human Suffering.* Abingdon: Routledge-Cavendish.

Vieira Velloso, J. G. (2013) "Beyond Criminocentric Dogmatism: Mapping Institutional Forms of Punishment in Contemporary Societies". *Punishment & Society* 15(2): 166–186.

Villanueva, J. (2017) "Pathways of Confinement: The Legal Constitution of Carceral Spaces in France's Social Housing Estates". *Social & Cultural Geography* 19(8): 963–983.

Von Benda-Beckmann, F., and K. von Benda-Beckmann (2014) "Place That Come and Go: A Legal Anthropological Perspective on the Temporalities of Space in Plural Legal Orders", in I. Braverman, N. K. Blomley, D. Delaney, and A. Kedar (eds) *The Expanding Spaces of Law: A Timely Legal Geography.* Stanford, CA: Stanford University Press: 30–52.

Wacquant, L. (2007) "Territorial Stigmatization in the Age of Advanced Marginality". *Thesis Eleven* 91(1): 66–77.

(2008) *Urban Outcasts: A Comparative Sociology of Advanced Marginality.* Malden, MA: Polity Press.

Walby, K., and R. Lippert (2012) "Spatial Regulation, Dispersal, and the Aesthetics of the City: Conservation Officer Policing of Homeless People in Ottawa, Canada". *Antipode* 44(3): 1015–1033.

Wanger, B. K. (1987) "Limiting Preventive Detention through Conditional Release: The Unfulfilled Promise of the 1982 Pretrial Services Act". *Yale Law Journal* 97: 320.

Webster, C. M., A. N. Doob, and N. M. Myers (2009). "The Parable of Ms Baker: Understanding Pre-Trial Detention in Canada". *Current Issues in Criminal Justice* 21(1): 79–102.

Wiber, M. G. (2014) "Syncopated Rhythms? Temporal Patterns in Natural Resource Management". *Journal of Legal Pluralism and Unofficial Law* 46(1): 123–140.

Williams, S. (2016) "Situating Drugs and Drug Use Geographically: From Place to Space and Back Again". *International Journal of Drug Policy* 33: 1–5.

Winter, J. (2018) "Zoned Out: Critics Say Police-Imposed Area Restrictions Put Vulnerable People at Risk". 24 April. *Toronto Star.* www.thestar.com/vancouver/2018/04/24/zoned-out-critics-say-police-blockades-put-vulnerable-people-at-risk.html.

Wyant, R. E. (2016) "Bail and Remand in Ontario", Ontario Ministry of the Attorney General. www.attorneygeneral.jus.gov.on.ca/english/about/pubs/wyant/#_Toc46854411.

Zedner, L. (2016) "Penal Subversions: When Is a Punishment not a Punishment, Who Decides and on What Grounds?" *Theoretical Criminology* 20(1): 3–20.

Zick, T. (2006) "Speech and Spatial Tactics". *Texas Law Review* 84(3): 581–651.

(2009) *Speech Out of Doors: Preserving First Amendment Liberties in Public Places.* Cambridge: Cambridge University Press.

Index

accumulation of cases, 73, 87–88
  per individual, 87–88
ACD. *See* adjournments in contemplation of
  dismissal
activism, 193–196, 198
  spatiotemporal political infrastructures of
    activist politics, 197–198
actuarial spaces, 144
Adam, 171, 176–178
addiction, 34–35, 95, 174–175, 177–178, 224. *See*
    also drug related offences
  conditions of release and, 158
  drug overdose, 179
  Indigenous people and, 224
  legal bracketing and, 162
  non-addicted drug traffickers, 141
  poverty and, 159
  spatiotemporal dependencies and, 174
  trauma and, 164
  withdrawal, 178, 215–216
adjournments in contemplation of dismissal
  (ACD), 109
adjudicative model, 108–109, 125
administration of justice (AJO), 83–84, 100–101
  increases in number of, 101
  marginalized people and, 85
  Montreal and, 112–123
  offences against, 85–89, 97–98, 224
administrative law, 132–133
Adrian, 181
adversarial procedure, 120
AJO. *See* administration of justice
alcohol, 159–160, 183–184
alleged offenders, 36, 147, 215–216
Allen, J., 28
Anita, 193–196, 204

Anne, 122
anti-Olympics movement, 10, 114, 142–143
APEC. *See* Asia-Pacific Economic
  Cooperation
area restrictions, 12, 79–84
  breaches from, 84–88
  drug offences in DTES and, 141
  in DTES, standardized templates for, 154
  for Marius, 199
  for Martine, 2–5
  reoffending and, 157
  for Steve, 199–200
arrests, 192–193, 221–222
  house arrests, 10, 13, 126–127, 193, 196–197
  mass arrests, 9–10, 24–25, 130–131, 190
  of protesters, 130–131
Asia-Pacific Economic Cooperation (APEC)
    Summit, 113–114
Assize of Clarendon, 41–42
Attorney General of Ontario, 10
autonomy, 110–111

bail, 30, 41–43, 50–52, 54, 62–63, 68–69, 74. *See*
    also Vancouver, British Columbia
  breaching, 122, 184
  cash, 65
  community supervision and, 59
  conditions, 10
  conditions of release, law of bail and, 38–39
  conditions of release and, 64–69, 75
  days between bail release order and case
    conclusion, 120–121
  defence lawyers and, 116
  drug related offences and, 107
  failure to comply with, 86
  frequency of conditions at, 75

247